A STRANGER KILLED KATY

A STRANGER KILLED KATY

The True Story of Katherine Hawelka, Her Murder on a New York Campus, and How Her Family Fought Back.

By WILLIAM D. LaRUE

CHESTNUT HEIGHTS
PUBLISHING

Published by Chestnut Heights Publishing

ISBN 978-1-7322416-4-0 (hardback)
ISBN 978-1-7322416-2-6 (paperback)
ISBN 978-1-7322416-3-3 (ebook)

Library of Congress Control Number: 2020924238

First edition. Epilogue, April 2021.

Contact the author at williamlarue.com

Front cover: Katherine Hawelka and Clarkson University's Walker Arena. (Hawelka family/Potsdam Police Department photos.)

Back cover (print versions): Brian McCarthy leaves Potsdam Village Court, escorted by Potsdam Police Investigator John Perretta, left, and Officer Gene Brundage on Friday, August 29, 1986. (Mary Ellen Banta, The Post-Standard photo.)

Cover design by www.ebooklaunch.com

Typesetting services by BOOKOW.COM

Contents

Chapter 1

The Attack at Walker Arena

ROBERT J. Warren Jr.'s headlights caught something strange in the inky darkness as he drove southwest on Route 11 in upstate New York at around 10:15 on the evening of August 28, 1986. Warren hit the brakes on his GMC pickup and managed to screech to a stop a few feet before he would have struck a man sitting partly in the roadway.

The 24-year-old Warren had been heading home to Morristown, New York, after dropping off his wife at her parents' house in nearby Winthrop. He was now alone in the truck as he studied the man, who looked to be in his mid-20s with a medium build, dark hair, a scruffy beard, a dark jacket and beige work boots.

Seconds later, the man jumped up and ran over to the truck.

"Do you have a problem? What are you doing?" Warren asked.

The stranger in the road said he was going to the village of Potsdam, about 10 miles up ahead, and asked if Warren could give him a lift. In the mid-1980s, it wasn't considered uncommon or particularly unsafe to pick up a hitchhiker heading toward Potsdam, home to a college and a university. In this rural region just south of the Canadian border, public transit was all but nonexistent. Young adults often used their thumbs to get from one distant town to another.

Warren invited the man to get in.

The hitchhiker climbed onto the passenger seat and introduced himself. Warren only caught his first name: "Brian." The man smelled of booze, but he seemed friendly, if perhaps a bit wired. As Warren resumed driving toward Potsdam, his passenger did most of the talking, making a point to brag that his family was prominent in the Potsdam area and owned numerous businesses there. Warren heard him say something about being related to the Snells.

The hitchhiker also let it be known he had spent much of that day drinking, snorting coke and smoking marijuana, and he still had about 4 ounces of pot on him.

"Do you want to smoke a joint?" he asked.

Warren shook his head. "No," he said, "I don't do that anymore."

Warren was a bit amused by all of this until the hitchhiker confessed he had a violent confrontation that evening at Chateau's Restaurant and Bar in Winthrop. He got into an argument with a man who accused him of stealing three dollars left on the bar. Then, the hitchhiker said, he "shot him in the leg," adding that this "guy would be dead by 4" that morning.

As if to offer proof, he said he was packing .25-caliber and .357-magnum handguns. He asked if Warren wanted to see one.

Warren's hands tightened on the steering wheel. "No," he said.

By the time the pickup entered Potsdam's village limits around 10:30 p.m., Warren couldn't wait to get rid of his passenger. Warren pulled the vehicle to the curb at the corner of Elm and Market streets near Robinson's Market in the heart of downtown. After quick goodbyes, the hitchhiker jumped out, crossed Market Street, and disappeared into crowds of young people heading in and out of the restaurants and bars.

Thoroughly shaken, Warren decided he had to warn the cops before this man killed someone. Although there was a village police station around the corner on Raymond Street, Warren continued on Route 11, going past the Clarkson University campus and driving south for several more miles until he pulled into the driveway of a New York State Police barracks. It was just before 11 p.m.

A trooper on duty made Warren write out a statement describing the encounter with the hitchhiker. Warren wrote down as much as he could recall. Warren didn't have a last name for "Brian," but he remembered other details, such as the reference to the Snells and how the man was wearing a silver-colored watch with a silver elastic band.

At that point, state police had no report about any bar altercation or anyone being shot that night in Winthrop. And with Warren's somewhat vague description, police didn't have much to go on. However, troopers said later, they relayed Warren's statement to Potsdam police and kept an eye out for anyone matching the hitchhiker's description in hopes of questioning him.

Unfortunately, the timing couldn't be worse for locating a stranger in Potsdam. Thousands of out-of-towners had arrived that Thursday for the fall semester at Clarkson and at the State University College at Potsdam, adding another 8,000 or so students to the village's permanent population of about 10,000. With most classes not starting before Tuesday, thousands of students had descended on downtown bars and restaurants.

Police patrolled the village streets until well after midnight, but none of the officers recognized anyone matching the description of the hitchhiker.

In the hours that followed, police would wish so desperately they had.

Potsdam Police Officer John Kaplan began his shift the evening of August 28, 1986, at around 8. He zipped up his denim jacket, grabbed a two-way radio, and headed out the door of the police station. Kaplan walked briskly to Market Street, the main thoroughfare in the business district, to begin his patrol of downtown and nearby streets. By then, the sun had disappeared behind the long row of sandstone and brick buildings, and the temperature had dipped to 50 degrees Fahrenheit. A light breeze made it seem even chillier.

The 25-year-old rookie cop, who grew up in Potsdam and graduated from Potsdam State in 1982, was assigned this evening to work a "foot beat." With his youthful looks and casual clothing, he blended in easily with the college students. He could remain unnoticed until he had to respond to an incident. Backing him up were two uniformed officers circling the village in a marked patrol car.

Kaplan spent much of his time on the lookout for underage drinkers trying to slip into the bars. The previous November, the New York State Legislature raised to 21 the legal age to purchase alcohol in New York. Underage drinkers tried to get around the law by using fake IDs—or by borrowing a legitimate ID from someone 21 or older.

Strangely, while it was illegal for bars to serve an underage person, it wasn't against state law at the time for someone under 21 to drink the alcohol. The students only got in trouble for underage drinking when they used a fake ID; for that, they could face a $100 fine. It could turn into a felony charge if they altered the birthdate on a driver's license. When Kaplan saw someone using a fake or borrowed ID, he confiscated it, but he didn't always ticket the offender. He often issued a warning if the person seemed genuinely remorseful and promised not to try this again. Like many police officers in the 15-member department, Kaplan wasn't a big fan of the new drinking law. If people were old enough to vote or to serve in the military, Kaplan thought they should be old enough to legally buy a beer. But the law was the law, and Kaplan knew it was his job to enforce it within reason.

Kaplan and the other officers had a busy evening keeping order. The village police blotter for that Thursday and Friday showed numerous arrests, including ones for disorderly conduct and for holding an open container of alcohol outside of a bar. Things quieted after the bars closed at 2:30 a.m., and the streets quickly became all but deserted.

Shortly after 3, Kaplan spotted a blonde woman and a dark-haired man sitting on the stone wall in front of Trinity Episcopal Church on Maple Street. They appeared to be students resting for a moment on their way to Clarkson's main "hill" campus a quarter-mile away.

Kaplan arrived back at the police station just before 3:30 and began filling out some paperwork. Patrolmen Dale Culver and David Bartlett were there already, processing a few people who had been jailed earlier in the evening.

In a short while, Kaplan planned to call it a night.

Then at 3:41 a.m., the police emergency phone rang, and everything changed.

Dispatcher Paul E. Howard picked up the call. On the other end, a man identified himself as Kim Avadikian, a guard on the Clarkson University security staff. He said that "a girl had been raped and injured," Howard would recall, and that Avadikian needed officers and the rescue squad right away. The security guard gave the location as a service road next to Walker Arena, the building where the ice hockey teams played.

After hanging up, Howard told patrolmen Kaplan, Culver and Bartlett, and Sergeant James Lewis to stop what they were doing and to go right away to Walker Arena to investigate a possible rape and beating of a girl. Howard also alerted the Potsdam Volunteer Rescue Squad by activating pagers of the three members on call that morning for ambulance runs.

With the university campus only a half-mile from the police station, it took officers less than a minute to drive to the scene. As they pulled onto the service road, Avadikian ran up to one of the two patrol cars and pointed to the southeast corner of the arena.

"She's over there," he said.

He then quickly pointed about 50 feet away to a metal staircase that reached from the ground to the second floor of the arena. Barely visible underneath was the figure of a man.

"He is over there," Avadikian said.

The officers split up. Kaplan and Bartlett raced toward the stairs. Culver and Lewis went straight to the arena's southeast corner, where a woman was lying face-up and motionless on the grass. Her face was bruised and swollen, with blood pouring around her head and congealing in her blonde hair. It appeared, too, she had been sexually assaulted; all she was wearing was a sweater and blouse, which were pulled up above her breasts.

A second Clarkson security guard, Donald Shanty, knelt over the woman, his hand holding her head. He told the officers that he and Avadikian found her this way after checking on a loud noise outside the arena. When he noticed she was making gurgling sounds, Shanty turned her head to one side to keep her from choking on her blood.

Sergeant Lewis got on his two-way radio and contacted Howard.

The attack was "more than a simple assault," he told the dispatcher. The sergeant instructed Howard to contact Potsdam Police Chief Clinton R. Matott, Lieutenant Terry McKendree and Investigator John Perretta, and ask them to come to the scene. This assault looked to Lewis like it could turn into a homicide.

An officer placed a blanket over the victim. Two state troopers arrived, including one who brought a camera he was asked to pick up from the Potsdam police station. An officer began snapping pictures of the unconscious woman, Shanty still holding her head.

By now, officers Kaplan and Bartlett had the man in custody at the staircase. He was lying motionless on his stomach, squeezed under the bottom steps, looking like he was either unconscious or trying to hide. Kaplan reached down, grabbed the man's shirt and dragged him partially into the open to get a better look. The man appeared to be in his early- to mid-20s with a beard and straight brown hair that fell to his collar. He wore a dark jacket, a T-shirt, jeans, beige Timberland work boots, and a watch with a silver-colored wristband.

Kaplan turned the man to his side. Immediately, the man let out a moan.

"I'm hurt! My back!" he said.

"What's wrong?" Kaplan asked.

"My back! Don't move me!"

Kaplan rolled him back onto his stomach, but not before he spotted blood on the front of the man's shirt.

The officer fished a wallet out of the man's back pocket and handed it to Bartlett, who opened it and pulled out a driver's license. In the dim light, he read the name on it: Brian Milton McCarthy, of Potsdam, born September 14, 1962. He would be 24 years old in about two weeks.

"Are you Brian McCarthy?"

"Yes," McCarthy answered, then added, "How's the girl?"

"How do you know about a girl? What girl?" Kaplan asked.

"I heard her screaming. I got kicked in the back."

Kaplan pulled up McCarthy's shirt to look for bruises or other wounds, but couldn't find any.

"Where does your back hurt?"

McCarthy indicated he had pain up near his shoulders. He explained that a man in a black jacket attacked him as he was coming to the girl's aid.

The officers thought the story sounded fishy. Just to be safe, Kaplan and Bartlett placed handcuffs on McCarthy until police could sort out what occurred. Kaplan then left the stairs to check on the victim and to update Sergeant Lewis on the identity of the man.

By then, police found in the woman's possessions an Elmira College student identification card for Kathryn Ryan, age 21. Although it was dark, and the victim's face was beaten and bloodied, officers quickly matched her to the smiling blonde woman in the ID photo.

Police were puzzled, though, how she ended up at 3:30 in the morning outside Walker Arena. Was she using a nearby shortcut that Clarkson students often took when walking from downtown to the hill campus? Had she been walking alone? Was she even a student at Clarkson?

The southeast corner of Clarkson University's Walker Arena is roped off by police several hours after the attack there on August 29, 1986. Officers found Brian McCarthy under the exterior stairs closest to the corner. (Potsdam Police Department photo.)

Police also had questions about McCarthy. What was he doing outside Walker Arena at that time of the night? How did he end up under the stairs? Why did he have blood on his shirt without any visible wounds? And if someone attacked him from behind, as he stated, how did he know his assailant was a man wearing a black jacket? Officers also noted that he had the same first name and general description as the hitchhiker named "Brian" they had been seeking.

For Officer Kaplan, everything immediately pointed to McCarthy as being the only suspect in the attack. Kaplan wasn't the only one who thought that way. If authorities searched for any other suspect, police and court records would make no mention of it.

After Kaplan returned to the stairs, Bartlett decided to check on the woman. He picked up a flashlight he found on the ground next to security guard Shanty. When Bartlett turned the beam at the woman's face, he was alarmed by the extent of her injuries and labored breathing.

He radioed dispatcher Howard.

"If the (rescue) squad is already en route, tell them to step it up fast," Bartlett said.

Like the two other Potsdam Volunteer Rescue Squad members on call that morning, Brian E. Kurish was at home sleeping when his pager beeped, alerting him to a medical emergency. The 25-year-old Kurish was experienced in ambulance runs, having joined the rescue squad when he was a Potsdam State student. He remained as a member on a regular rotation after getting his degree and joining the college's housing staff.

Kurish was scheduled as the crew chief on the morning of August 29, 1986, joined by volunteers Joan Fonda and Christopher Taylor. Within minutes of being awakened, they drove themselves to squad headquarters at 21 Cottage Street, received from Howard the emergency location, and departed in an ambulance driven by Kurish.

At 3:50, Kurish pulled onto the service road next to Walker Arena. Officer Bartlett ran over, explaining they now had two people needing attention. After a quick check, Kurish decided whatever injuries McCarthy had weren't critical. Kurish leaned back into the rig and radioed for Howard to dispatch a second ambulance to the scene. McCarthy would have to wait.

Kurish raced to join Fonda and Taylor in aiding the woman. Her respiration was shallow, her pulse was weak, and her pupils were dilated and showing no response to light. Kurish knew she might not live if they didn't stabilize her quickly and get her to the emergency room at Canton-Potsdam Hospital, the village's 70-bed acute care facility.

The ambulance crew cleared her airway, placed an Ambu bag over her face, and squeezed oxygen into her lungs.

Suddenly, at 3:51, the woman "coded"—she stopped breathing, and her pulse dropped to zero. The crew immediately began CPR, with one volunteer using chest compressions to try to restart her heart and another pumping oxygen with the Ambu bag.

Kurish decided not to waste a second trying to insert a breathing tube. The crew lifted the woman into the back of the ambulance and climbed aboard. By this time, Rescue Squad Chief William Corbett had arrived at the scene and got behind the wheel. At 3:52, the ambulance sped away, its emergency lights flashing, as it raced to the hospital on the other side of the village.

At that time of the morning in Potsdam, there were no other vehicles in the way. The ambulance breezed through red lights and against the one-way traffic pattern to shave vital seconds off the trip. Patrolman Culver rode in the back, reaching out at times to keep a crew member from falling over as the vehicle took sharp turns.

At 3:54, the ambulance backed up to the emergency room entrance. The vehicle's rear doors swung open. The crew—still performing CPR and using the Ambu bag—wheeled the woman into the emergency room, where the hospital's medical personnel took over.

In a stroke of good fortune, the hospital earlier in 1986 had beefed up its ER to ensure it always had a doctor on call. When the staff heard a critically injured woman was on the way, it rounded up nurses from several floors to assist.

As the ER worked to revive the woman, Kurish and his crew remained at the hospital to fill out paperwork. Soon, the medical staff emerged with news they had restarted the woman's heart and got her breathing again, although she was still unconscious in critical condition. They were now stabilizing her for transportation to advanced care nearly 75 miles away at the House of the Good Samaritan, a hospital in Watertown, New York.

At about 4 a.m., a second ambulance arrived at Canton-Potsdam Hospital, this one with McCarthy inside. The handcuffs were off, but he was strapped to a backboard and wearing a neck brace. The crew wheeled him to the back of the ER, away from the woman still receiving care. A nurse explained that a doctor would come by to see him once one was available. Patrolman Bartlett, who escorted McCarthy in the ambulance, stood on guard nearby.

The collection of police evidence began immediately. Nurses changed the woman into a hospital gown after carefully removing her blouse and sweater, placing both into a clean paper bag, which they turned over to Officer Culver. The medical staff also administered a "rape kit," combing her pubic area for foreign hairs, using swabs to collect bodily fluids, and taking blood and saliva samples.

Police bagged the victim's other clothing found at the scene, including Levi blue jeans, bra and panties, white socks, and white shoes with laces on the front and a waffle design on the sole and heel. These items would be sent to the state police laboratory in Albany to test for foreign clothing fibers, to dust for fingerprints and to examine for other trace evidence.

Police sealed in manila envelopes several items found with the victim's clothes. They included a five-dollar bill, a one-dollar bill, a Pulsar gold watch, an opened package of Parliament brand filter cigarettes and a King Edward matchbook. Also collected was a single gold earring with a wreath design; the police inventory report did not note whether she was wearing it, or what might have happened to the other one.

At the same time, the rescue squad crew began filling out a one-page "Pre-Hospital Care Report." For personal information about the victim, all it had at that point was Kathryn Ryan's name and birthdate from the Elmira College ID card. Under this information, the crew members listed the victim's visible injuries, the treatment, the time she "coded" and their efforts to revive her. The report did not mention finding any odor of alcohol, although it noted an "unidentified bar stamp on right hand."

To avoid giving the woman's name over the police radio, Patrolman Culver called dispatcher Howard on the phone to ask him to look up Ryan's home address and phone number from the state driver's license database. Culver knew Chief Matott would want to quickly notify the victim's family and to get its consent to continue life-saving measures.

Back at Walker Arena, Officer Kaplan, Sergeant Lewis and the two state police officers roped off a large area to preserve the crime scene. Even in the dim light, officers could see a red stain splattered about seven feet up the arena wall next to where police found the young woman.

After the ambulances left, Shanty and Avadikian briefly excused themselves to go inside the arena, where Shanty took a few moments to wash the blood off his hands. The two security guards soon returned outside and gave a brief account of what they saw. Police told them to go to the Raymond Street station and wait there until an officer could take their sworn statements.

Potsdam Police Investigator John Perretta was awakened at 3:45 a.m. by the dispatcher's call that he was needed to investigate an assault at Walker

Arena. Perretta decided to head directly to Canton-Potsdam Hospital to collect evidence, take photographs and talk to witnesses.

At age 40, Perretta was among the senior members of the department, having joined it in 1970 following service with the U.S. Air Force. With his tinted glasses and collar-length haircut, and wearing a striped polo shirt this morning, Perretta cut something of a mod figure as he entered the emergency room just after 4:10 a.m.

After determining that the victim was in no condition to be interviewed, Perretta walked to the back of the ER, where he found McCarthy's 5-foot-10-inch frame stretched out on a gurney.

When he heard Perretta, McCarthy looked up.

"John, you got to help me," he said.

Perretta had known McCarthy since at least 1984 when the investigator arrested him and a 17-year-old girl for breaking into Potsdam's Arlington Inn apartments and stealing food. Long before that, McCarthy had a reputation in the police department as an unemployed drifter, drug user and petty thief often in trouble with the law.

Just a month before the attack at Walker Arena, McCarthy got into a dispute with a 35-year-old insurance agent at a Market Street bar in Potsdam. The drunken confrontation spilled into an alley, where McCarthy beat the man so severely that police initially thought the victim was a college-age student who fell from a third-floor roof. McCarthy lucked out when the insurance agent declined to press charges.

When he saw Perretta, McCarthy began to repeat his story about how someone attacked him as he was trying to help a girl outside Walker Arena.

"Just a minute," Perretta said, pulling out a laminated card printed with the Miranda Warning, which he always read to suspects before questioning.

"You have the right to remain silent and to refuse to answer any questions," he began. "Anything you do say may—"

McCarthy interrupted, "Be used against you in a court of law," calling up the words from memory.

Perretta continued, "As we discuss this matter, you have the right to stop answering my questions at any time you desire."

McCarthy interrupted again.

"I know 'em," McCarthy said impatiently, referring to his legal rights.

Perretta went ahead anyway and finished reading from the card, then asked McCarthy if he understood his rights.

Perhaps finally sinking in that police considered him a suspect, not a victim, McCarthy had one response: "This is a lot of bullshit."

Perretta put away the card. If McCarthy wasn't going to waive his rights, Perretta wasn't going to waste time talking to him. The investigator noted to himself that McCarthy, although angry and agitated, didn't show signs of being intoxicated.

Perretta took out a camera and proceeded to take several shots of McCarthy. Perretta got several closeups of McCarthy's blood-spattered boots and a knuckle on his right hand that appeared to be discolored.

One photo caught McCarthy with his left eye open and his left arm resting near his face, staring into the camera while he carefully extended his middle finger.

Police Chief Clinton Matott walked into the hospital at about 4:20 a.m. and immediately took charge of the investigation. Matott had been with the Potsdam Police Department for almost his entire working life. He joined the department in 1957 and worked his way up in the ranks until 1980 when he was appointed chief. At 54 years old, his full head of white hair and a penchant for three-piece suits added to his look of authority.

Those who worked for Matott marveled at the professionalism and discipline he brought to the small department. He made it a priority to use the latest technology and modern investigative techniques. As Perretta would remember years later, Matott often preached that "you win more cases by being smart than you do by being strong."

After being briefed by officers, Matott turned his attention to notifying the victim's family. By then, dispatcher Howard had located a telephone number and a home address for Kathryn Ryan's mother in Cazenovia, New York, a village about 20 miles east of Syracuse. Shortly before 5 a.m., Matott and a hospital doctor found an empty office to place the call.

A few minutes later, Matott stormed out with the ID in hand and headed to the injured woman's bedside. He returned to the lobby with an announcement.

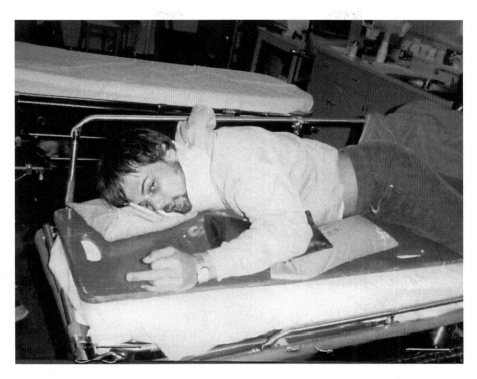

Brian McCarthy raises a middle finger in the direction of Potsdam police Investigator John Perretta inside the emergency room at Canton-Potsdam Hospital on the morning of August 29, 1986. (Potsdam Police Department photo.)

"This can't be Kathryn Ryan," Matott said quietly. "We just spoke to her mother, and she spoke to her daughter, and she's in California. There's no way she could be in Potsdam."

Matott had a new lead, though. Ryan's mother said her daughter's 19-year-old cousin, Katy Hawelka, was a student at Clarkson. She said the two looked a lot alike. If true the victim was Katy, Matott speculated she had borrowed her older cousin's ID to gain entry into the bars.

Matott got back on the phone and informed Howard the victim had a "phony ID." The chief had a new name for the dispatcher to look up. In minutes, Howard passed on to Matott an address and telephone number for Katherine Mary Hawelka, born June 18, 1967, registered with an address in Syracuse. She was described in the Department of Motor Vehicles records as 5-foot-6 with blue eyes and blonde hair.

Before he made another wrong call to next of kin, Matott told Howard to find someone from Clarkson University to confirm that Katherine Hawelka was a student there. The chief also wanted her address in Potsdam so an officer could check if she was missing.

As Howard began this assignment, he logged a message from the Potsdam Volunteer Rescue Squad: At 5:15 a.m., an ambulance had begun transporting the woman to Watertown.

Howard picked up a Clarkson staff directory. As he thumbed through, looking for an official he could call, the phone rang. It was Seth Chichester, director of the physical plant at Clarkson. Chichester had heard about the assault and was calling for information.

Howard asked Chichester to suggest the name of a university official who could confirm if Katherine Hawelka was a student. Chichester recommended calling Donna Brockway, an administrative secretary in the registrar's office. When Howard reached Brockway, she gave him another name: Nathan Snell, the assistant registrar.

Over the phone, Snell agreed to come down to the police station, meet with Chief Matott and escort him to the campus to check the registration records. It is unclear from police records if Howard told Snell the name of the suspect—or if police were aware that Snell was the brother of Brian McCarthy's mother, Florence. Even for a small community like Potsdam, it was an eerie coincidence that police had turned to an uncle of the suspect to help identify the unrelated victim.

At about 5:45 a.m., Matott and Snell arrived on the Clarkson campus. Snell quickly pulled up records confirming Katherine Hawelka was a sophomore in the university's School of Management. Her student application from 1984 gave a phone number for her home in Syracuse, where she lived with her mother, Terry Connelly, a sales representative for Pitney Bowes. The application listed her father, Joseph E. Hawelka, as a dentist in Oneida, New York. Her parents, records also showed, were divorced.

Snell found the address of campus housing where Katy was staying. Matott radioed Howard to send an officer to Woodstock Village, Apartment 5C16. Officer Kaplan, still on duty at Walker Arena, received the assignment. He reported back in a short while to say Katy wasn't there. She had not returned since leaving about 8 the previous evening to go downtown.

Now confident police had the correct identification, Matott picked up the phone shortly before 6 a.m. and, for the second time that morning, got ready to notify a parent that her child was the victim of a violent attack.

A day earlier, Terry Connelly had traveled north to Potsdam to drop off Katy for her second year at Clarkson. Terry wasn't surprised to see Katy all smiles as she packed her belongings into the back of her mother's car. Terry described her second-oldest daughter— a trim and stylish teen with blonde hair that softly curled onto her shoulders—as "never-have-a-bad-day-Kate." (Although born Katherine, the teen preferred Katy or Kate, but never Kathy.)

Shortly before the 140-mile trip, Katy's doctor gave her permission to re-move a protective walking boot. She began wearing it that summer after injuring her right foot while stepping off a curb near Syracuse University. The foot was still tender, and Katy limped a bit as she came out of the fam-ily's two-story Colonial with boxes of clothes, towels, sheets, family photos, and other belongings destined for her apartment at Clarkson.

For the ride to Potsdam, Terry agreed to let Katy drive the family's dark gray 1984 Chrysler New Yorker. Terry, 43, sat in the passenger seat, while Katy's younger sister Carey, 17, squeezed into the back with all the bags and boxes.

It was a delightful road trip, except that Katy, in her eagerness to get to Potsdam, got stopped by a state trooper on Interstate 81, just south of Wa-tertown, and was issued a ticket for speeding. As they resumed the journey, Terry made a mental note to remind Katy not to forget to pay the fine.

Just past Watertown, the trio left the interstate and continued north on Route 11, a two-lane highway with pastoral views of rolling hills, dairy farms, and vast fields dotted with bales of hay and small herds of Holsteins. Every few miles, Katy slowed for a hamlet or village, where numerous buildings with peeling paint hugged the roadway.

In the afternoon, the trio crossed a bridge over railroad tracks and entered the village of Potsdam along Maple Street. Clarkson University's main cam-pus immediately loomed to their right, its brick and red sandstone buildings rising above carefully manicured lawns. A couple of turns more, and they

In this photo from summer 1986, Katy Hawelka shows off a walking boot she wore after injuring her right foot. (Hawelka family photo.)

arrived at Katy's assigned residence at Woodstock Village, a complex of 10 apartment buildings near the rear of the campus.

After dropping off Katy's belongings, the three got back into Terry's car and headed downtown to the Super Duper supermarket to pick up groceries for the apartment. As they rode through the village, with its clean streets and quaint boutiques, Terry was happy her daughter chose to go to college in this oasis away from big-city crime and congestion. Potsdam looked like the safest place in the world.

Terry and Carey hugged Katy goodbye outside her apartment, and Katy said she was already looking forward to coming home to Syracuse for the Thanksgiving break.

Back in Syracuse that evening after the 280-mile roundtrip, Terry went to bed exhausted.

It was still a half-hour before sunrise on Friday, August 29, 1986, when the phone extension rang in Terry's second-floor bedroom. As she reached to pick up the line, Terry wondered who possibly could be calling so early. In their bedrooms down the hall, the ringing awakened Carey and her brother Joe Hawelka Jr., 16. He lived during the school year with his father in Verona Beach, New York, but the boy decided to spend this summer with his mother, Carey and Katy in Syracuse. Their oldest sister, 21-year-old Betsy, worked in Florida.

At first, Carey and Joe Jr. only heard the muffled sound of their mother talking to someone. Then her voice got louder, quickly shifting in tone. It sounded like she kept asking the caller to repeat what he was saying.

Then they heard her scream.

The two teens leaped from their beds and raced to their mother's bedroom, where they stood quietly outside the doorway until she finally hung up the phone.

Terry was crying so hard she could barely get out the words.

"Something's happened to Katy," she said. "Your sister was attacked."

"Who was that?" Joe Jr. asked.

"A police officer." She couldn't remember his name.

"What did he say?"

He said that Katy was going to the hospital in Watertown because someone attacked her on the Clarkson campus. He also said that the police had arrested someone. Terry couldn't remember anything more, except she needed to get to House of the Good Samaritan.

Terry picked up the phone and called Joe Sr. at his home, telling him everything she could remember. He assured her that he and his wife, Donna, would come right away to Syracuse, and the three of them would drive together to the hospital. The children could come up later.

Terry hung up the phone and dialed neighbor and close friend Isabel McConnell, a retired schoolteacher, who promised to check in on Carey and Joe Jr. Terry must have sounded like a nervous wreck because McConnell came over right away with a Valium.

"Everything is going to be all right," McConnell assured her.

Joe Sr. and Donna arrived at Terry's house at about 7:30 a.m. Katy's father didn't say a lot, but Terry got the impression he was holding back something. Armed with his medical training, she suspected later, Joe Sr.

probably called a doctor at Canton-Potsdam Hospital and learned Katy's injuries were much worse than what the police told her.

Before leaving for Watertown, Joe Sr. telephoned Betsy in Florida, asking her to take the next available flight to Syracuse.

"Your sister has been in an accident," he said. "You need to come home."

Betsy pressed for details, but all he would say was that Katy's injuries were "serious."

Carey and Joe Jr. sat on the stairs nearby as their father placed other phone calls, including one to his dental office, which he told to cancel his appointments.

"Katy has been in a serious accident and is on life support and possibly in a coma," they heard Joe Sr. say.

Carey and Joe Jr. looked at each other with expressions of disbelief. Life support? Coma? This was the first they heard just how critically Katy was injured.

After their father hung up the phone, the two teens left the stairs and began asking him questions. Realizing they overheard a conversation he intended to be private, he handed Carey the keys to his car, and told her and her brother to fill up the vehicle with gasoline.

After they left, Joe Sr. telephoned his brother and sister-in-law, Bill and Cathy Hawelka, in Auburn, New York, and Terry's brother, Don Ryan, and his wife, Carol, in Oneida, to let them know Katy was in the hospital.

Once off the phone, Joe Sr. suggested that Terry ask her parents, Frank and Alice Ryan, to join them at the hospital. Terry thought that was a bad idea. She worried the stress would be too hard on her parents, especially her father, who was especially close to Katy.

Shortly after 8 a.m., with Joe Sr. behind the wheel of his dark brown Cadillac Coupe De Ville, the vehicle sped north on Interstate 81 toward Watertown. In the back seat, Terry silently prayed while taking comfort in McConnell's assurances that Katy was going to be okay. Terry could imagine Katy, all banged up and bandaged, already smiling and joking with doctors and nurses.

Katy had everything going for her. She was young, healthy, smart and resilient. Best of all, Terry thought, her daughter was one tough cookie. If anyone could overcome this, it was Katy.

Chapter 2

Growing Up Hawelka

FIVE days before Christmas 1975, Joe Hawelka Sr. and his second wife, Janice, carefully bundled up Betsy, 10, Katy, 8, Carey, 6, and Joe Jr., 5, at their home east of Syracuse in Oneida County. They squeezed everyone into a red-and-tan Dodge Charger for the 60-mile drive to a holiday celebration with Grandma Helen Hawelka in Auburn. One reason Betsy would remember the day is that she got to wear her new white coat with fake fur on cuffs and collar.

The Saturday morning newspaper warned that several inches of snow were possible that day, with winds of up to 20 miles per hour and temperatures falling well below freezing. The bad weather held off, however, as 36-year-old Joe Sr. drove to Auburn, where the family enjoyed a great feast and delighted in swapping early presents.

Darkness had fallen by the time they began the long drive home, but conditions were still decent until shortly after Joe Sr. turned onto the New York State Thruway and hit a blinding storm dumping about a foot of snow. Unknown to them, Hancock International Airport in Syracuse had canceled flights, and police were advising people to stay home.

For close to two hours, it was slow, touch-and-go driving as the children's father battled to keep the vehicle from sliding off the road or into another car.

It was relief all around when Joe Sr. reached the driveway behind his two-story home in Sylvan Beach, a village along the southeast corner of Oneida Lake, just adjacent to the hamlet of Verona Beach. The beautiful A-frame house, a former camp insulated for year-round living, sported a log exterior, a cobblestone fireplace, and bay windows overlooking the lake.

Joe Sr. and the children's stepmother immediately herded the young-sters off to their bedrooms on the second floor. After placing presents from Grandma Hawelka under the freshly cut Christmas tree in the living room, Joe Sr. headed outside with a shovel to clear the driveway of snow before going to bed.

Several hours later, at about 4:20 a.m., a pungent odor and a soft crackle woke up Joe Sr., who jumped out of bed, raced to the staircase, and peered over the railing. He was stunned to see flames shooting up from the Christ-mas tree and from the curtains over the bay windows. With choking smoke filling the first floor, he decided there was no way to escape down the stairs safely.

Joe Sr. ran back to his bedroom and alerted Janice, and together they rounded up the children, who were clad only in their pajamas. With every-one in the parents' bedroom, Joe Sr. picked up the phone. Fortunately, the connection still worked. Joe dialed the Sylvan Beach-Verona Beach Volun-teer Fire Department, where the dispatcher assured him trucks would be there soon.

Smoke began to billow up into the second floor, and the children started yelling that they could hear the fire growing louder. "I knew the Christmas tree was on fire," Betsy would remember. "The pine was popping because it was so engulfed in flames."

It was now clear they didn't have time to wait for the firefighters. Joe Sr. quieted the children and told them that he had a plan: They were to climb onto a second-floor ledge behind the rear window, then jump into the driveway. He assured them they would be okay because he would jump first and then catch them as they followed one by one.

While Janice gave her husband a side-glance that said she didn't know if she could make a 30-foot leap, Katy and the other children lined up as he instructed. If their father promised to keep them safe, they had no doubt that's what he would do.

Joe Sr. was born on September 19, 1939, in Syracuse but grew up in Auburn, where he was an honors student, class president, and a star in basketball and baseball at Holy Family High School. He and his younger brother, Bill, helped their father, also named Joseph, to operate the family's auto parts store on Dill Street. Along with their mother, the former Helen Mosher, they lived at 105 Swift Street on Auburn's south side.

The Hawelkas traced their roots to some of the earliest settlers in Auburn, a city whose famous former residents included Abraham Lincoln's secretary of state, William H. Seward, and abolitionist Harriet Tubman. In 1850, Frank Hawelka emigrated to Auburn from Germany, eventually serving as a soldier with Lincoln's Army during the Civil War. Another ancestor, Margaret Sheehan Hawelka, was a descendent of John O'Connor, who hosted the city's first Catholic Mass, according to her 1944 obituary.

Auburn also holds a notable place in the history of America's penal system. Located in the middle of the city behind massive concrete walls is Auburn Correctional Facility, New York's oldest operating state prison and the site in 1890 of the world's first execution by the electric chair.

After graduating from high school in 1957, Joe enrolled at Niagara University near Buffalo, New York, where his excellent grades quickly won him a spot on the school's dean's list. He later was inducted into the Alpha Zeta chapter of Delta Epsilon, a national honor society for Catholic colleges and universities.

In September 1959, he was away at the university when he learned his 56-year-old father and 16-year-old brother were involved in a traffic altercation just outside of Auburn. The elder Hawelka was driving on Bluefield Road in the town of Aurelius with Bill and two 14-year-old boys when a car pulled in front and forced them to stop. Three men jumped from the other vehicle and attacked Joe's father and the boys, beating the elder Hawelka so severely that he suffered a partial loss of hearing in one ear. Then the three men fled.

The attackers might have gotten away except that another driver took down their license plate number, and police arrested all three. Two pleaded guilty and received jail time. The third, Francis M. Golembeski, fought the charge of third-degree assault.

On October 20, 1959, about 50 people crowded into the second floor of the East Aurelius firehouse for the three-and-a-half-hour trial, according to the *Auburn Citizen-Advertiser*. Cayuga County Assistant District Attorney Charles W. Avery told the jury of four men and two women that the assault was a "vicious, unprovoked beating." Avery wondered if such random violence signaled that "it had gotten to the point in Cayuga County and in your town where a man has to carry a gun in his car" to defend himself.

It took the jury 15 minutes to find the defendant guilty. Golembeski was sentenced to 18 months in the penitentiary and ordered to pay a $750 fine.

Five months later, on March 17, 1960, the elder Hawelka was working in his auto parts store shortly before 9 a.m. when he suddenly fell ill and was taken by ambulance to Auburn Memorial Hospital, where he passed away. His obituary didn't list a cause of death or indicate if his passing was related to the attack the previous year.

After her husband's burial at St. Joseph's Cemetery just outside of Auburn, Helen Hawelka took over Auburn Unit Parts, which she ran with Bill Hawelka's help while Joe continued his studies at Niagara University. After graduation, Joe enrolled at the School of Dentistry at the University of Buffalo, with plans to eventually return to Auburn to set up a dental practice.

In 1963, as he was attending dental school, Joe became engaged to an Auburn woman working for Prudential Insurance. Announcements in the newspapers set a wedding date for that July 8. The wedding never happened.

Joe broke off the engagement after meeting a 19-year-old student attending Rosary Hill College, then a women's school near Buffalo. Her name was Theresa "Terry" Ann Ryan.

Terry was born July 22, 1943, in Oneida, New York, where she and her brother, Don, grew up in a well-to-do Irish-Catholic family that lived on Main Street. Their father, Frank Ryan, operated the A.F. Ryan & Sons Dodge and Plymouth dealership in Oneida. Their mother, the former Alice Cross, who studied at St. Joseph's College of Nursing in Syracuse, was employed for a while as a stenographer for a retail supplier. She also did volunteer work for St. Patrick's Church, the Catholic Daughters of America, and the St. Patrick's School Mothers Club.

Frank Ryan doted on his baby daughter, calling her "Miss Muffin." The nickname, or variations of it, would stick. Even into her adulthood, close friends and family affectionately addressed Terry as "Muffy" or "Muff."

At Oneida High, Terry was a majorette, played basketball and volleyball, joined the French Club, Dramatic Club and Science Club, and helped to plan the junior prom. An inscription with her yearbook photo quoted Shakespeare: "As merry as the day is long."

In early 1963, Terry found herself prepared to marry a young man studying law at Syracuse University. But just as Joe's engagement fell victim to his sudden romance with Terry, so did her wedding plans with the law student.

On June 6, 1964, Joe Hawelka and Terry Ryan were married at St. Patrick's Church in Oneida, with the bride wearing a "sheath gown of silk organza decorated with re-embroidered Alencon lace and lace beading," and carrying white roses and carnations with ivy, according to the Auburn newspaper. An accompanying photo showed Terry peering into the camera with a soft smile and expressive eyes, a spitting image of teenage Katy in photos two decades later.

Joe graduated that spring with his Doctor of Dental Surgery degree, and the newlyweds moved to Illinois, where he began a dental internship at the University of Chicago.

Before long, Joe gave up his goal of moving back to Auburn. After talking about it with others, he became convinced there were more opportunities to repair teeth and fill cavities in his wife's hometown. When he finished the internship in Chicago, Joe and Terry moved to Oneida.

While Joe set up his dental practice there and threw himself into community volunteer work and weekend golf outings, Terry's life was taken over by diapers and late-night feedings. She gave birth to Betsy in March 1965, followed by Katy in June 1967, Carey in June 1968, and Joe Jr. in July 1970. By the early 1970s, Terry had grown weary of long stretches when she felt like a single mother because of Joe Sr.'s absences. She confided in friends that it was no accident that she gave birth to each of her three youngest children about nine months after golf seasons ended.

When Joe Sr. and Terry divorced in 1972, though, it was an amicable split. The four children would live in Oneida with their mother, although their father had generous visitation rights. Each weekend he usually had at least two children with him, and he sometimes had all four. The children seemed to adjust well to the divorce, perhaps because they were so young at the time, and their parents handled the split without obvious strife.

In 1974, after Joe Sr. married the former Janice Bonanza, the newlyweds moved into the converted camp at Sylvan Beach, where the children would have memories of enjoying swimming, boating, fishing, touch football and other games at the lake.

In these lazy summer days, if you saw one Hawelka child, you also saw two or three others nearby. One time, Joe Jr. stepped into deep water and struggled to keep his head above the waves. Suddenly, he felt the arms of Katy and Carey grabbing him from behind and pulling him up to safety. Betsy, as the oldest, was more babysitter than a playmate to her siblings. But all of the Hawelka children looked out for each other at home, in their neighborhood, and while attending Catholic elementary school. Joe Jr. would have memories of sitting on the handlebars of Katy's bicycle as they rode to Grandma Ryan's house, his sister teaching him how to spell H-A-W-E-L-K-A so he would know it before starting kindergarten.

One Christmas, Carey found herself with almost no presents under the tree. As the children began opening the gifts, Katy noticed Carey was being short-changed. So, she handed some of her gifts to her younger sister until Terry realized the mistake and retrieved Carey's presents that Santa had hidden too well in the closet.

On December 21, 1975, the house fire in Sylvan Beach tested, like nothing before, how much the Hawelkas had come to count on each other. As the smoke seeped into the second floor, Katy and Carey noticed their brother was missing.

"Joey, where are you?" they yelled.

"I'm here," he said, poking his head out from under the bed in the rear bedroom. When they pulled him out, the 5-year-old explained he was staying low to avoid the smoke, just like the man in a television commercial instructed children to do.

Joe Sr. opened the bedroom window and stepped onto the roof over the house's rear entrance. A chill of about 10 degrees Fahrenheit bit into his face as he peered down at the bare driveway far below and wished he hadn't shoveled away a cushion of snow a few hours earlier.

He eased himself to the edge of the porch roof and hung off for a second before dropping awkwardly. He felt a sharp pain in his left leg, and he knew immediately he had broken something.

Smoke was growing thicker and the flames were getting closer. Joe Sr. yelled up to Janice to lower each child one-by-one as far as she could, then drop them into his arms. The children agreed among themselves to line up by age, with Joe Jr. going first.

Janice lay on her stomach and dangled her stepson as low as she could until she dropped him to her husband below. She did this next with Carey, Katy and Betsy. The children were barefoot and cold, but none was injured.

It was now Janice's turn. For a minute, she just lay there, paralyzed by fear. Joe Sr. begged her to jump, promising he would catch her. Finally, with the flames at her back, she eased herself off the ledge. As she dropped into her husband's arms, she slightly injured her back. Joe Sr. felt another sharp pain, this time in his right foot.

He told the children to try to stay warm in the car while Janice ran to neighbors, knocking on doors for help. But with most beach homes vacant for winter, no one answered. After what seemed like an excruciatingly long time, fire trucks arrived. By then, flames engulfed the house. The Hawelka family warmed themselves in the cabs of the fire trucks while watching the volunteers battle the blaze.

Joe Sr. was in excruciating pain, he could barely walk, Janice was hurt, too, and their beautiful home was in ruins. But as he pulled Carey onto his lap in the fire truck, all he felt was immense happiness because everyone was alive.

Carey looked up and notified her father she had to pee.

Joe Sr. told her, "It's all right. Just go." And as she relieved herself, soaking their pajamas, he sat in the fire truck and smiled.

It took about 40 volunteers until about 6 a.m. to bring the fire under control. The only thing left standing was the stone fireplace and a section of the back wall. All the contents were gone, including Grandma Hawelka's presents and Betsy's beautiful white coat with its fake fur.

Terry was awakened around 5 a.m. by a telephone call asking her to pick up her children at the fire station. As she drove to Sylvan Beach, she passed an ambulance with her ex-husband going the other way to the hospital.

At the station, the children's pajamas reeked of smoke, but they otherwise seemed okay. Terry drove them home, gave them baths, and sent them back to bed. Only then did she notice she was operating on adrenaline. When that began to wear off, she realized how close she came to losing every one of her children that morning, and she wept at the thought.

The next day, the front page in *The Daily Press* in Utica carried the headline "Family Leaps 30 Feet to Safety from Burning Home." The news article noted how Joe Sr. had "smashed his right foot and broke his left leg but still managed to catch his wife and four children who leaped after him early Sunday."

In an interview from his bed at Oneida City Hospital, he saved the praise for the youngsters.

"The children were great," he said. "They remembered what they saw in those (fire-emergency) ads on television and stayed on the floor and did what the adults told them to do."

Joe Sr. spent several weeks in the hospital. When the children came to visit, he gave each a small amount of cash to buy a replacement Christmas present. Katy decided on a small toboggan because she wanted something all of the children could enjoy together.

The fire soon was largely forgotten as the children returned to school and to various youth activities. Katy joined the Brownies, and she and Carey took dance lessons, while Betsy became a cheerleader for the Oneida Pop Warner football team. In 1976, the family made news again when *The Post-Standard* reported that Betsy and other neighborhood children held a "carnival for Debbie" at Terry's Oneida home, raising $14 to help a 12-year-old local girl with cerebral palsy travel to Florida for an operation.

Katy and her siblings continued to live in Oneida until 1977 when Terry married insurance agent Martin M. Connelly, and they moved with the children into a home in the historic Sedgwick neighborhood in northeast Syracuse.

In 1980, after divorcing Janice, Joe Sr. married the former Donna Bielby, and they moved to Verona Beach, where Joe Jr. went to live with his father and to attend school.

Terry found that the children seemed to quickly adapt to new homes, new stepparents, and new schools, throwing themselves into community activities, getting good grades and staying out of trouble. One day, though, a teacher at Lincoln Junior High in Syracuse called Terry, asking for a meeting to discuss something Katy had done. All that the teacher would say over the phone is that the girl had been "insubordinate."

Chapter 3

Positively Katy

INSUBORDINATE? That didn't sound at all her daughter. However, Terry Connelly was eager to meet the teacher who made that claim about Katy and to clear up the matter, as long as the principal also attended.

When they got together, the teacher explained that she thought Katy didn't like her. Several times in class, the 12-year-old pointed to some mistake the teacher made. The final straw occurred when Katy raised her hand to correct something the teacher wrote on the blackboard.

"Was she right?" Terry asked.

"Yes," the teacher said. "But I think she did it to embarrass me."

Terry agreed Katy should try to be sensitive in correcting others. But the way Terry saw it, the girl wasn't the one at fault here.

"If you're teaching them something that isn't correct, I think Kate has a point," Terry said.

The principal seemed to agree, and that was the end of that. Terry received no more calls from the teacher or bad reports about Katy. And Terry felt vindicated in learning that, when Katy graduated from eighth grade, she was among several students at Lincoln Junior High who were honored with its Good Citizenship Award for class effort and participation, positive attitude, and favorable rapport with others.

Jim Damiano, a neighbor who attended Lincoln Junior High in the eighth grade, was among those who had only positive thoughts about Katy. His youthful eye quickly noticed this cute, blonde classmate with a quick smile and lots of friends.

When someone told him, "Katy likes you," he found it hard to believe until he got up the courage to say "hi," and she agreed to be his girlfriend. In

Katy Hawelka, from elementary school to 12th grade. (Hawelka family photos.)

1980, rock group REO Speedwagon had a hit with "Keep on Loving You," and Katy would often playfully sing it to Damiano, inserting "Jim" for the word "you" in the lyrics.

"She was cute and super sweet, and she was super smart," said Damiano, whose relationship with Katy evolved by high school into a lasting platonic friendship.

Katy was still in junior high when a neighborhood parent, Mary Ellen Andrews, needed a babysitter. Terry suggested Katy, but Andrews wasn't sure she wanted to leave her newborn girl in the care of a 12-year-old.

"Mary Ellen," Terry said, "I'm five houses down. So, if Katy needs anything, I'll be around."

Andrews and her husband, Russell, decided to let Katy babysit one evening while they went out. When they returned, the baby was freshly changed and asleep, and Katy had taken it upon herself to fold the family's laundry and do other household chores.

After that, until Katy left for college, she regularly babysat for the Andrews' daughter and a son born later. The children adored Katy, and the parents treated her like a member of their family, inviting the teenager to join them on vacations and other outings.

At Syracuse's Henninger High School, Katy stood out as an honors student, took advanced courses, and always got good grades. In her senior year, she packed her schedule with business-related classes, including advanced accounting, math 13-calculus, business English, economics, and business law. She was a member of the Student Council for three years and president of her class in her junior year. She was a cheerleader, treasurer of

Kappa Epsilon Phi sorority, and a member of pep club, concert band and yearbook staff. She also attended the Henninger Faith Center, which was run by the Catholic Church and provided religious and educational services to students.

A close friend and neighbor, Lisa Campolo, who was a year below Katy in school, loved hanging out with her because she was this force of positivity.

"Oh, that's gorgeous," Katy inevitably would say when Campolo dressed in a new outfit. "That looks so good on you."

Katy was so genuinely nice that even her mother found it hard to refuse when her second-oldest daughter asked to do something.

Martha Gualtieri, another of Katy's childhood friends, recalled one time when Katy asked if Gualtieri and her twin sister, Amy, could do a sleepover. Terry didn't think that was a good idea, noting Carey had friends staying for the night.

"We already have eight kids in the house tonight. We don't need anymore," Terry said.

Katy insisted they could squeeze in two more. Terry then pointed out they didn't have enough breakfast for everyone. "We don't need to eat breakfast," Katy said.

Terry finally caved, and the Gualtieri twins slept over.

"Terry was tough, but she could be a pushover when Katy wanted things like that," Martha Gualtieri said with a laugh.

In high school, Katy attended dances and parties, had a boyfriend her senior year, and enjoyed a typical teen social life, including the little traumas that most youngsters go through during the awkward transition toward adulthood.

One icy Saturday in March, Katy arrived with the Henninger band in downtown Syracuse to play the clarinet at the St. Patrick's Parade. Katy suddenly realized she forgot to bring gloves, and there was no time to go back and get some. The band instructor kindly loaned her a nice leather pair with fur linings.

"You got to be careful," Terry told her daughter as she marched off. "You can't lose these gloves."

When the parade ended, Katy approached her mother with a forlorn expression. The girl had misplaced the gloves.

FROM LEFT, high school friends Lisa Campolo, Amy Gualtieri, Martha Gualtieri and
Katy Hawelka visit a Florida beach in 1983. (Martha Gualtieri McLain photo.)

"Oh, Kate! Really?"

"Mom, I don't know what happened to them."

Terry went out that day and bought a replacement pair for the instructor.

At age 16, Katy found a job at Peter's Groceries supermarket in the Shop
City strip mall, which was within walking distance of her home. The shopping center, which also had a McDonald's and a department store, became
a popular hangout for Katy and her friends from Syracuse's northeast side.

Katy loved to shop. In high school, she favored a "preppy" look that was
popular in the early 1980s, often wearing an oxford shirt with a sweater or a
polo shirt with the Lacoste crocodile on the front. Katy also had a fondness
for Stan Smith-style white leather shoes.

Once, Katy and a friend boarded a municipal bus to downtown Syracuse
to buy school clothes. Katy was excited because it was her first time taking
the bus without a parent along to supervise.

When Katy returned home, Terry asked, "Oh, Kate, what did you get?"

Katy looked down at her empty arms.

"Oh, where's my stuff?" the girl asked.

"I don't know where your stuff is."

"I must have left it on the bus."

Terry joked that she hoped there was "somebody wonderful wearing new underwear riding around Syracuse somewhere."

After sharing this story years later, Terry laughed and worried she was "making Katy sound like such a ditz. She wasn't. She was a smart kid."

In the early 1980s, being the oldest Hawelka child, Betsy had her own circle of friends, and she would recall that she considered herself "too cool" as a teen to hang out with her siblings. On the other hand, Katy and Carey thoroughly enjoyed each other's company. More than sisters, they were also best friends, sharing advice and confidences about everything from personal fashion to romance. When a boy asked Carey to attend Katy's junior prom with him, Katy not only was excited for her sister but insisted they make it a double-date.

In fact, until she left for college, Katy hardly went anywhere without inviting Carey to come along.

"My friends couldn't believe that my sister and I were close, and that she drove me to school every day," Carey said. "Many of them had older sisters who wouldn't even acknowledge them in the lunchroom hallway."

In the summer of 1983, just before the start of Katy's junior year, the Gualtieri twins, their 19-year-old sister, Joan, and their mother moved to Clearwater, Florida. Katy presented each twin with a small plaque she cut out of wood in the shape of a letter—a large "A" for Amy and an "M" for Martha—on which Katy penned personal messages, including "Friends Forever."

Early that October, Katy heard the awful news that Joan Gualtieri was killed in an accident on her way home from her shift as a waitress at the Brown Derby restaurant in Clearwater. A motorcycle she was riding was struck from behind by a 1978 Dodge driven by a 26-year-old accountant, who was later found to be legally intoxicated.

Shaken by the death, Katy joined the Henninger chapter of Students Against Drunk Driving and, when she got her driver's license, she designated herself as an organ donor. In the 1985 Henninger yearbook, in a section for Senior Comments, Katy printed the twins' initials and quoted lyrics from the Genesis song "Squonk" with a message of self-empowerment —that people don't stand a chance if they don't "stand up."

While against drunken driving, Katy was like many underage students in the early 1980s who sneaked a beer now and then when parents weren't around. The legal drinking age in New York state had been 18 until lawmakers raised it to 19 in 1982, but it wasn't until it increased to 21 in fall 1985 that police began to widely enforce it.

"We used to have fake IDs and go up to (bars near) Syracuse University," high school friend Campolo said. "It was just the thing we did, and we thought it was okay because everybody our age was doing it. We weren't bad kids. It was the way it was. It was a different time. If you were caught, it wasn't like today where you'd lose everything."

As her senior year began, Katy set her sights on an undergraduate degree in business or finance, possibly at Syracuse University, but her heart was set on attending Clarkson University in Potsdam. After Clarkson, she hoped to earn a master's in business administration, perhaps at the acclaimed Wharton School at the University of Pennsylvania.

"She had some pretty good goals," Terry said. "She just wanted to be in business and working with numbers, that kind of thing. She knew she wanted a good-paying job as soon as she possibly could out of school."

On December 10, 1984, in careful penmanship, Katy filled out a three-page application for admission to Clarkson's freshman class in fall 1985, setting herself on a path toward what a university official would later call the "darkest day" in the school's history. A bold statement considering that Clarkson was founded out of another fatal tragedy more than 90 years earlier.

Chapter 4

Walker

O N the morning of August 14, 1894, Potsdam businessman Thomas S. Clarkson III and four of his employees began maneuvering into place a 4,400-pound steam pump at a sandstone quarry he owned about three miles south of the village. It was a dangerous task. But the 57-year-old Clarkson, despite being born into a family with vast wealth, was a hands-on guy raised by his father to learn a trade and embrace physical labor.

For years, Clarkson and his brother, Levinus, operated a family farm in the village. Later, they ran a series of local quarries where workers mined Potsdam sandstone, a handsome but durable pink-red rock used for the construction of many buildings in the United States and Canada.

On that Tuesday in 1894, Thomas Clarkson and the quarry employees nearly had the steam pump in position when it began tipping toward him. He tried to step out of the way but tripped and fell, and the massive pump pinned him to the ground. After much effort, the workers raised the pump high enough for Clarkson to crawl from underneath.

The weight of the pump broke Clarkson's right thighbone and crushed the leg below it. The accident also left deep bruises on his left leg and right hip. The workers carefully lifted him onto a bed in a spring wagon and transported him to his Potsdam homestead, where Clarkson, who was single, lived with his three sisters.

Two physicians soon arrived to treat his injuries.

"They dressed his wounds and left him as comfortable as could be expected, though he slept but little the first night," the *St. Lawrence Herald* reported, noting Clarkson declined painkillers. "He has since rested well, and his legs swell but little. All are hopeful, but at best the injuries are very serious and painful, and recovery will necessarily be slow."

Despite the optimistic early reports, his condition quickly worsened, and Clarkson fell into a coma and died at 4:30 a.m. Sunday, August 19, 1894. He was interred in the Clarkson family vault in Bayside Cemetery in Potsdam.

Not long afterward, sisters Lavinia, Frederica and Annie Clarkson decided that establishing a technical school in Potsdam would be a proper memorial for their brother, as he had been a vocal proponent of advanced education.

The sisters allocated $8,000 to buy land along Main Street to construct what initially would be known as the Thomas S. Clarkson Memorial School of Technology, soon renamed the Thomas S. Clarkson Memorial College of Technology. The school opened in 1896 with undergraduate degrees in electrical and mechanical engineering for the men and domestic science for the women. The school later added chemical and civil engineering, but it dropped domestic science from the curriculum after it stopped admitting women in 1907. It would not accept female undergraduates again until 1964.

As the college grew, so did its men's intercollegiate hockey program. In 1938, Clarkson constructed its first indoor ice arena on land that later expanded to become its main hill campus on the west side of the Raquette River. The concrete block structure, then known as Clarkson Arena, featured a 183-foot-long rink and bleachers for 1,500 spectators. For decades, the massive arena also hosted many campus events, including graduation ceremonies. Its indoor acoustics were so perfect that it would lure many concerts, including ones performed by students at the elite Crane School of Music at the State University College at Potsdam.

On September 21, 1974, hundreds gathered inside the arena in early afternoon to inaugurate Robert A. Plane as the university's 12th president. Plane's 58-year-old predecessor, John W. Graham Jr., gave a speech that concluded that Plane "has the makings of a truly great college president." Graham predicted that Clarkson would do well in the years ahead.

Seconds after he finished his remarks, Graham stepped from the podium and fell to his knees before the stunned audience. Recognizing that Graham was suffering a heart attack, physician Hans Lee, head of the coronary

From about 1980, Clarkson University's Walker Arena, home then of its Division I men's ice hockey team. (Potsdam Public Museum photo.)

care unit at the Potsdam hospital, rushed onstage to begin CPR. Just as he reached Graham, Lee collapsed with a heart attack of his own.

The Potsdam Volunteer Rescue Squad rushed both men to the village hospital, where Graham was pronounced dead upon arrival at 3:19 p.m. The 64-year-old Lee died at 3:45 p.m.

Graham had been right about Plane. Clarkson did thrive under the leadership of its new president, who led the college in one of its most dynamic periods of growth. Clarkson constructed numerous buildings, including an engineering laboratory, and it renovated others, including the ice hockey arena, renamed Walker Arena in honor of longtime hockey booster G. Murray Walker. The college also expanded its endowment from $5.5 million to over $19 million.

Katy Hawelka and others who applied to Clarkson in the mid-1980s had a vastly expanded choice of majors over those offered to previous generations. It included business, biology, industrial hygiene, industrial management, technical communications, marketing, and computer science. In 1984, the school changed its name to Clarkson University to better reflect the diversity of its offerings, to raise its profile in higher education and to attract more students. By then, the student population had grown to about 4,000, including 800 women.

Of all its accomplishments during the Plane era, Clarkson drew the most national publicity for its decision in 1983 to provide each incoming student with a personal desktop computer. The only "catch" was that the student had to pay a $400 annual surcharge and wouldn't officially own the computer until graduation.

Clarkson distributed the first computers on August 25, 1983. Freshmen and transfer students stood in line at Walker Arena to pick up brand-new Zenith Z-100s, a video monitor and six software packages. Reporters from *Life* magazine, *USA Today*, CBS News and NBC News were among those on hand to marvel at how this small university in Potsdam was the first institution of higher education to supply its students with personal computers.

Clarkson stored the computers at Walker Arena under tight security, as each one with accessories had a retail value of about $4,000. The university became acutely aware of the risk of theft in January 1983 when it reported to Potsdam village police that a Z-100 was stolen from the office of an instructor evaluating it. Once the full shipment arrived at Walker Arena, the university hired a part-time security guard to watch over the Z-100s at night. Publicly, though, it downplayed the possibility of anyone stealing the computers once they ended up in dorms. A *United Press International* wire story about the computers paraphrased a Clarkson spokesperson saying that the school "never had a theft problem because of its rural location."

Katy was delighted in early 1985 when Clarkson sent her an acceptance letter. By the time she graduated from Henninger in June, she had notified the university she would join its freshman class on a path to graduate in spring 1989.

Terry wasn't sure that getting a Zenith computer factored at all into her daughter's decision. Katy mostly talked about Clarkson's strong business program, and she was happy her acceptance came with generous financial aid. Katy also liked the idea of going to a school where she would be part of reshaping male traditions and stereotypes. As she told her sister Carey, "It is kind of like women still breaking the barriers."

Over the summer of 1985, Katy received her dorm assignment—a room on the third floor of Cubley dormitory—and contact information for her

Katy Hawelka poses with sister Carey, left, and their mother, Terry, at Katy's graduation from Henninger High School in Syracuse in 1985. (Hawelka family photo.)

roommate, Nicole Caruso. She chatted over the phone a couple of times with Caruso, a resident of Clifton Park, New York, who planned to major in management information systems. They decided which items each one would bring, as there wasn't a lot of space in the room, which came furnished with beds, dressers and desks.

As Katy arrived on campus and unpacked in late August, the big story was that year's retirement of university President Plane and the hiring of his successor, Allan H. Clark, who previously was dean of the school of science at Purdue University. A gala weekend celebrating Clark's inauguration included an all-campus picnic in the parking lot in front of Walker Arena.

At a press conference afterward, Clark said his goals as president included developing Clarkson's undergraduate programs, enrolling more women and finding ways to adjust to a new drinking age of 21 going into effect that December. "We have to take some positive steps and try to construct a social life for students that is not so dependent on alcohol-related events," Clark said.

For a small university in a small town, Clarkson offered a vigorous social life, with its numerous fraternities and sororities, sports that included Division I ice hockey, an ice carnival, lots of student clubs and organizations, and a busy nightlife in downtown Potsdam.

Katy and Caruso quickly became such good friends that they regularly swapped clothes—although Caruso liked to kid that Katy never quite trusted her to handle their laundry. Wherever they went, Katy lit up a room with her loud, hearty laugh, which decades later remained indelibly etched in Caruso's memory.

"I can still hear her laugh. It was very distinctive," Caruso would say.

Down the hall on their dorm floor, a different situation played out for Nanci Parks, a freshman from Penfield, New York, who was majoring in accounting. As she confided to Katy during their first week on campus, Parks was having trouble with her roommate.

"Why don't you move in with us?" Katy asked.

Caruso had no objection, and neither did the resident assistant in charge of the floor, so the three students soon squeezed into a dorm room designed for two. They slapped on a fresh coat of paint and hung curtains, and Parks kept it brightened with flowers that her father often sent.

Katy and Parks became all but inseparable their freshmen year. If you saw one, it was likely you'd see the other, often wearing matching pink T-shirts designed by their dorm floor with the image of a teddy bear. Even on holidays and breaks, Parks and Katy hung out together.

"I never had a sister. She was like a sister," Parks said. "She was just fun and personable. She was very bubbly. I think that's why we clicked. We were like Frick and Frack. If we weren't together, people would say, 'Where's Katy?' or 'Where's Nanci?' Because we were always just together. For whatever reason, there was no drama. Believe me, with 18-year-old girls, there can be drama. But to this day, I cannot give you an example of us getting irritated with each other, or anything like that."

Katy and Parks became friends with several players on Clarkson's men's hockey team and attended all of its home games at Walker Arena. When the team traveled to Boston in March 1986 to play in the ECAC Tournament, Katy and Parks made the trip, staying in a hotel room that Parks' father booked.

Katy Hawelka, bottom left, attends a birthday party for a friend on October 17, 1985. Clarkson University roommate Nanci Parks, right, joins the celebration. (Nicole Caruso Pfeifer photo.)

During freshman year, their favorite hangouts on weekends included the Rusty Nail, the Whiskey One, and Bogie's, which were three taverns along Market Street in Potsdam. Katy and Parks would usually walk there and back because neither had a car, and there was no regular bus service.

"The biggest thing was the dancing. I remember there would be live music, and Katy and I would dance the whole night," Parks said. She and Katy "would study like crazy during the week, and then weekends were when we partied."

On Parents' Weekend in October 1985, Katy's mother drove to Potsdam and stayed overnight in the dorm room with Katy and Parks while Caruso was out of town. Katy and Parks even took Terry to a fraternity party, where somehow Katy's mother got a gash on her foot. To stop the bleeding, they used a sanitary pad, sparking giggles from those who saw it.

"I remember to this day Muff being such a great sport," Parks said. "We wrapped that (pad) around her foot, and she was laughing as much as the rest of us. Terry is a tough lady. She always was. But, God, we had a lot of fun with her."

As for Clarkson's academic side, like many first-year students, Katy had trouble adjusting to the rigorous demands of classes. Good grades didn't come as easily as they did in high school.

"She didn't like the classroom," Parks said. "You know, we had 8 o'clock classes, and we both would grimace. But that was Clarkson. You had to buckle down."

In their second semester, Katy and Parks aligned their class schedules with the idea it would help each other academically. It did help, but by spring 1986, Parks had enough of Clarkson. She wearied of the classwork, missed her family, and hated the 200-mile bus trip to Penfield, which was excruciating when she became sick with mononucleosis and had to take the long ride home.

Parks' parents were okay with her leaving Clarkson, but they insisted she transfer to the nearby St. John Fisher University in Rochester, where her older brother had received a degree.

Katy was stunned when Parks told her she was transferring.

"Who am I going to room with?" she asked.

Parks and Katy soon came up with a solution: Katy would also transfer to St. John Fisher. That was the plan when classes wrapped up in May, and Parks thought it was still in the works just before the fall semester.

However, Katy called Parks in August to say she was staying at Clarkson. Exactly why, Parks wasn't sure. Terry would say that Katy looked at the big picture and decided what she wanted most remained in Potsdam, including a strong business program and enough financial aid to afford a four-year education.

Katy confided in her younger sister, though, that she desperately wanted to transfer to St. John Fisher, but their parents wouldn't allow it. Joe Sr. and Terry thought the friendship with Parks wasn't a valid excuse for Katy to give up on Clarkson. "I remember her (Katy) being very upset they would not allow her to transfer," Carey said. "I know Katy didn't change her mind."

For whatever reason, Katy was back at Clarkson in August 1986, vowing to bear down in her sophomore year, study harder and make it work. With all her close friends already set with roommates, Katy was assigned to a Woodstock Village apartment she would share with three other female students.

Temperatures in Potsdam reached a high of only 60 degrees with occasional sunshine on Thursday, August 28, 1986, as Katy arrived for her second year at Clarkson. Terry and Carey helped Katy haul belongings into the apartment, then went grocery shopping with her before saying goodbye and heading back to Syracuse. By now, first-year students were already flocking to Walker Arena to pick up their personal computers, now upgraded to Zenith Z-2000s. In the village, Clarkson students also lined up at the university-owned Weston's Bookstore on Market Street to pick up textbooks and other supplies.

As darkness fell, Katy dressed in blue jeans and a warm sweater, tucked her cousin's identification card into a pocket along with a few dollars, and headed downtown with some of her new roommates.

Just after 11 p.m., she was enjoying a beer at Bogie's when she spotted Clarkson student Todd Kilburn, a junior engineering major from Rutland, Vermont. They had been friends since Katy's freshman year. Kilburn told her he had been in Potsdam for several days helping to clean and repair the Sigma Delta fraternity house, where he was living this academic year. At Bogie's, they chatted the rest of the evening over several beers.

They left together when the bars closed at 2:30 a.m. After chatting with a friend for several minutes outside Bogie's, Katy and Kilburn headed for the Clarkson campus. Although Sigma Delta's frat house was in another direction, Kilburn agreed to walk with Katy as she began the slow, one-mile trek to the Woodstock apartments.

Katy was still limping from her summer foot injury, and she asked to stop several times to rest, including once around 3 a.m. at a stone wall in front of Trinity Episcopal Church between two bridges over the Raquette River. When they resumed the walk, they stopped again just beyond the second bridge, near a Kentucky Fried Chicken restaurant, where Kilburn excused himself. While Katy waited along Maple Street, Kilburn walked to a nearby fence to relieve himself. He noticed another male doing the same thing a few feet away.

Behind the restaurant was an open gate leading to a campus shortcut that students often took to trim a few steps off the walk from downtown. When they got to the gate, Katy told Kilburn she could walk the rest of the way by herself. Kilburn told her he didn't mind continuing to Woodstock Village, but she insisted she would be fine by herself now that she was on campus property, just a few yards behind Walker Arena.

With that, Kilburn gave Katy a light kiss goodbye and walked back across the bridges before heading up Main Street toward the frat house. On the way, he passed the North Country Savings Bank, which displayed the time on a large sign. Kilburn later recalled it was about 3:30 a.m.

A party was still going on at Sigma Delta when he arrived there. Kilburn had one beer and went to bed, unaware that his friend Katy never made it past Walker Arena.

Chapter 5

Campus Security

CLARKSON University security guards Kim Avadikian and Donald Shanty were waiting at the Raymond Street police station when Potsdam Police Lieutenant McKendree arrived there at 4:30 a.m., about an hour after the attack on Katy. From the trauma etched on the guards' faces, McKendree knew, even before talking to them, that they had witnessed something horrifying.

"They looked very concerned," McKendree commented later. "Not something they ever expected they would have to deal with."

It had taken about 45 minutes for McKendree, who lived south of Potsdam in the small hamlet of De Kalb Junction, to get dressed and make the drive to the police station. He initially planned to go to Walker Arena but changed his mind after learning Sergeant Lewis and others had the crime scene secured and needed someone to take statements from the guards.

McKendree had been a member of the Potsdam Police Department since 1978 when he went to work as "para-police" officer under a federally funded training program. The department hired him as a full-time patrolman a year later. In January 1986, the village promoted him to lieutenant, the No. 2 position in the department behind Chief Matott.

McKendree had a small office in a corner of the police station, a one-story building constructed in 1957 with cement-block walls and bright fluorescent lights that gave the place a spartan look that was standard architecture at the time it was built. The middle of the building included a row of jail cells, alongside several small offices, a large conference room, and a command post overseeing the main entrance.

At 4:45 a.m., McKendree began taking the men's statements.

Avadikian, 31, had been hired as a temporary night watchman assigned to protect the Zenith personal computers being stored at Walker Arena. This was his second year assigned to this task, which paid $4.50 an hour. Clarkson at other times hired him for miscellaneous jobs, including cleaning buildings and writing parking tickets. His job application showed he previously worked in Potsdam for his family's restaurant, the Quonset Steak House, where he was a manager.

Avadikian's overnight shift that began at 11 p.m. Thursday, August 28, had been mainly uneventful until about 3:25 a.m. when he heard a noise he said "sounded like someone hitting one of the doors somewhere on the outside of the arena." He immediately radioed Shanty, who was Clarkson's only other security guard on duty at the time.

Shanty, 30, had been a full-time "fire/night watchman," as Clarkson classified him, since 1984. He previously worked as a laborer for a local lumber company. His job description at Clarkson involved working 11 p.m. to 7 a.m. five nights a week, sharing duties with another full-time watchman on Friday, Saturday and Sunday nights. Clarkson paid Shanty $7.02 an hour.

One of Shanty's primary responsibilities involved checking campus buildings for doors left unlocked and lights that weren't turned off. He also ticketed illegally parked vehicles, kept an eye out for fires, and reported vandalism and other crime. If he discovered petit larceny or another minor offense, he was told to report it to Clarkson administrators. If it was an emergency or a major crime, Shanty was to immediately phone the Potsdam Police Department, which patrolled the campus for several hours a day.

It was Clarkson's opinion that it didn't have enough crime to justify a full-time security force of its own, even though the nearby campuses of SUNY Potsdam, St. Lawrence University, and SUNY Canton each had one by the mid-1980s.

When Avadikian alerted him to check out the noise, Shanty was making a building check of Moore House, one of the university's dormitories.

"Kim said that it sounded like someone was banging on the doors of Walker Arena, and asked me to come down and check to see what was going on," Shanty said in his police statement. "I got in my vehicle and drove to

Walker Arena. As I was on my way down to Walker Arena, I looked at my watch and saw that it was 3:30 a.m."

Shanty said his initial thought was to "scare off anyone who may have been around the building."

He drove down the service road between Walker Arena and the physical plant, then turned around in a parking lot. It was then that the vehicle's headlights lit up the southeast corner of Walker Arena, where Shanty spotted "a guy with his pants down, and I could see his rear. It appeared he was having intercourse with a female. I could see one of her legs bent up in the air."

This male, who had dark hair and a medium build, looked up briefly at Shanty before turning his head back down and resuming the sexual act.

Shanty wasn't sure what to do. He thought he might try to chase away the couple, or he could radio Adavikian to call the village police. However, Shanty chose a third option: He decided to drive from the scene and talk about it with Avadikian.

"I didn't think too much of the guy and girl being there," he told McKendree, "because in the two and a half years that I've been working as a security guard for Clarkson, I have seen students having sex in unusual places before, and therefore I really didn't think too much of this at the time."

Shanty said he drove to the arena's front entrance and told Avadikian that "there was only two people having sex," and he didn't see anyone "bothering the doors."

In his statement, Avadikian recalled Shanty's words a little differently: "He said all that he saw was a male and female out back of the building, and the guy was putting it to her."

At Shanty's invitation, Avadikian joined him in the car. Shanty drove again to the southeast corner, where his headlights found the man and woman "still in the same spot as when I first saw them, and this time Kim saw them."

According to Avadikian, the man "laid still" when the lights hit him.

Still uncertain what they should do, Shanty once again drove away. He parked the vehicle and talked it over with Avadikian about whether to call the police.

"Don stated that he hated to call for nothing," Avadikian said.

After another minute or two, Shanty said, they decided to return to the scene and "park with our headlights on them so they would get up and leave." If the couple didn't go then, Shanty would ask Avadikian to go back inside and call the police. He would have to use the phone since their two-way radios didn't connect to the station.

For the third time that evening, Shanty drove onto the service road and once again aimed the vehicle's headlights on the arena's southeast corner.

This time, the scene was different.

"When we got back to that spot, we saw that the male subject was gone, and the female was still laying there," Shanty said. "It was at this point that we realized something was wrong."

Shanty pulled the vehicle as close as he could. In the headlights, the two guards were shocked to see blood all around the woman's head. She wasn't moving.

"Call the police!" Shanty shouted as he ran toward the woman.

Avadikian raced several hundred feet up the service road to the arena's front entrance, went inside the office, and called the Potsdam Police Department, requesting officers and an ambulance. By then, it was 3:41 a.m. —about 16 minutes after the time Avadikian heard a noise and about 11 minutes after Shanty first arrived at the scene.

As he waited for help, Shanty said, he noticed that "the female was having a hard time breathing. She was laying flat on her back, and I think her airway was filled with blood." He turned her head to the side a little "to try to let the blood flow out of her mouth."

Shanty checked her pulse, which to him seemed to be steady. Even so, he radioed Avadikian to tell the police and rescue squad "to hurry because she was breathing awful slow."

After hanging up with police, Avadikian returned to the southeast corner just as patrol cars were arriving. As he passed metal stairs to his left, about 50 feet from where the guards found the injured woman, Avadikian noticed a man "laying right up tight underneath the first step."

Avadikian ran over to officers, pointing to the woman in the corner and to the man lying motionless under the stairs. He watched as officers split up, with two helping the woman and two converging on the man, whom they soon identified as Brian McCarthy.

"They told this person not to move, and they stood around him," Avadikian said.

After an ambulance rushed the woman to the hospital, Shanty walked over to the stairs to look at McCarthy. Shanty told officers that McCarthy appeared to be the same person he had seen on top of the woman.

The guards cleaned up after that and went directly to the police station.

Even before McKendree finished typing their statements, he knew some would criticize the two guards for not immediately coming to the woman's aid. McKendree chose a more sympathetic opinion, realizing that Shanty and Avadikian weren't police officers trained to recognize an assault in progress, let alone know how to respond to it. He thought Avadikian and Shanty deserved some praise for discovering the attack before McCarthy could flee the scene, then contacting authorities and providing aid to Katy.

"In hindsight, you wish they had done something" to stop the attack, McKendree said. "But I think the whole thing of being Clarkson and being Potsdam, and not expecting something like this could happen. I think they just didn't believe what they saw."

In the emergency room at Canton-Potsdam Hospital, Chief Matott and other officers were busy for more than two hours after the attack, collecting evidence and, eventually, identifying the victim as Katy Hawelka.

The police also kept a close eye on McCarthy, who was waiting for his own medical exam while repeatedly asking, "How's the girl?"

After a while, he asked if he could leave.

"You're not going anyplace," Investigator Perretta said.

"Well, am I under arrest?"

"You can consider yourself under arrest."

McCarthy grew quiet after that.

At 5:15 a.m., after sending Katy off to the Watertown hospital, the medical staff at Canton-Potsdam Hospital finally turned its attention to McCarthy. A doctor, a nurse, and a member of the Potsdam Volunteer Rescue Squad carefully removed his clothes, handing each item to Patrolman Bartlett to preserve in clean paper bags. This included Timberland work boots, Lee corduroy pants, a sweatshirt jacket, and a yellow T-shirt printed with the logo for rock band Queen on the front. Police also collected two light-green hospital sheets on which McCarthy had been lying.

Found in McCarthy's pants pocket were six one-dollar bills, two quarters, a dime and three pennies. He also had a brown Rolfs brand wallet with his driver's license and a Marine Midland ATM card, a matchbook from Maxfield's restaurant in Potsdam, a silver neck chain, and a Pulsar quartz watch with a silver-colored watchband. Police sealed these items in envelopes. Police did not find McCarthy in possession of drugs or weapons.

At 5:30 a.m., police escorted McCarthy to the hospital's radiography department for X-rays, since he had complained of a neck and back injury. When the film was processed, and after a thorough exam of McCarthy, the ER doctor told police he found no injuries.

At 6:30, Perretta collected "combing samples" of pubic hairs from McCarthy to compare with any foreign hairs found on the victim. Not long after that, police loaned McCarthy a pair of pants and a jacket, placed him in handcuffs, and transported him to the Potsdam police station.

At 6:54, before getting coffee for himself and meeting with Chief Matott to discuss the case, Perretta took the handcuffs off McCarthy and locked him in a 9-by-5-foot jail cell.

"Why am I being arrested?" McCarthy finally asked.

Perretta had a one-word answer: "Assault."

Perretta checked in on McCarthy at 7:43, according to jail logs. McCarthy kept shouting about something.

"Calm down," Perretta told him.

When dispatcher Howard checked at 8:07, he found McCarthy asleep.

By now, the Potsdam community was waking up to news about an attack on a female student outside Walker Arena. Chief Matott wasn't releasing many details to the news media, but he confirmed that a sophomore at Clarkson was beaten and raped, and that police had an "individual in custody." He did not release the names of Katy or McCarthy.

However, Clarkson officials issued a statement identifying Katherine Hawelka of Syracuse, New York, as the student beaten outside the arena. Although the statement didn't mention the alleged rape, newspapers withheld publishing her name because of their policies not to identify living victims of sexual assault.

In its first edition Friday, the *Watertown Daily Times* described "unconfirmed reports" that the suspect was a Potsdam-area resident and that he injured himself running into a staircase or wall while trying to flee the scene. The newspaper added that House of the Good Samaritan in Watertown had confirmed at 9:12 a.m. that the victim was in critical condition and heading at that moment into surgery.

Not for the last time, the news media would learn developments in the case ahead of Katy's parents, who would not arrive at the hospital until she was leaving the operating room.

Chapter 6

The ICU

IT was close to 10 on Friday morning when Katy's parents walked into House of the Good Samaritan, where a receptionist directed them to a second-floor waiting room in the intensive care unit. Terry's brother, Don Ryan, was already waiting there with their mother, Alice.

As Joe Sr. and Terry stepped off the elevator, nurses wheeled past them a gurney with an unconscious female patient connected to multiple tubes and lines. Her face was so swollen and bruised it looked like she had been in a horrible car accident.

"That's Katy," Terry said quietly as the patient passed them.

"That's not her," Joe Sr. assured her.

Katy's mother didn't press the point, but she thought to herself: *Yeah, it is.*

After the family spent several minutes in the waiting room, a doctor came by, looking grim. Katy was alive, he told her parents, but she was unconscious and hooked to life support. She suffered a severe beating to her head and upper body, and there was the likelihood of permanent brain damage. However, it was too early to know if she would recover. The doctor did offer the parents a sliver of hope. The medical staff detected slight movement in one of Katy's pupils, indicating she might have brain activity. Doctors would need to run more tests.

The doctor said family members could see Katy, but the ICU would restrict them to two visitors at a time, and then only for short periods.

When Terry and Joe Sr. made their first visit, there was no more denying that the injured patient on that gurney had been Katy. Deep bruises covered her upper body, and her nose was swollen and purple. Her eyes bulged in their blackened sockets. Nasal packing controlled bleeding, and intravenous catheters fed her nutrients. An endotracheal tube connected to a ventilator delivered oxygen to her lungs.

Doctors had stitched up several cuts to her scalp and face, including ones on her forehead and the bridge of her nose. They also had inserted a pin to repair her fractured right index finger, which Terry saw as a hopeful sign surgeons thought she might recover since they bothered to fix such a relatively small injury.

Terry kept repeating to herself: *Katy could pull through this. She's a determined kid. She's a fighter.* However, this was easier for her to believe before she saw her daughter in the ICU. Even if Katy did wake up, it seemed her daughter's life would never be the same. Terry imagined Katy requiring months, if not years, of rehab and special care.

As she held her daughter's hand, Terry wept as she asked herself what kind of monster would hurt Katy. Terry was told that a suspect was in custody in Potsdam. Was this someone Katy knew? Why would he attack her? Terry had a million questions, but she decided for the moment she needed to focus on Katy's medical care and recovery.

Over the next few hours, Terry's mother often accompanied her daughter to Katy's room every time the medical staff allowed two family members to visit briefly. Terry wouldn't recall making many of these visits with Joe Sr., who mostly sat in stoic silence in the waiting room, fully aware from his medical training that patients with Katy's kind of traumatic injuries rarely survived.

In Syracuse, Carey and Joe Jr. waited anxiously by the phone, desperate for news from Watertown, and wondered when their parents would allow them to see their sister. Soon, Terry's house was filled with Katy's friends and others who heard the news, and the telephone seemed to be constantly ringing with people trying to learn what happened.

As the hours passed, Carey placed a call to the home of Katy's former Clarkson roommate Nanci Parks, now a student at St. John Fisher in Rochester and living with her parents in Pittsford.

Carey was crying, telling Parks that lack of news from Watertown couldn't be a good thing.

"Something's wrong, and my parents won't tell me," Carey said.

After the phone call, Parks went downstairs and told her parents she needed to get to the Watertown hospital, right away.

Later Friday, Betsy arrived in Syracuse on a flight from Florida, still under the impression Katy had been in an accident. As she picked up her sister at the airport, Carey informed Betsy that someone beat up Katy at Clarkson, and she was now in the ICU in Watertown.

Betsy was stunned. "It was so different from what I had imagined, you know, for four hours on a plane of what was going on, and I had no idea the severity of it," she remembered. "It was just bizarre to me. I'm like, 'What are you talking about?' Like, I was totally clueless."

Betsy quickly decided that she would go see Katy, but Carey told her that their parents wouldn't allow it. Betsy was sure they would make an exception for her because she was 21 and old enough to decide for herself. But when Joe Sr. called Terry's house with an update, he told Betsy she needed to stay in Syracuse to take care of Carey and Joe Jr.

In Potsdam, Clarkson University officials were in full crisis mode by late Friday morning. The top administrators, gathered at meetings, weren't available to talk to reporters. However, the university had counselors ready for students and staff who needed to "sort out their feelings," Gary Kelly, director of counseling services, told the *Ogdensburg Journal*. He added that counselors would discuss with students "decision-making in terms of whether to be outside alone, especially at night, and if they've been drinking."

The only other initial comment from the university came anonymously from an employee who acknowledged to the newspaper that the area near the site of the attack wasn't well-lit.

At the Potsdam police station, the investigation into the assault on Katy sparked what Lieutenant McKendree called an "all-hands-on-deck" kind of morning. Potsdam officers came in on their days off to help. Other police agencies stopped by to offer assistance.

New York State Police spent part of the morning following up on the report filed the previous evening by Robert J. Warren Jr., the driver who heard hitchhiker "Brian" claim he shot someone that night at Chateau's Bar and Restaurant.

Troopers quickly determined that the hitchhiker was lying; there was no shooting in Winthrop. But when shown a lineup of photos, bar owner John Edward Chateau identified McCarthy as a patron involved in an argument between 9 and 10 the night before. Chateau told police the dispute began after a Winthrop man sitting at the bar briefly left to play a video game or the jukebox. When he returned, the man noticed that three dollar bills he placed on the bar were missing, and he accused McCarthy of stealing it. The dispute escalated into shouting and a shoving match. Chateau ordered McCarthy to leave, which he did with a friend without further incident.

As police continued to take statements and to collect evidence, officers checked on McCarthy in his cell every five to 10 minutes. Potsdam Patrolman Mike Knowlton found McCarthy sleeping at 8:07 and 9:26 a.m., awake at 9:33, then asleep a few minutes after that. McCarthy was awake again at 10:05 and "asking about girl," according to a notation in jail logs.

At about 10:15, Chief Matott asked Knowlton to remove McCarthy from the cell and bring him to the chief's corner office for questioning. Matott was sitting behind his desk when McCarthy entered the room, still wearing the jacket and pants that police provided him earlier, but minus handcuffs or shackles.

After Knowlton left, Matott invited McCarthy to take a seat. Lieutenant McKendree, the only other person in the room, sat next to McCarthy.

Matott asked if McCarthy wanted coffee. McCarthy said no.

McKendree studied McCarthy, who was sitting straight and looking alert, showing no sign of impairment from alcohol or anything else. If anything, McCarthy exuded confidence, as if he were an innocent man eager to tell his story and be on his way.

Matott had two cassette recorders sitting on his desk, one a miniature model and one of standard size. The chief asked McCarthy if it was okay if they taped the conversation.

McCarthy said he didn't mind.

Matott pressed "record" on the miniature player. McKendree did the same for the larger one.

It was 10:23 a.m., about seven hours after the attack on Katy, and police were ready to give McCarthy a chance to tell them how he ended up under the stairs at Walker Arena.

Chapter 7

"Sure, I Have Nothing to Hide"

MATOTT leaned slightly toward the tape recorders whirring on his desk and announced, "Today is August 29, 1986. Present in my office: Chief Matott, Potsdam Police Department, and Lieutenant Terry McKendree and Brian Milton McCarthy. The interview with Brian McCarthy is in reference to the assault and rape which occurred around 3 a.m. this morning."

Matott had chosen his words carefully. He didn't want to spook McCarthy into silence by directly accusing him of being the assailant or by warning him Katy was so critically injured that she might die from her injuries. By taking a nonconfrontational approach, Matott hoped McCarthy would confess, or at the very least talk his way into incriminating statements.

Matott read McCarthy his Miranda rights. Hours earlier, McCarthy interrupted John Perretta when the investigator tried to do the same. This time, McCarthy sat and listened.

When Matott finished, he asked, "Do you understand these rights I have read to you?"

"Uh," McCarthy mumbled.

"Speak up," Matott said.

"Yeah, I do."

Matott asked McCarthy if he was willing to talk.

"Sure, I have nothing to hide."

Matott shifted to a gentle, almost fatherly tone.

"All right, Brian," he said, "do you want to tell us what happened last night behind the arena at about 3 o'clock this morning?"

"I was walking in front of the—in front of the Walker Arena and I stopped by the bushes and I was taking a leak," McCarthy began. "I started walking up towards the parking lot, or I was walking across the parking lot, and I started walking up towards the road because I was going to go to Hannawa." McCarthy was referring to Clarkson Avenue, which turns into County Road 138 leading to Hannawa Falls, a hamlet about three miles south of Potsdam.

As he was walking past the arena, McCarthy said, he "heard somebody scream, and I just stopped for a minute, and I thought it was just somebody playing."

McCarthy then "heard somebody scream again, and they screamed again, and screamed again. And they yelled something—I don't know what they yelled—and I ran over there."

"You ran over where, Brian?" Matott asked.

McCarthy said he ran over by some "steps."

"No, wait," he said, correcting himself. McCarthy said he first "went into where the building dips in," a description that fit the southeast corner of Walker Arena where Katy was found injured. However, he saw nothing there, he said, so he walked back out to the road. McCarthy said he didn't hear anything more. "So, I walked over by these steps, and I turned around and looked back, and looking back, and that was it. That is all I remember."

"And did you see any girl while you were there?" the chief asked.

"No, I didn't see anybody there."

McCarthy interrupted himself again: "Wait. I remember a black jacket. That is all I remember, a black jacket. I remember seeing white on its cuffs right here in the sleeves, whosever's jacket it was," McCarthy said, pointing to his wrist area. "It might have been the girl's, I don't know. I can remember seeing a black jacket, and it had white stripes on the jacket right here. That was all I saw."

"Now, where, where was this jacket you saw?" Matott asked. "Somebody wearing it? Was somebody wearing this jacket?"

"As far as I can remember. I am not going to say for—it had to be. Where else would I see it?"

"Well," the chief answered, "I didn't know if it was laying on the ground or whether you saw something with it on or—"

"Oh, no, it wasn't on the ground."

"Did you see anything at all on the ground?" Matott asked.

"I don't know," McCarthy said.

Matott pressed for a definitive answer. "No? Is that a no? Is that what you are saying?"

"No, I didn't see anything on the ground," McCarthy said.

Matott began another question, but McCarthy interrupted again.

"I am trying to think what I did," he said. "I walked around the corner. I don't know. I just went out. I was gone. I don't know what happened. I saw stars, and then everything went black. And I could taste the grass. And that was the last thing I remember. I got hit. I was—see, I know I got hit, I know I got hit."

"Where did you get hit?"

"On my neck, on my shoulder, my back somewhere, I don't know. It all hurts, on my neck, down my back and my shoulder blade. In between my shoulder blade, it hurts," McCarthy said, holding his neck. "They took X-rays at the hospital, and they can't find anything broken."

The police chief returned to the black jacket.

"Then you are trying to tell me now that you just came around the side of the arena and you saw somebody in a black jacket. Is that what you said?"

"No, I didn't see—I am saying that I saw a black jacket."

"Well, somebody had to be wearing it, right?" Matott asked.

"That was all I remember because I went black. But I can remember seeing a black jacket," McCarthy said. "I can remember seeing the white stripes on his wrist."

McCarthy quickly corrected himself.

"On *the* wrist, whoever was wearing the jacket, or something," he said, removing his reference to the gender. He then tried to explain his changing story. "I don't know, it was all confused."

Matott finally dropped the subject of the jacket.

"What is the next thing you remember?" the chief asked.

"Somebody shining a flashlight in my face. Somebody grabbed my arm, and it hurt real bad. I asked him to just leave me alone," McCarthy said, apparently referring to Patrolman Kaplan, who pulled him from under the outdoor staircase.

McCarthy said he then "heard a bunch of radios" before an ambulance took him to the hospital.

"And then (Investigator) John Perretta tells me that I am being charged with, uh, assault or something. And then you are telling me I am being charged with rape."

Matott hadn't said anything about charging McCarthy with rape. But since McCarthy raised the subject, the chief decided to pursue it.

"Well, Brian," Matott asked, "how do you explain the fact that a couple of security officers from Clarkson College said they saw you having intercourse with this girl just prior to that? On the ground behind the arena."

"Why would I have intercourse with her?" McCarthy said, "*I don't even know this girl.* I have no idea what she looks like. No, I don't explain it, because I wasn't."

Matott pressed McCarthy to explain why police found him under the staircase.

"Underneath where?" McCarthy asked.

"The steps that go up the side of the building there, to the arena. How did you get from there underneath those steps?"

"I don't even know where I was. I have no idea where I was."

"And you say that you never went around the end of the building?" Matott asked, referring to the corner of Walker Arena where Katy was found.

"No," McCarthy answered.

"At no time?"

"No, I did not go around the end of the building. I went probably a quarter of the way down," McCarthy said.

McCarthy returned on his own to the question about arena stairs.

"Oh, those are the steps you are talking about," he said. "I went underneath those steps and went around and came back. I stood out by the road, and I didn't hear anything, so I walked back up on the sidewalk by the arena."

So, Matott asked, you never saw the girl?

"No, I didn't see anything," McCarthy said. "Then somebody tells me that I beat up some girl and that I did this to a girl and that girl and, shit, I didn't even see no damn girl."

"You didn't see any girl anywhere around there?"

"Nope."

"On the ground or walking or anything else—you didn't see any girl?"

"Oh," McCarthy said, "I saw girls walking. Yeah, there was girls walking through there. Walking, coming out, you know where they cut through that short path, whatever it is, and they come out on the backside of Walker Arena."

McKendree remained silent, letting Matott ask all the questions. But the lieutenant noted to himself how McCarthy kept amending his answers in a way that suggested he was making up details as he went along.

Matott pressed McCarthy on his familiarity with the shortcut that students took behind Walker Arena.

"Do they cut through there all the time?"

"I don't know," McCarthy said. "I am not sure. I haven't been in Potsdam for a while."

"How many girls went through roughly while you were out there?"

"Oh, I was walking across the parking lot in front of Walker Arena. There were two girls in there walking out by the road going—going to Clarkson. They went up the hill."

"You saw girls walking through. Did you see any guys walking through there?" Matott asked.

"I don't know," McCarthy said. "It is kinda hard to tell sometimes. One of them might have been a guy. One of them might have even been a girl. But there were two of them together. I assume it was two girls, so I don't know. I have no idea who it was. I really don't care to know who it was. I don't even know who this girl was that got beat up."

He then added, "Is she going to be all right? Somebody told me she is pretty bad."

"Yes, she is in the hospital. That is all I know about it," Matott said.

Matott asked again about the shortcut near the arena.

"When was the last time that you came up through that road?"

"In back of Walker Arena?"

"Yeah, cross through behind Walker Arena," the chief said.

"God, I don't know. It's been a couple months now."

"That was the last time you went through, a couple of months ago?"

"Yeah, I would say," McCarthy said, "I would say it was more than a couple of months ago. I haven't been in Potsdam in two months—well, I can't say that. I came in the other night to get some groceries, but—"

"Where have you been living?"

McCarthy said he was staying at a house under construction near a boat landing in Madrid (locals pronounce it MAD-rid), a small town about 10 miles from Potsdam. McCarthy said he was doing work there for the owners.

"Do the owners of the property know that you stay there?"

"Oh, yeah. Oh, yeah, yeah. You can call them and ask them. All of my stuff is out there."

"Do you have a car, Brian?"

McCarthy said he didn't own a car, although he was supposed to buy one later that day.

"How did you get to Potsdam?"

McCarthy said he had been drinking with friends in North Lawrence. One of his friends gave him a ride part of the way to Potsdam, and he had hitchhiked the rest.

Matott asked McCarthy where he had been drinking, not letting on that police knew about the dispute the previous evening at Chateau's in Winthrop and about McCarthy's alleged threat while hitchhiking to return and kill another patron.

"Well," McCarthy said, "we stopped in North Lawrence, and we stopped in—let's see, Brasher Falls. No, wait. Is that right? No, Winthrop. Winthrop. We stopped in Winthrop. Winthrop is before Brasher, right? Yeah, we stopped in Winthrop. And we went in there and had a drink."

"Who is 'we'?"

"This friend of mine and myself."

"What is your friend's name?"

"Joe. Joseph Lopez."

After they left the bar, McCarthy said, Lopez drove him part of the way to Potsdam. McCarthy said he then walked at least a couple of miles before hitchhiking the rest of the way.

Matott asked McCarthy if he had a conversation with anyone at the bar in Winthrop.

"Uhhhh," McCarthy said, "yeah, I did—an argument with a guy. He accused me of stealing three dollars of his off from the bar."

Matott wanted to know if McCarthy told anyone that he was "going to come to Potsdam and kill somebody before the night was over."

"No, I don't believe so, officer. No, I didn't."

"You are sure?"

"I am absolutely positive I did not tell anybody I was going to kill somebody before the night was through, or whatever you said. No way. No way."

After arriving in Potsdam, McCarthy said, he went to see a friend, Dick Hayes, who lived in an apartment behind Morgan's ice cream parlor along Main Street. Because Hayes was "upstairs talking to some girls," McCarthy said, he left and went to a bar, had a couple of drinks, and played some pool before returning to Hayes' apartment.

"We had a couple of beers," McCarthy said of his visit with Hayes. "We were trying to get my dog back from him, but he wouldn't let me have my dog."

Matott asked how much McCarthy had to drink that evening.

"Ten or 12 cases, who knows?" McCarthy said. "I have no idea how much I drank. I didn't sit down and keep track. I probably drank maybe two six-packs—yeah, about two six-packs, maybe three, before I got to Potsdam, and then I sat over to Dick's, and we had a beer and … I didn't even finish the beer."

McCarthy said he left the apartment "about 4 in the morning" and started toward Hannawa.

"And Brian, you still maintain that, uh, you never saw a girl last night?" the chief asked. "You still deny that you were having intercourse with a girl behind the arena last night? Is that what you are telling me, that that never happened?"

"No, not to my recollection, it didn't happen because I—I don't understand how all of this could of happened," McCarthy said. "Here, if I'm out, if I am laying on the ground, how am I supposed to be doing this? I am telling you I got hit. I got hit last night by something. I don't know what it was. It might have been a fist. It might have been a piece of metal."

"But you have no marks on you," Matott said.

"What?"

"But you have no marks on you."

"I don't have any marks on me?"

"No, you have no marks that show you have been hit. How do you get hit that hard without having a mark?"

"Well, I have a good lump on my head, I don't know what that causes," McCarthy said. "Maybe I fell, I don't know. I have no idea, I really don't. . . . My neck is not sore like this all the time."

By now, McKendree and Matott had noticed that McCarthy was trying to keep his right hand out of sight. It was swollen, and his index finger had a purplish color—the kind of injury someone might get if he punched something. Or someone.

"Let me see your knuckles," Matott said. "Are your knuckles sore?"

"No."

"Isn't that knuckle on your right hand swollen up?"

McCarthy held his hand with the pinkie side up. He said he had some swelling there because "I have bad circulation in my fingers."

"No, no, I am talking about the back knuckle, way back over—"

"Over here?" McCarthy asked, studying the side with the index finger.

"Yeah," Matott said.

"Nope. It is not sore at all."

"It is all swollen," Matott said.

"It is all colored, isn't it?" McCarthy conceded.

Matott thought it looked swollen, too.

"What caused that?" the chief asked.

"I probably slammed my fist last night."

"What did you slam your fist on?"

"Dick's door. Or part of the door. I tore the door down last night."

Matott didn't ask McCarthy why he would want to tear down Hayes' door, but the chief made a mental note to have an officer check the apartment for damage.

"Brian, I want you to give this a little bit of thought before we wrap this up," Matott said.

"All right."

"Is there anything else that you want to tell us about last night? Especially in reference to the situation by the Clarkson arena."

"I wish that I—you know, if I did it, I would admit to doing it, but I did not do it, so I am not going to admit to doing it. That is all I can say."

"Okay," the chief said, "the time is 10:54, and this is Chief Matott, Potsdam Police Department, and this concludes the interview with Brian Milton McCarthy."

After he and McKendree turned off the tape recorders, Matott informed McCarthy that he was being charged with rape and assault. McCarthy said nothing more as Officer Knowlton escorted him back to his jail cell.

Even without a confession, the chief decided police had enough to bring charges based on the statements of the security guards, the blood on McCarthy's boots and shirt, his injured hand, and the fact he was found nearby. McCarthy's evasive answers and outright lies also gave the police more reasons to believe he was behind the attack on Katy. When Officer Knowlton checked out Hayes' apartment on Main Street, he found no damage to the door that McCarthy claimed he tore down.

As Investigator Perretta began drawing up paperwork for an afternoon arraignment, Matott fielded more calls from the news media. He told reporters that McCarthy had been formally arrested just after 11 a.m. in the attack on the female Clarkson student, whose name at that point was still being withheld by the police.

"She was beaten pretty badly," Matott told the *Watertown Daily Times*. "The motive, as far as I know at this point, was rape." He added that McCarthy and the victim were not romantically involved or have any other known relationship.

As for rumors around Potsdam that McCarthy may have knocked himself unconscious by running into stairs trying to flee, Matott said, "We're assuming something like that happened prior to our arrival."

If convicted of the two felony charges of rape and assault, Matott noted, McCarthy faced a possible sentence of up to 25 years in prison.

In his cell, McCarthy accepted a breakfast of coffee and an English muffin. At 11:23, his mother, Florence, and one of her other sons arrived at the police station to see him. The three met privately in the cellblock. Brian

McCarthy was crying so much, his mother testified later, that she had a hard time understanding what he was saying.

Chapter 8

Brian Milton McCarthy

POTSDAM insurance agent Leonard F. Page was not surprised to learn of Brian McCarthy's arrest for the attack on Katy Hawelka. A month before, in July, Page got into a heated argument with McCarthy at the Backstreets bar on Market Street. The dispute quickly spilled into a nearby alley. When the village police responded, they found the 35-year-old Page beaten so severely that officers weren't sure at first that he would survive. McCarthy lucked out. Not only did Page live, but he declined to press charges.

After the attack on Katy Hawelka, Page declined to talk to reporters about his own encounter with McCarthy. But in an interview with the Potsdam *Courier & Freeman* newspaper, Page suggested it was inevitable that McCarthy was going to injure someone, whether or not the victim was female or walking alone at night.

"This is not the first time he's been in trouble," Page said. "All we can do is pray this fellow gets help. He needs it. Anyone who does that has more than minor problems. The sad thing is, this fellow's parents are really nice people."

Brian Milton McCarthy was born in 1962 in Meriden, Connecticut, the second oldest of six children in a Catholic family whose roots went back several generations in the Potsdam area. His mother, the former Florence Snell, graduated from Parishville-Hopkinton Central School, where her father, Milton, a farmer, was president of the school board. She was a basketball cheerleader, a member of the yearbook staff, and a St. Lawrence County dairy princess before attending Le Moyne College in Syracuse. She married Edward McCarthy on February 27, 1960, at St. Mary's Catholic

Church in Potsdam. He was a graduate of the nearby Colton-Pierrepont High School, where he competed in football, basketball and track, acted in school plays, and was a member of the yearbook staff. After graduation, he enrolled at what is now the University of Massachusetts at Amherst's Stockbridge School of Agriculture, where he became a certified arborist.

On Sunday, October 28, 1956, while Edward McCarthy was attending school in Massachusetts, a small kerosene stove flared up inside a two-room house trailer in South Colton where his father, Clement, was living alone. The 56-year-old man tried to open a window but was overcome by smoke. A coroner ruled that he died of accidental suffocation.

After Edward and Florence McCarthy were married, they made their home in Connecticut. Then in the late 1960s, they moved to the Adirondack Mountains village of Saranac Lake, New York, where Edward went to work for Niagara Mohawk Power Corp. on a tree-trimming crew. A former neighbor who knew the family in Saranac Lake remembered Brian McCarthy as a "lively" kid and "maybe a little more full of it than most children."

He was "sometimes a little hellraiser as a kid, but it was mischief" and nothing serious, said Mrs. Dean T. Gilbert, according to the *Watertown Daily Times*.

In the early 1970s, the McCarthys moved again, this time to Route 72 in Parishville, near a hamlet known as Parishville Center. They settled into a two-story home, built of Potsdam sandstone in 1823 and owned by the Snell family since 1917. The house later would join the National Register of Historic Places.

The McCarthys quickly wove themselves into the fabric of the community. The children took swimming lessons at Parishville Beach. The family attended St. Michael's Catholic Church in Parishville, where Ed McCarthy joined the church board. He later became a member of the Parishville school board. News accounts from the 1970s also show that the couple regularly donated money to local groups, including the Potsdam Junior Hockey Association, where their sons played on youth teams.

Brian McCarthy was in his mid-teens when his behavior turned from mischievous to criminal. He began smoking pot, skipping school, and getting in trouble with the law. His parents got him into counseling, but as his behavior in his late teens became a threat to the family, they kicked him out of the house. Even so, McCarthy's troubles stayed out of the newspapers for a long time because courts sealed his juvenile criminal record.

That changed after McCarthy turned 18. He was arrested on February 12, 1981, for petit larceny after he was caught shoplifting at the Potsdam Super Duper, the *Courier & Freeman* reported. In the same incident, police additionally charged McCarthy with escape after he fled the patrol car.

While his siblings' names would often appear in the newspapers for their academic achievements and other accomplishments, Brian McCarthy's only showed up in the police blotter listings. Also in 1981, McCarthy was charged with third-degree burglary on July 27, petit larceny on August 1, theft of services and possession of marijuana on August 30, third-degree possession of a forged instrument on October 9, and second-degree forgery on December 8. In cases where dispositions were reported by the media, he typically pleaded guilty in exchange for a small fine and restitution. In addition that year, McCarthy left high school before obtaining his diploma.

He kept his name out of the Potsdam newspaper in 1982. But McCarthy was arrested again in 1983 in the town of Pierrepont on a charge of petit larceny. He was fined $80 and ordered in July to pay restitution. Two months later, after moving nearby to Sylvan Falls, he was charged with petit larceny, fined $50, and ordered to pay restitution.

Having worn out his welcome in several North Country communities, McCarthy departed upstate New York in late 1983, landing in Houston, Texas, where he crashed at the apartment of a couple he knew there.

One day at the apartment complex pool, McCarthy struck up a conversation with a high school girl, Mary Colb, who lived there with her mother, brother and sister. At 16, Colb was blonde and pretty with shining blue eyes and an easy laugh, although she tended to cover her mouth to hide her slightly crooked teeth.

Colb had an immediate crush on McCarthy. He was five years older, but she didn't care; she thought McCarthy was handsome and quite a gentleman, always polite and soft-spoken around her. She would recall that their relationship became sexual, although the age of consent in Texas at the time was 17.

"I was star-struck," Colb said. "He was cute, and I was in such love. I was so gullible when I was 16."

Being inexperienced in such things, she missed the warning signs about McCarthy, such as the fact that he didn't seem to have a job, that he drove a junker, and that he spent most of his time hanging around the apartment watching TV, drinking beer and smoking pot. McCarthy never spoke much to Colb about his past troubles in New York, other than to mention he was the "black sheep" in his family.

Everything was going fine until one day in early 1984 when McCarthy and his male roommate got into an argument with Colb's older half-brother, William Rye, in her presence. Rye warned McCarthy to stop seeing the underage girl.

After Rye left, McCarthy and his friend followed. When the two returned to the apartment, Colb noticed the roommate had blood on his hands and shoes. Fearing the worst, she raced back to her apartment to find her brother bleeding and his jaw broken. Rye told her that McCarthy and his friend punched and kicked him. But when Colb confronted McCarthy, he denied he had anything to do with her brother's injuries.

"I didn't touch him," McCarthy said, blaming his roommate for the attack.

Colb chose to believe McCarthy over her brother. "Never once in the whole year and a half I knew him (McCarthy) did he even raise his voice to me," she said. "He never lifted a hand to me. Nothing violent towards me whatsoever."

Perhaps fearing her brother would call the cops, McCarthy told Colb he was heading back to Potsdam, and he invited her to join him, even though it was the middle of the school year.

For several days, McCarthy drove his beat-up car north while Colb handed him cans of beer and freshly rolled marijuana joints. "He said, 'I'm driving, so if you want to smoke, you've got to learn how to roll them.' That's how I learned to roll weed. I had to roll the whole way while he drove," she recalled.

McCarthy first headed to his parents' house in Parishville. But after his mother refused to let Colb inside, she slept a couple of more nights in his car. One of McCarthy's friends eventually allowed them to stay in a rustic cabin, where the water coming out of the faucet looked brown.

To get money to buy food, Colb said, they committed several burglaries, including one at a church, where they stole quarters from coin-operated washing machines. Potsdam police finally caught up with them on July 12, 1984, when they were arrested for stealing food from the Arlington Inn apartments on Market Street and a keg of beer from a private residence. Police charged them with second-degree criminal trespass, possession of stolen property, and petit larceny. Potsdam Village Justice Kathleen Martin Rogers granted them conditional discharges on all counts, records show.

It wasn't long afterwards that Colb, now 17, woke up crying and telling McCarthy how much she missed her mother.

"We'll call her," he said quietly.

Colb's mother was so relieved to hear from her daughter that she agreed to buy bus tickets for both of them to Virginia, where the family was now living. She insisted, though, that McCarthy had to find a place of his own.

McCarthy and Colb continued to see each other until, suddenly, he just disappeared. She learned later that he was jailed on January 13, 1985, in Richmond after police caught him stealing a 1985 Ford automobile. In a deal with the prosecution, McCarthy pleaded guilty on March 14 to a reduced charge of unauthorized use of a motor vehicle. Circuit Court Judge James L. Lupkin sentenced McCarthy to two years in prison, to be followed by supervised probation for three years.

However, shortly after sentencing, McCarthy applied for early release under Virginia's Community Diversion Incentive Program, designed for non-violent offenders who agreed to do volunteer community service, submit to probation supervision, and to stay out of trouble.

McCarthy had served only 10 months behind bars when he was released on October 25, 1985, under the program. Because McCarthy wanted to return to the Potsdam area, Virginia authorities reached an agreement to transfer his probation supervision to New York State.

He was soon in trouble again. McCarthy was arrested for petit larceny in Potsdam on March 4, 1986, and for that was sentenced to 60 days in jail. Apparently unaware McCarthy was on probation, New York authorities never notified Virginia of this conviction, which would have triggered a review and his possible return to prison for up to four years. Virginia officials also didn't know that McCarthy was charged with harassment in Potsdam in May 1986, or that he got into the fight with insurance agent Page in July. During this time, McCarthy consumed alcohol and illegal drugs, despite signing probation papers agreeing to stay out of trouble.

A few days after the attack on Katy, Colb finally learned of McCarthy's whereabouts when her sister showed her a story in *The New York Times* reporting on his arrest.

"I still don't know to this day if Brian beat my brother," Colb recalled in 2020, noting her brother passed away several years earlier. "But after what happened to Katy, I kind of think maybe he did. My brother was beaten the same way he hurt that poor little girl. The way he hurt that poor little girl, I can't even think about, it upsets me so bad. I kind of feel like writing to him and just going, 'What were you thinking? What the hell?' Because that's not the person I knew."

McCarthy was still serving time in Virginia in fall 1985 when his parents organized a late-summer "work party" to put siding on a Parishville neighbor's home. A dozen volunteers took part, including the McCarthys' four other sons, several of Florence McCarthy's brothers, and a family friend, Lawrence Manor, who was a senior investigator with the New York State Police Bureau of Criminal Investigation.

The family was so close to Manor that, on the morning that Katy was attacked, Florence McCarthy placed a personal call to him around 10:30 at the state police barracks.

She told him she heard that Potsdam police had a suspect in custody.

"Is it Brian?" she asked.

"Yes," Manor answered.

At the time, Florence McCarthy was an office worker at Clarkson University. Not only was her son accused of raping and brutally assaulting Katy, he allegedly chose to do so on the campus where she worked.

After talking to Manor, Florence McCarthy headed to the Potsdam police station, where she talked with her son and agreed to bring him a change of clothes.

Manor showed up at the police station around noon, looking to talk to Chief Matott about the case. Matott invited the trooper to join him for lunch at McNamara's restaurant, located just around the corner from Walker Arena.

As Matott ate his meal and Manor sipped coffee, they talked about the physical evidence, the statements from witnesses, and that morning's police interview in which McCarthy denied he attacked Katy. Matott expressed disappointment he couldn't get McCarthy to tell the truth.

Investigator Manor looked up from his coffee. He pointed out that he was friends with McCarthy's parents.

"Maybe I should talk to him for a while," Manor said.

Chapter 9

"What Are You Doing?"

IT was about 1:30 p.m. Friday, August 29, 1986, by the time Potsdam Police Chief Matott and state police Senior Investigator Manor returned from their lunch. Manor waited in the chief's office while Matott fielded more calls from the press and handled a few other tasks. Investigator Perretta, still busy drawing up the arraignment papers, took a break to briefly talk with Manor.

In the cellblock, McCarthy slept on and off.

At 2:04 p.m., McCarthy was awake and asking about his friend Joseph Lopez, according to jail logs. Eight minutes later, McCarthy demanded to know the whereabouts of the clothing his mother was supposed to get for him.

At 2:15, done with other tasks, Matott asked an officer to escort McCarthy back to the chief's office. When McCarthy arrived, Manor was waiting in the room with Matott. The chief told McCarthy that he wanted him to speak with Manor privately. Matott then left, shutting the door behind him and leaving the two alone.

About 10 minutes later, Matott's office door swung open, and Manor emerged to say that McCarthy "told me he wants to change his statement. He will tell the truth about what he remembered." Matott did not ask Manor what he said to change McCarthy's mind.

With Potsdam Police Lieutenant McKendree joining Matott and Manor in the chief's office, the officers again turned on the tape recorders. Matott repeated the date and now noted it was 2:37 p.m.

He also repeated the Miranda Warning.

"Do you understand these rights?" Matott asked McCarthy.

"Yes, I do."

"You do understand that you do not have to talk to me?"

"I understand completely," McCarthy said.

"Is it your request that at this time that you do not have a lawyer?"

"Yeah, that's my request."

McCarthy was wearing the same jacket and pants he had for the first interview that morning. However, McKendree noticed the suspect's demeanor was quite a bit different. Gone was the cocky air of self-confidence. McCarthy sat slumped in his chair, often just staring at the floor.

Matott asked McCarthy to "narrate in your own words" what happened.

"Are you aware of the incident that I am talking about?"

"Yes, I am."

"Do you wish to tell me about it—what happened?"

"The truth, yeah," McCarthy answered.

"Go ahead and proceed, Brian."

McCarthy once again recalled how he had been walking west on Maple Street when he cut across the front parking lot at Walker Arena. He said he then headed back east along the building's south side. Unlike his first statement, though, he didn't claim he made the detour because he heard screams.

Near the arena, he saw a "guy and a girl" sitting on the grass, laughing and talking. McCarthy said he sat on a rock and watched until the two parted.

"I heard something, 'See you later' or 'Goodbye' or something," he said.

McCarthy started to resume his journey, he said, when he nearly bumped into the "girl" at the southeast corner of the arena. He was referring to 19-year-old Katy Hawelka, although neither he nor the officers spoke of her by name during the interrogation.

"As I was walking out," McCarthy said, "the girl was squatting in the corner peeing. And when I walked by, I didn't say anything. I didn't really see her at first because she was sitting in the dark. Then I got right on top of her. She scared me, and I said, 'Oh, excuse me.' And she said, 'That's okay.'"

At that point, McCarthy said, the girl had her right boot off, and she only had one leg in her pants. He said he also noticed "she had blood on her."

He started to walk away, McCarthy said, but then turned around, "went over, and I pushed her into the wall and just—"

McCarthy paused.

"I don't know how to say it."

"Just tell us just exactly what happened," Matott said.

"I tried to take advantage of her," McCarthy said. "I tried, but I couldn't, I couldn't do anything. I just went nuts. I went crazy."

"Then what happened?" the chief asked.

After about two or three minutes, McCarthy said, a car drove by, turned in the parking lot, and stopped. The vehicle soon left, then returned a few minutes later with two people inside. After they left again, McCarthy decided to get out of there.

"When I was leaving, this car drove up and put the headlights right on the girl, and then I heard a bunch of guys—or two guys—say something about, 'Oh, call an ambulance' or something, and I ducked down right there by the stairs. And that is where they found me."

Just like that, Matott had obtained a confession, although he thought McCarthy was lying about some details. The police chief didn't buy that McCarthy's only violence against Katy was to shove her once before trying, but failing, to rape her. The chief also found it hard to believe Katy was bleeding before McCarthy attacked her.

"Okay," Matott said, "now let's get back to when you went over and pushed the girl against the wall. What did you do? What exactly did you do, Brian?"

McCarthy said she had been leaning up against the arena, her back partially to him.

"She couldn't—I don't think she could see me, and when I walked up, she was holding onto the wall or something. She must have been drunk, I think, I don't know. She was staggering. And I just pushed her into the wall, and right, right, right into the wall hard with her face."

"How many times did you do that?" Matott asked.

"Just—I just pushed her once into the wall. And she fell down, and just —I tried to take advantage of her, but I couldn't do anything. I was just too—I don't know—I was too crazy or something. It was weird."

"Did you have intercourse with her?"

"No, I tried," McCarthy said. "I sure did try, but I—I just, I don't know."

"In other words, what you're saying is that you couldn't have an ejaculation?" the chief asked.

"Right."

"Or you couldn't have an erection?"

"Yeah, both."

Matott asked McCarthy if he beat or kicked the young woman. The chief knew from Katy's injuries that her assailant did a lot more than shove her face once into a wall.

"No, I didn't kick her at all," McCarthy said. But after she "passed out or whatever it was," he said, he dragged her by her feet away from the arena wall. Doing this, he dropped her head "real hard," McCarthy said, and then "I saw blood start coming out of her face."

"I just looked at her and I—I said, 'I know I didn't do that.' I just know that I did not beat that girl like that. She had already been hit, repeatedly, before I had seen her there. Yes, I tried to take advantage of her. But ... somebody started to do the same thing before I did, and I—I just, I got caught."

Matott asked him to describe this guy he claimed he saw talking with the girl. (At this point, police weren't aware that Clarkson student Todd Kilburn had walked Katy from downtown to the gate behind Walker Arena just before the attack.)

McCarthy described the man as about 6-foot-1 or 6-foot-2 with dark hair, probably brown, "cut just a little bit shorter than mine." McCarthy didn't think the man had a mustache or other facial hair. He was wearing sneakers and dark-colored pants, possibly jeans; McCarthy said he couldn't be sure because it was still dark. McCarthy also said the guy wore a dark jacket with stripes on the wrist. McCarthy heard the girl ask him something about a fraternity, perhaps one named Theta Kappa or Delta Kappa.

McCarthy added that he heard the guy yell something before he began walking back toward downtown Potsdam.

"But did they seem to be parting in friendly terms when he left?" Matott asked.

"No, because the boy, because the guy yelled, you know."

"But you said, you said one of them said 'goodbye,' you know."

"Yeah, and then I heard—I heard the guy yell, and probably three minutes later, he walked by, and he was walking like he was pissed off at somebody, you know. . . . He was walking really stiff-legged, you know, like he was mad or something."

To the officers in the room, McCarthy still seemed to be making up details as he went along.

Matott returned to asking McCarthy about his attack on Katy.

"So how many times, Brian, did you, did you push this girl's face into the wall?"

"Well, once real hard that I meant to, and the other time, I didn't—I didn't mean to do it. I was just, I was trying to get her out of the corner, trying to sit her up or help her or whatever, and I dropped her. And her face and her head hit the wall real hard, real hard."

"Did she say anything to you?" Matott asked. "After you originally pushed her face into the wall, did she say anything to you? Did you have any conversation with her?"

"She just, she just asked, 'What are you doing?' And that was it. That was all she said. She just said, 'What are you doing?'"

Matott asked who removed the victim's clothing.

"Um, I pulled her shirt up, but her right boot and her right pant leg were off when I, when I walked up. She was trying to do this, trying to pee in the corner or whatever."

"Did you take the rest of her clothes off? Did you take her pants the rest of the way off?"

"Yeah," McCarthy said.

"And her other boot?"

"Yeah. I pulled her boot off and her pants."

"Was she conscious at this time?"

"Yes, she was mumbling," McCarthy said, "but I couldn't make any sense of it."

"You couldn't make any sense out of what she was saying?"

"I had no idea what she was saying."

Matott pressed McCarthy once again whether he did more to injure Katy than to push her face into the wall and accidentally drop her head. McCarthy finally conceded that he did.

"I know that I kicked her, but I wasn't intending to kick her. I was just moving her, because I was pissed off, you know. I wanted her to get up and whatever," he said. "She just, she wouldn't get up. She just laid there."

Matott asked if McCarthy hit her with his fist.

"No, I didn't. I never touched her with my fist the whole time," McCarthy said, adding that he bruised his right hand when he fell against the wall. "That is why it is all black and blue. Because I never hit that girl. I swear to God I never hit her, not with my fist I didn't hit her."

And kicking her in the face was a mistake?

"Right. When I was trying—no, when I walked up, she was, she was standing there trying to hold her, whatever, shit together trying to pee, and one boot was like, was like, I don't know, it looked like she kicked it off or something. It was gone, you know. It was over there."

At this point in the interrogation, even McCarthy seemed to be baffled by what he did, or perhaps he had just grown weary of defending himself.

"I don't know why I did it. I have no idea why I did it," he said.

Matott pressed on.

"When you were attempting to have intercourse with her, did you have the impression that she was conscious or unconscious?"

"I had the impression she was conscious. Because she was mumbling something. I couldn't understand what she was saying. I had no idea what she was saying."

Matott returned to the beginning of the attack.

"Now, when you pushed her face into the wall the first time, would you describe to me how you—what did you do, run up behind her and just push her face?"

"Yeah. Yup."

"Were you running when you pushed her face into the wall?"

"I had all my weight behind me."

"So, you really slammed her face into the wall real hard then?"

"Yeah. I used both hands."

Matott began to ask another question, but McCarthy interrupted. "I hit her in the mid-section and her—she kinda snapped her neck, you know, her neck went back like that when she hit the wall."

McCarthy was no longer even trying to downplay the brutality of his attack on Katy.

After that, Matott asked Manor if he had any questions.

The state police senior investigator wanted to know if the victim really did say, "That's okay," when McCarthy surprised her at the corner of the arena.

"Yeah," McCarthy said. "She said, 'Oh, that's all right.' You know, she was just hanging onto the wall, peeing."

"She was not upset you were there?" Manor asked.

"No. It didn't seem to bother her at all," McCarthy said. "She didn't scream. She didn't yell. She didn't say anything. I mean, I scared her. I know she scared me, because I didn't see her. And I know that I scared her, and she didn't say anything."

Manor asked McCarthy if perhaps he kicked his victim a couple of times on purpose, maybe because he was sexually frustrated.

"No, I didn't," McCarthy insisted. "But I was, I was rolling her, and pushing her and just, I was really, really mad. I was like picking her up and throwing her, and I was just using every bit, every bit of my strength in my body to move that girl, just—just to shake her insides out."

Manor pressed McCarthy on when he realized he severely injured the girl.

"You knew that you had hurt her, once you did this, of course, right, with blood coming out and so forth?"

"I didn't really," McCarthy said. "I didn't really realize what I was doing until, like, when I looked down and I grabbed her by the shirt, and I pulled the shirt up, and I looked, and blood was just—it was all over her. It was all over her shirt and all over her face and in her hair."

Manor also asked McCarthy if he was trying to hide when police found him under the stairs.

"No, I was laying there because I was scared. I didn't know what, you know, I had—I just raped this girl."

McCarthy immediately corrected himself again. "I just *tried* to rape this girl, and I couldn't do anything. . . . I was paralyzed. I just—I just laid there."

McCarthy then added that he ended up under the stairs because he struck his head on "the railing or something."

Before wrapping up the interrogation, Matott asked the suspect if he had anything else he wanted to say.

"Yeah. I am being truthful with you," McCarthy said. "And I am not the only one that tried to do this to that girl, that night."

"Do you swear this is the truth?" Matott asked.

"I swear to God," McCarthy answered.

At precisely 3 p.m., Matott ended the interview.

After he and McKendree turned off the recorders, McCarthy again asked, "How is the girl?"

Matott replied that he hadn't checked on her recently, but he knew that "she was seriously ill and that she was in the hospital."

McCarthy asked if he could be told if her condition changed.

"If there was any change," Matott said, "you would be the first to know."

Back in his cell, McCarthy smoked a cigarette and waited for his family to deliver his clothes, which finally arrived at 3:45 p.m.

Meanwhile, Matott told the Syracuse *Post-Standard* that McCarthy was scheduled to be arraigned that afternoon in Potsdam Village Court on charges of first-degree rape and assault.

"He confessed to it about an hour ago," Matott said.

The Post-Standard and other news media would infer from Matott's statement that McCarthy had confessed to both of the charges, when, in fact, he had admitted to assault but denied raping Katy. Reporters would repeat this mistaken assumption more than once in the coming weeks.

Shortly before 4:30 p.m., officers escorted McCarthy in handcuffs to the village court on Park Street for an arraignment before Justice Kathleen Martin Rogers. By now, McCarthy was dressed in blue jeans, a checked cotton dress shirt, a gray down jacket and unlaced sneakers.

Brian McCarthy arrives at Potsdam Village Court for his arraignment on Friday, August 29, 1986. Escorting him are Officer Gene Brundage, left, and Investigator John Perretta of the Potsdam Police Department. (Melon Grover, Watertown Daily Times photo.)

Clarkson President Clark and Terrence Taylor, Clarkson's director of university relations, were among those seen in attendance.

Rogers set McCarthy's bail at $50,000, which she said was the amount recommended by District Attorney Charles A. Gardner. "I feel the $50,000 is appropriate under the charge and because of the fact that you have a criminal record," Rogers told McCarthy.

The judge also scheduled a preliminary hearing for the following Thursday, September 4. Before then, she said, McCarthy would be eligible to apply for free legal assistance through the county's Assigned Counsel Program.

After the arraignment, an officer walked McCarthy to a patrol car, which immediately transported him to the St. Lawrence County Jail in nearby Canton.

Clarkson University released a statement in which Clark said it was "our most urgent hope" for Katy's recovery. "Her friends and teachers at Clarkson are deeply saddened by this terrible event. It is hard to understand why someone so young and innocent should be the victim of such violence. There is little we can say or do to relieve the anguish felt by the community. We ask everyone to hope and pray for her and her parents."

That afternoon's *Ogdensburg Journal* gave a sobering outlook for Katy's recovery. Without attribution, the newspaper said her injuries were so severe "they could cause loss of brain function." The *Watertown Daily Times* quoted an unidentified hospital official in Watertown who said that the next 36 to 48 hours "are crucial to her survival."

If she died, the newspapers also noted, police were prepared to charge McCarthy with murder.

Chapter *10*

Friends and Family

Todd Kilburn might have been one of the last Clarkson University students to hear the news about the attack outside Walker Arena. Because he slept in late that Friday morning, then got busy doing chores at the Sigma Delta fraternity house at 6 Prospect Place, Katy's companion the night before wasn't on campus to hear announcements.

It wasn't until later in the day that a fraternity member mentioned Katy had been attacked as she was walking home from downtown the night before.

"No way," Kilburn said. "That can't be true." He knew he had escorted her back to campus after the bars closed, and she was fine. But as he picked up a newspaper and read details, he realized that she must have been assaulted just after they parted ways at the gate behind Walker Arena. A stomach-turning combination of horror, sadness and second-guessing overwhelmed him: *Why didn't I try harder to insist on walking her back to her apartment?*

Kilburn decided the next day that he needed to go to the police after reading that authorities were trying to determine the victim's whereabouts before the attack. At 2 p.m. Saturday, Kilburn got a friend to walk with him to the Potsdam police station.

Lieutenant McKendree was on duty when the dispatcher notified him there was a Clarkson student at the front desk saying he escorted Katy back to campus before the attack. McKendree immediately ushered Kilburn into his office, told the friend to leave, and proceeded to read Kilburn his legal rights, a standard procedure in such cases.

"I do remember it was very surreal," Kilburn would say. "Getting your rights read to you, it does very weird things. I understand it now, but I didn't at the time."

In his statement, Kilburn recalled how he and Katy spent time talking and drinking beer at Bogie's until closing time at 2:30, then slowly made their way toward the Clarkson campus. They stopped several times, including occasions when Katy needed to rest her sore foot, and once when he walked to a fence to urinate. As he was doing the latter, he recalled seeing a man he didn't know doing the same thing nearby.

When they got near the arena, Kilburn said, Katy told him "she didn't want me to walk her all the way back to Woodstock because it would be too long a walk back for me."

Other than Katy's limp, Kilburn said, she showed no sign of being impaired.

"When I left her at that gate" behind Walker Arena, Kilburn said, "she was in good enough condition to walk back to the dorms, or I would not have left her to go by herself. At that time, she was walking and talking quite well. Her speech was not slurred, and it had been at least an hour since her last drink."

Piecing together the facts in Kilburn's statement with what McCarthy admitted, along with other evidence, police had a plausible theory of what occurred:

McCarthy first noticed Katy and Kilburn as the two crossed the bridge near the Kentucky Fried Chicken somewhere around 3:15 a.m. McCarthy may even have been the other man Kilburn saw urinating on the fence. Kilburn, who wore a black fraternity jacket with white stripes like the one McCarthy described, chatted briefly with Katy as they arrived at the edge of campus property.

When Kilburn left, McCarthy raced around the front of Walker Arena, then cut back along the south side, expecting to ambush Katy as she walked along the poorly lit shortcut there.

However, he didn't count on Katy stopping to pee at the arena's southeast corner. In the darkness, McCarthy nearly bumped into her. This would explain his odd story to the police that he told her, "Oh, excuse me," and she replied, "That's okay." She must have thought he stumbled upon her by mistake.

Momentarily unsure what to do, McCarthy started to walk away but changed his mind, turned around, and rammed Katy's face into the arena wall with his body's full weight. As she attempted to fight him off, he pummeled her with his fists and kicked her with his heavy boots until she no longer resisted. He then sexually assaulted her.

This theory was just a theory, but it made more sense to McKendree than McCarthy's claim that he came upon Katy by accident, then assaulted her after someone else did.

The problem was, only two people witnessed the assault. One was McCarthy, who couldn't be relied upon to tell the truth. The other was Katy, who was unconscious in an intensive care unit, with a face so disfigured that her mother placed a high school photo next to the bed so the nurses would know what her daughter had looked like.

On Saturday, as Katy's parents camped out at the Watertown hospital, numerous friends and family showed up for support. Others came by to gather information for the police investigation.

When she saw a New York state trooper, Terry suddenly remembered the traffic stop two days earlier on Interstate 81 when Katy was driving to Clarkson.

"What do we do about this speeding ticket?" Terry asked.

The officer gently assured her not to worry about it.

"The least of the problems," he said.

Terry nodded in agreement. She never heard anything more about the ticket.

Two of Katy's close friends from high school, Jim Damiano and Lisa Campolo, drove from Syracuse to House of the Good Samaritan, only to be disappointed they weren't allowed into Katy's room in the ICU. "You don't want to see her anyway," Terry told them quietly, adding that Katy "isn't looking too good."

Katy's former roommate, Nanci Parks, who arrived with her parents, shared a long cry with Terry, telling each other they still had hope Katy would recover. Terry believed it was a miracle Katy was alive, considering her injuries. Maybe she would surprise them with another.

Terry thought it was a good idea when someone on the hospital staff asked if the family wanted a priest to stop by to say prayers and counsel the family. Not long afterward, a casually dressed young man showed up at the ICU. Terry almost mistook him for a teenager.

"Who's that?" Terry asked a staff member.

"He's the priest."

"I want a real priest, like a Roman Catholic priest," Terry said.

Assured the man was a Roman Catholic priest, Terry said she wished he looked more like the ones she remembered.

"Okay," she said. "But I was expecting some older guy with a collar. I wasn't expecting a 12-year-old in sandals."

Several Clarkson officials, including President Clark and Dean of Students Cooper, came by the hospital. Cooper spent much of the weekend with the family, assuring Joe Sr. and Terry that they had the university's full sympathy and support.

Seventy miles away in Syracuse, Betsy Hawelka was growing more frustrated by the hour. Although her father called with updates from the hospital, her best information about the criminal case was coming from TV newscasts and local newspapers. Saturday morning's *Post-Standard* led its front page with the headline, "Student 'Critical' After Rape, Beating." The paper continued to identify the assault victim as a Clarkson sophomore from Syracuse but withheld her name.

Betsy found some of the coverage puzzling, including the newspaper's account of how McCarthy allegedly attacked Katy in a "secluded, dimly lit area used by students as a shortcut from downtown Potsdam to their dorms." The news article also described the path behind Walker Arena as "overgrown" and "poorly lighted." Betsy thought this didn't sound like a route her sister or anyone else would want to take, especially at night.

On Sunday, the Syracuse *Herald American* published an update with the headline "Syracuse rape victim clings to life." A reporter spoke to several of Katy's friends at Clarkson, who said they often used that shortcut. However, none thought she would "take the chance of walking through the brushy, dimly lit area in the company of a strange man."

In the story, university spokesman Taylor defended campus security. He noted that students "are given strong advice on how to handle themselves. . . . In that context, although I'm certain they don't single out that area, they are advised to avoid areas that can be a problem."

By Sunday morning, Betsy decided she needed more answers, and she knew she wasn't going to find them at her mother's home in Syracuse.

"Well, I'm not staying here," she told Carey and Joe Jr. "I'm going to Clarkson."

Betsy borrowed her mother's car and began driving north toward Potsdam. As she neared Watertown, she made a spontaneous decision to detour to the hospital, hoping her parents would change their minds and let her see Katy. To her disappointment, the closest they let her get to Katy was standing outside her door. Betsy was glad, though, that she made the stop, as she was able to spend time with her parents and to learn more about Katy's medical care.

A short while after that, Betsy resumed the drive to Potsdam, where her first stop was Katy's apartment at Woodstock Village. Betsy had been worried someone might steal Katy's possessions, but she found everything as her sister left it, including clothes, dishes, and other items in bags and boxes. It looked like the only items Katy had unpacked were some family photos, which she had put up on a wall.

Betsy questioned Katy's roommates about what they knew. They said they accompanied Katy downtown on Thursday night, but they split up after that and never saw her again.

A resident assistant for the apartments said she heard that a Clarkson student, Todd Kilburn, had walked Katy back to campus.

How do I find him? Betsy asked.

"I'll call him," the resident assistant said.

When the phone rang at Sigma Delta, Kilburn was working up a sweat helping to get the fraternity house into shape.

The resident assistant told him Katy's sister was at the Woodstock Village apartment and wanted to talk to him.

"I have to take a shower and clean up first," Kilburn said.

"We don't care about that. Just come now," the RA said.

When he arrived, Kilburn repeated for Betsy what he told police a day earlier about spending time with Katy at Bogie's before he accompanied her back to campus. He said he would have walked with her to Woodstock, but Katy insisted on going alone.

"She said, 'I'm fine to walk.' And I said, 'Are you sure you're okay?' And she's like, 'Oh, yeah. I'm on campus now. I'm fine.'"

Betsy spoke to Kilburn for several minutes, prodding him to recall every possible detail. She would later describe it as a "grilling." But at that point, Betsy's need to know trumped her sympathy for any emotional distress Kilburn was feeling.

After leaving Woodstock Village, Betsy drove down Clarkson Avenue to Walker Arena to see for herself the corner where McCarthy ambushed Katy. By then, the university had washed away the blood and cleaned up the area, and the rope police used to block off the area was gone. Some students were once again strolling by the arena on their way from downtown.

Betsy walked behind the arena to check out that shortcut. Betsy had been under the impression that it was some overgrown, isolated path. Instead, the route passed through an open gate, across a parking lot, and onto a sidewalk. To Betsy, it seemed reasonable that students would assume Clarkson intended for them to walk this way back to campus.

After a couple of hours, Betsy left Potsdam and returned to the Watertown hospital. She would be present when her parents learned that Katy had run out of miracles.

Chapter 11

Life Support

A T about 3 p.m. Sunday, August 31, 1986, doctors at House of the Good Samaritan informed Terry and Joe Sr. there was nothing more the hospital could do to bring back their daughter. Katy Hawelka's heart was pumping blood, and oxygen still flowed through her lungs, but tests showed she had suffered brain death.

"She's never going to regain consciousness," one of the doctors said.

To diagnose brain death, the hospital had followed the latest guidelines under New York state law. The patient's pupils had to be fully dilated without constriction in light. The eyes must not have moved when touched. When doctors injected cold water in the ear, the body must have showed no reaction. There had to be no movement in any part of the body.

In Katy's case, doctors also relied on an electroencephalogram, or EEG, that showed a flat line while measuring her brain activity. For a final confirmation, they would run another EEG the next morning. If that result were the same—and the doctors believed it would be—they would recommend that Katy's parents permit them to disconnect the ventilator and other machines keeping her body alive.

By the mid-1980s, courts had granted, and New York state legislators had enacted laws, giving next of kin this right to disconnect life support if the patient had irreversible brain damage. However, Katy's mother couldn't stop thinking about all those stories of patients who surprised everyone by coming out of a coma.

Terry and Joe Sr. would wait for Monday's test results before telling doctors what to do.

Meanwhile, the St. Lawrence County District Attorney's Office jumped into the process by asking doctors not to take any steps to disconnect life support until prosecutors made sure they followed the correct legal procedures for cases involving a homicide. The DA's office didn't want Brian McCarthy's attorney to argue that Katy would have recovered if left on the machines.

Terry had an issue of her own. She knew Katy was a designated organ donor who wanted her last act of life to be a gift that might save someone else's. So, Terry was crushed when doctors said they weren't allowed to harvest Katy's organs due to it being a homicide. Someone suggested authorities were afraid McCarthy's lawyer might say Katy wasn't dead if her organs were alive in someone else. The truth was, authorities wanted all of Katy's organs intact so that an autopsy could document her injuries and determine the cause of death.

The next morning, Monday, September 1, as most of America celebrated Labor Day, doctors ran the second EEG and confirmed the earlier test: Katy was legally brain-dead. They urged the parents to end life support. By then, Katy's parents had already agreed between themselves to follow whatever the doctors suggested. "I think I was in such a state they could have told me anything, and I probably would have bought it because they were the doctors, and I wasn't," Terry said.

However, Terry and Joe Sr. asked to delay removing the life support until Monday afternoon when the whole family could be present at the hospital.

Since the morning of the attack, Joe Jr. had wanted to join his parents at the hospital. When he was told on Monday that he and Carey could finally do so, the teen initially concluded that it meant Katy's condition had improved. But on the long drive to Watertown, an older family member gently suggested otherwise.

"Have you ever contemplated she's not going to make it?" Joe Jr. was asked.

It was only then that Katy's brother understood that they were traveling to Watertown so the whole family could be present when Katy died.

By 1 p.m., the family was all in one place for the last time while Katy was alive. But even as her parents made a final visit to the ICU to hold her hand and to say goodbye, they insisted that Betsy, Carey and Joe Jr. remain outside. Carey would remember peering through a window and seeing only the foot of Katy's bed. Like her sister and brother, Carey didn't argue with their parents about their decision, but she was upset about it anyway.

"It's something I will always regret," she said. "But being 17 at the time, who was I? I was a child. I didn't have the voice to say, 'Hey, I really need to see her.' I was in shock and just did what I was told to do."

At about 1:45 p.m., doctors announced they were ready to disconnect life support. They asked the family to wait in the first-floor chapel while the medical staff unplugged the machines. The staff said it could take hours, maybe even a couple of days, before Katy's heart stopped.

As her family waited in the chapel, Betsy walked to the lobby and sat alone, just staring ahead at the glass doors. She thought someone from the family should be in the room when doctors disconnected life support. However, Betsy understood the pressure her parents faced to go along with whatever the doctors requested. No parent gets a manual on the right thing to do when your child is declared brain-dead. "It's almost like my parents were on autopilot where you're just trying to do what people tell you to do," Betsy said. "It's such a gruesome experience, and no one is in their right mind in thinking anyway."

At 1:58 a.m., the medical staff unplugged Katy's life support.

About 20 minutes later, a doctor came by the chapel and gently shared the news that Katy had gone quickly. The official time of death was 2:16 p.m., September 1, 1986.

"You did the right thing," a doctor assured Terry and Joe Sr., adding that the hospital would "take care of it from here."

Terry interpreted that to mean that the family members were expected to leave. No one suggested they go back in and see Katy one last time. There was nothing more to do except to go home and begin making funeral arrangements.

A short while later, Clarkson Dean of Students Cooper, whom the family had welcomed to wait with them in the chapel, issued a statement announcing Katy's passing. Students would begin fall classes the next day knowing that one of their own would never join them.

"There is no adequate way to express how deeply saddened the entire campus feels about Katherine's death," the statement said. "In a small community like Potsdam, crimes of this ferocity are rare, and when they happen, they touch everyone. This only adds to the depth of our grief. Our hearts go out to her family and her classmates."

Potsdam police did not wait long to respond in their own way to Katy's death. Within an hour, they additionally charged McCarthy with second-degree murder, which carried a maximum sentence of 25 years to life in prison. (At the time, a first-degree murder charge was possible in New York only if the victim was a police officer or prison guard. The state had no death penalty in place or a sentence of life without parole.)

At 4:30 p.m., police removed McCarthy from his county jail cell and returned him to Potsdam to appear before Village Justice Rogers, who arraigned him on the new charge and revoked his bail. The proceeding was otherwise unremarkable, except when Rogers made the routine request for police to remove the suspect's handcuffs. An officer guarding McCarthy insisted on keeping them on, saying he was doing so for the protection of the suspect and others.

Not long after Katy's family returned to Syracuse, Joe Sr. turned to his teenage son and said, "Let's go for a ride." They didn't talk much during the drive, which was okay with Joe Jr. He just wanted time, finally, to spend with his father.

When they reached the suburban community of Fayetteville, Joe Sr. pulled into the driveway of the Eaton-Tubbs-Schepp Funeral Home on East Genesee Street.

As they sat in the car, he said quietly to his son, "I used to drive by this funeral home, and I never remember seeing people there." That was the thing about funeral homes: It wasn't a place people visited unless they had to do so.

The two went inside, where a funeral director greeted them with quiet condolences and began collecting information for Katy's calling hours, services, burial, and obituary.

When the discussion turned to the choice of casket and gravestone, Joe Sr. excused himself to use the bathroom. While he was away, the funeral director continued to discuss options with Joe Jr. until the teenager stopped him.

"I'm only 16. You should be talking to my Dad about this," the boy said.

The funeral director patted his shoulder and said, "Your dad is in the bathroom because he can't handle this. You're going to have to do it."

Joe Jr. went ahead and made arrangements for his sister's funeral, trying to make sensible and dignified choices he thought his father would approve. When they were finished, Joe Sr. came out of the bathroom and signed off on everything.

On the way home, he turned to his son and thanked him for doing a good job.

Joe Jr. would look back later and decide this was the day his childhood ended. From that point onward and for many years, he would experience dark fantasies about what he would do if alone in a room with Brian McCarthy.

Katy's mother would recall that she suffered from anger, too, not only at her daughter's killer but incredibly at the neighbor who promised everything would turn out all right.

For a long time, Terry resented Isabel McConnell for "lying" to her by saying on the morning of the attack that Katy would be okay. Terry remained friends with her, though, and McConnell died in 2016 at age 98, never knowing Terry had once harbored a grudge against her.

"I loved her dearly, and I never told her," Terry said. "I never said a word to her that, damn it, she lied to me. She was my good friend, and she lied to me."

Chapter 12

Cause of Death

JEFFERSON County Assistant Medical Examiner Joven G. Kuan delayed Katy's autopsy until nearly six hours after her death so that police Lieutenant McKendree and Investigator Perretta could drive from Potsdam to attend the examination in the ground-level morgue at House of the Good Samaritan. McKendree brought a camera and took photos as Kuan directed and as he, himself, saw fit, while the pathologist offered a running commentary.

The only other person in attendance was Medical Examiner Virgilio A. Alon, who supervised the procedure.

One of the first things Kuan noted was the remnants of Katy's extensive medical treatment, including the presence of a breathing tube, intravenous lines, sutures, and bandages.

Later, it would take him five single-spaced typed pages to fully list his findings, including what he immediately noticed were "numerous external body injuries." Many were classic defensive wounds, including a compound fracture to Katy's right index finger, possibly from trying to block a punch or kick. Bruises on her forearms were similar to ones seen when a beating victim tries to protect her face. Bruises on her inner thighs were of the type that often occurred during rape. The toll also included two black eyes, swelling and bleeding of the nose, and bruising to Katy's face, neck, and shoulders.

However, none of these visible injuries caused her death.

During an internal examination, Kuan discovered a fracture to the hyoid bone, a horseshoe-shaped structure in the middle of the neck that often fractures when a person is strangled. It is almost impossible for it to break when someone is punched or kicked, since a blow to one side alone would cause it to flex in the other direction. Other evidence of strangulation included swelling and bleeding in Katy's throat, as well as damage to her lungs.

Kuan's exam of Katy's brain found a small bruise to the left frontal lobe that, absent other injuries, might have caused her some disability but wouldn't have led to her death. More importantly, her brain showed "neuronal necrosis," which in layman's terms means the neurons in the brain that control the electrical impulses died due to lack of oxygen.

Because there were no ligature marks on Katy's neck, Kuan came to the conclusion she was manually strangled. In other words, rather than use a rope or other object, her killer used his hands to compress her neck with such force that it interrupted the flow of blood to her brain. She would have fallen unconscious in less than 15 seconds once full pressure was applied. Continued lack of blood flow would have led to brain death in about four or five minutes.

Medical Examiner Alon, in filling out Katy's death certificate, ruled she died from asphyxia due to manual strangulation, with "minimal subdural hematoma" as a contributing factor.

The death certificate and autopsy report did not provide an answer to a critical question: Would Katy have lived if the two Clarkson University security guards had intervened to stop the attack? The report did not determine the order in which the injuries occurred. However, if Katy wasn't immediately strangled when she was first attacked, her injuries were not yet fatal when the first security guard reached the scene. Even if the strangulation began at the start of the attack, quick intervention might have saved her.

"I don't think there's any way of knowing," Alon told a reporter.

In the immediate aftermath of the attack, Potsdam Police Chief Matott and university officials described the guards in heroic terms, noting they had discovered the attack, called the police, gave initial aid to Katy, and pointed out McCarthy before he could flee.

The day after Katy died, this narrative changed dramatically when the Syracuse *Herald-Journal* obtained a copy of police statements by the two guards. In a front-page story with the sensational headline "Guards saw rape, did nothing," the newspaper revealed that guards Donald Shanty and Kim Avadikian had witnessed the attack but didn't intervene because they thought they were witnessing a couple involved in consensual sex.

National news organizations soon picked up this story of two university guards who reportedly ignored an alleged rape and murder in progress. Typical was this headline in the *Adirondack Daily News* over an Associated Press story: "Brutal rape witnessed by guards." The story included Shanty's admission to police, "I didn't think too much of the guy and girl being there because, in the two and a half years that I've been working as a security guard for Clarkson, I have seen students having sex in unusual places before."

An editorial in the Syracuse *Post-Standard* under the headline "Clarkson's Standards" said the newspaper was "troubled by the response of authorities to the incident. Surely Clarkson College is not an institution given over to free love and outdoor sexual acrobatics. . . . Parents and other college supporters won't like to hear that sex in the open is tacitly considered part of the college experience—at least by some in authority."

Some students also were critical of the guards.

"It was a public place. Consenting or not, they should have stopped it right away," Clarkson student Michael Cook, 20, told the *Herald-Journal*, adding that the guards shouldn't have assumed it was a couple having a sexual romp at 3:30 a.m. next to the campus hockey arena. "That (sex) isn't common outside on the campus grounds."

The New York Times sent a reporter to Potsdam, choosing a broader perspective about a village where its "sense of security has been shattered by a brutal rape and murder on the campus." But the newspaper also prominently noted the failure of the guards to intervene. Speaking to the *Times*, Chief Matott agreed the two displayed an unusually casual attitude toward public sex.

But, he added, "Mommies and daddies don't stop sex, and neither does a college."

Privately, Clarkson President Clark seethed about the critical news coverage and editorials. He thought the media acted more outraged by what they perceived as tolerance of public sex than about the report that a young woman was brutally raped and murdered.

In his first public statements, Clark defended the guards and said it was unfair to claim the university was lax in security based on a single tragic incident.

"Even President Reagan, the most protected man in the world, was shot and hurt," Clark told the *Watertown Daily Times*. "Despite the best preventative measures, tragedies like this happen. But at the same time, we've got too many people playing 'what if,' and there is a tendency to blame, to say, 'Because this is such a tragedy, it must therefore be someone's fault.' But it doesn't always work that way, and in life, there are things out of our control that are really no one's fault."

Clark did add that the university would review its security measures in the wake of the tragedy to see if they might be improved.

Clarkson Dean of Students Cooper told reporters that the university did not turn a blind eye to people having sex outdoors on campus, despite what Shanty said to police. In the two years that he had been dean, Cooper said, this was the first report to him about public sex on campus.

One other important voice also came to the university's defense. Wednesday afternoon, Joe Hawelka Sr. asked the funeral home to release a statement from the family.

"I have seen the newspapers today, and I have talked to the Potsdam police from the very first," Katy's father said. "I, her mother, and her whole family in no way feel that there is any fault on the part of Clarkson University or the village of Potsdam."

Terry would say later she had no memory of approving her ex-husband's statement. But she wasn't surprised he would defend the university at that point. Clarkson officials had gone out of their way at the hospital to comfort the family and to offer support. It was Joe Sr.'s nature to repay kindness with kindness.

At calling hours, Joe Sr. made a point to greet mourners who stood in a long line that went out the door of the Fayetteville funeral home and down the street. Many of them were Henninger teachers and other adults who were as tearful as Katy's friends.

Normally, Joe Sr. wasn't the kind of person to show physical affection for those outside his family, but he put that aside when someone approached him in tears at the funeral home.

Clarkson University President Allan H. Clark speaks to the university community during a campus telecast on Wednesday, September 3, 1986. (WSYR-TV, Channel 9 photo.)

"I don't know what to say," one might say.

"You don't need to say anything," Joe Sr. responded. "Thank you for coming, and give me a hug."

Wednesday evening, Clark gave a seven-minute address televised by the university's cable channel. He again defended campus security and the actions of the guards, noting Joe Sr.'s statement supporting the university.

Clark encouraged "sympathy for all touched by this tragedy—for Katy's family and friends, her roommates, for those who worked so hard to save her life. If you knew Katy, send a comforting word to her family. It means a lot to them."

He added that Clarkson would provide bus transportation for any university student wishing to attend her funeral, set for 10:30 a.m. the next day in the Syracuse suburb of Manlius.

Chapter 13

Mourning

Dressed all in white, Terry Connelly arrived at her daughter's funeral holding a single daisy, Katy's favorite flower. Terry also made sure that plenty of these flowers decorated St. Ann's Church, chosen for the Thursday service because it was located across the street in Manlius from where Terry's grandparents once lived. Betsy Hawelka carried a copy of one of Katy's favorite poems to read aloud at the service. Her sister Carey brought an audiocassette with a rock 'n' roll song that had a special meaning.

Katy's family was determined to see that her funeral would not dwell on the tragic way she died but instead celebrate how she lived. But the sadness was almost overwhelming at times. Joe Hawelka Sr. walked into the church with his arms wrapped tightly around his wife, Donna, as if trying to keep each other from collapsing. They joined the rest of the family as they took seats in front of the church, next to a white coffin that pallbearers slid from a black hearse and rolled inside on a silver-colored trolley.

"From what I recall," Betsy said, "I was just trying to keep it together. I don't think at that point there was a lot of ability to deal with it."

The service drew about 400 people, including students arriving on buses from Clarkson. Several university officials, including President Clark, drove to the church on their own, as did Brian E. Kurish and Chris Taylor, members of the Potsdam Volunteer Rescue Squad. Also making the trip was the Rev. John Hunt, pastor of the Catholic Newman Center in Potsdam, who was among at least four priests at the service.

Outside the church, news photographers kept a respectful distance, and later set up cameras in the back of the church. However, one person didn't get the message the family asked not to be photographed during the service.

In this screenshot from video, pallbearers escort Katy Hawelka's casket into St. Ann's Church in Manlius, New York, for her funeral service on Thursday, September 4, 1986. (WSYR-TV, Channel 9 photo.)

Not long after it began, a side door swung open, and someone with a camera peered in. Betsy rose in outrage to confront the intruder, but then sat down when she saw someone else intervene.

In his eulogy, the Reverend Fred R. Mannara, pastor at Our Lady of Lourdes Church in Syracuse, drew on his memories of Katy through his pastoral work with students at the Henninger Faith Center. He described her as someone with "that gracious smile, always a smile, faithful in class, beautiful, attentive, good."

Mannara told Katy's friends that he understood their "feeling of frustration, bewilderment and that eternal 'why?'" He had no answer to that, but he said just asking the question was healthy. "It's a sign of our love, our deep friendship, and our loss of Katy," he said.

Continuing to address the young mourners, Father Mannara encouraged them to follow Katy's example of embracing education "so you can continue

In this screenshot from video, priests officiate at Katy Hawelka's funeral on September 4, 1986, at St. Ann's Church in Manlius. (WSYR-TV, Channel 9 photo.)

to make life better for all of us—to dispel the darkness of ignorance (and) to bring about truth." He added, "She is no longer able to experience the joys of life with us, but now she will experience the joys of heaven . . . and the challenge here on earth must be ours."

After he spoke, Betsy walked to the altar to recite the poem Katy had shared with someone going through tough times. If you need a friend, the unknown writer said, "I will be here until the end." As she read the poem, Betsy became so overwhelmed by emotion that she couldn't continue speaking. Sister Linda Hogan of the Faith Heritage Center stepped forward and finished the reading for her.

After the service, vehicles lined up behind the hearse to take Katy's family and several of her closest friends to the burial at St. James Cemetery in nearby Cazenovia. In one car, Betsy, Carey, and Joe Jr. rode together. As they left the church, Carey put on the cassette with the song "You Can't

Always Get What You Want" by The Rolling Stones.

In 1984, not long after Katy got her driver's license, the family took a car ride from Syracuse to Florida to visit their grandparents Frank and Alice Ryan. Katy remembered to bring music. Hour after hour, mile after mile, whenever Katy drove, she played an album by The Rolling Stones so many times everyone thought she was going to wear out the tape. The album became, in effect, the soundtrack to their memories of that wonderful trip.

A few weeks before Katy's death, she and Carey watched the 1983 film *The Big Chill*, which has a memorable scene when "You Can't Always Get What You Want" is played at a funeral. Katy turned to Carey and remarked that song would be a great choice for any funeral.

Now, on the way to the cemetery to bury Katy, "You Can't Always Get What You Want" played, and her three siblings somehow smiled and wept at the same time.

After the burial, Terry invited everyone back to her home in Syracuse. Clarkson student Kilburn joined the university friends who showed up, although he was a little nervous if he would be welcome. But the family was exceptionally nice, never even hinting they found him at fault for not walking Katy back to her apartment.

"There weren't even nonverbal cues that I got, no looks of 'How dare you!' I got absolutely none of that," Kilburn said. "If I had been through what they went through, I don't know if I could have been as gracious as they were."

During the gathering, Terry invited some of Katy's closest friends to go to her bedroom and take an item of clothing or something else as a remembrance. High school pal Lisa Campolo picked out a little brown box in which Katy had stored flowers she wore to her prom. Nanci Parks, Katy's freshman roommate, took a jean jacket that the two had often swapped.

Almost an hour had passed when several people noticed that another of Katy's friends, Sarah Kharas, hadn't returned from the cemetery.

Finally, when Kharas showed up, she appeared flustered. Someone asked what was wrong.

"I can't say," Kharas said quietly. "I don't want to upset Katy's mom."

Terry overhead the conversation. She told Katy's friend that, whatever happened, she wasn't going to be upset with her.

In tears, Kharas said she was standing by the open grave to say a private goodbye to Katy when her keys slipped from her hand and fell under the coffin. Embarrassed, she had to find someone from the cemetery to lift the casket and retrieve her keys.

Terry smiled. "Sarah, that was Kate, you know, saying, 'You want to say goodbye to me, I'll grab your keys.' It was her way of saying, 'I'm going to be all right' and 'You're going to be all right.'"

Not long after Katy was buried, workers placed a stone marker etched with her name, the names of her parents, and a Christian cross separating "1967" and "1986." Later, the graveside would become home for stuffed animals, beer caps, flowers, photographs, and other gifts from her friends. Joe Sr. also planted a small bush, but he eventually was asked to remove it when cemetery officials said it grew too large.

"Everybody deals in their own way," Betsy said of the cemetery gifts. "It's not always been the best place or the most comfortable place. It's difficult for me to go there to this day."

On the day of Katy's funeral, one of Terry's friends took her aside.

"Terry," she said, "you need to get an attorney."

"What are you talking about?" Terry said. "I'm not looking to sue anybody."

The friend thought it wouldn't hurt to get some legal advice since it wasn't clear what role the family would play in the criminal case or who was responsible for paying the medical and funeral bills. Terry said she would think about it.

At that point, she was so numb she could do little more than take one day at a time. What she should do tomorrow or the day after that, she didn't know.

"All I wanted to do," Terry said later, "was to crawl into a hole and die."

Chapter 14

The Week After

Abulletproof vest bulged slightly under Brian McCarthy's tan sports jacket as police escorted him into Potsdam Village Court for a preliminary hearing on Friday, September 5, 1986, a day later than first planned. At the door, police used hand-held metal detectors to screen spectators, searched handbags and briefcases for weapons, blocked off the first two rows of seating behind the defendant, and stationed an officer directly behind him.

In the mid-1980s, this was unprecedented security for the Potsdam courtroom. Police Chief Matott explained afterward that he heard rumors someone might try to harm McCarthy, although police had not received a specific threat.

"We just want to make sure he's safe," Matott said.

Justice Rogers held the 9:30 a.m. hearing to determine if there was sufficient evidence to jail McCarthy until a St. Lawrence County grand jury could meet to decide whether to indict him in the murder of Katy Hawelka.

McCarthy sat quietly with eyes lowered and hands folded as the proceedings got underway with testimony by Clarkson security guards Shanty and Avadikian, who last saw the defendant when an ambulance whisked him from the crime scene.

Avadikian testified that it was shortly before 3:30 a.m. when he heard a noise, possibly someone shouting, outside Walker Arena before he summoned Shanty to check it out. Avadikian couldn't tell if the voice was male or female. "It was a strange noise, lots of echoes," he said.

Avadikian said he later discovered the defendant under nearby stairs, prompting the guard "to make sure (McCarthy) wasn't moving or anything"

Brian McCarthy wears a bulletproof vest as he leaves a preliminary hearing Friday, September 5, 1986, in Potsdam Village Court. Escorting him are, from left, Lieutenant Terry McKendree, Officer John Kaplan and Officer James Mason of the village police department. (Melon Grover, Watertown Daily Times photo.)

until police arrived. He recalled that an officer soon pulled the defendant "out from under the staircase, face down."

Both guards testified that McCarthy was the assailant they had seen on top of Katy.

The hearing's only other witness was Police Lieutenant McKendree, who began by describing the time and place of the attack and other details. But before he could answer questions about McCarthy's confession, defense attorney Charles Nash asked Rogers to close the hearing. If McCarthy's statements to police were later suppressed, Nash said, having their contents publicized now would make it difficult to find jurors who didn't know about them.

District Attorney Gardner objected, as did several media organizations, which argued that Nash had not shown "substantial probability" that banning the press was necessary to prevent publicity from having a prejudicial effect on McCarthy's rights.

Rogers decided to go along with Nash's request, ruling that "public access has to be balanced against the right of the defendant to be able to have a fair trial should he go to trial." However, she said she would release a transcript of the hearing once a trial judge ruled the confession admissible or, if not, once the criminal proceedings were over.

McKendree gave the rest of his testimony behind closed doors in the judge's chambers. About an hour later, Rogers returned to the courtroom to announce that she had "reasonable cause to believe" that McCarthy had raped and assaulted Katy. She sent him back to jail pending a grand jury convening later in the month.

The judge also signed an order requiring the St. Lawrence County Office of Health & Mental Health Services to evaluate McCarthy to determine if he was mentally competent to participate in legal proceedings.

Only a day before, the *Ogdensburg Journal* and the *Watertown Daily Times* published stories detailing some of McCarthy's erratic behavior in the hours before the attack. The owner of Chateau's in Winthrop told the newspapers that McCarthy had been involved in an altercation at the bar several hours before the attack on Katy.

The newspapers also reported how McCarthy, while hitchhiking to Potsdam shortly after visiting Chateau's, had allegedly threatened to kill a patron from the bar. State police Senior Investigator Manor told the *Journal* it wasn't clear if officers had enough evidence to arrest McCarthy, even if they had found him that evening. But Manor conceded that "there may have been an arrest, and that (murder) might not have happened."

Police also learned after Katy's death that McCarthy had been involved in an altercation after hitchhiking to Potsdam.

Potsdam State junior Thomas D. Rupert, 20, told police that a man confronted him and another student after they left Maxfield's restaurant and bar on Market Street just after midnight. He said this stranger shouted at them as they walked through the Clarkson Inn's parking lot on Main Street.

"Shut up!" Rupert recalled that the students yelled back.

When they reached the edge of the lot, the students noticed the man was following them. They stopped and waited for him to catch up. When this unkempt man in jeans and work boots identified himself as a police officer, they demanded to see his badge.

Patrolman James Mason escorts Brian McCarthy to a patrol car outside Potsdam Village Court following a hearing on Friday, September 5, 1986. (Bill Hart, The Post-Standard photo.)

The man put his hands behind his back.

"If you do anything, I'm going to blow you away," he said.

"Oh, and you have a gun?" one of the students taunted.

"Yes."

They demanded to see the weapon. Not in the light, the man said. Rupert and his friend walked to a darker spot near the parking lot.

It was then the man admitted he was lying about having a gun.

"Oh, you called my first bluff," he said. "Do you want to call my second?"

"Yeah, what is it?"

The man finally identified himself as Brian McCarthy and said he was working with three state troopers perched in the trees with high-powered rifles; they paid him $250 to watch the two students. McCarthy pulled out his wallet to show his driver's license confirming his name.

Still, the students didn't buy McCarthy's claim that he was working with the police. Finally, he admitted to them he was lying about that, too.

In an act of contrition, McCarthy pulled out a baggie containing what Rupert recognized as marijuana and asked if the two wanted to get stoned together. Rupert said they refused. But he agreed to walk back to Maxfield's to accept McCarthy's offer to buy him a beer. Rupert said McCarthy also bought one for himself. The two did not see each other after that.

These witness statements led Potsdam police Investigator Perretta to tell the *Adirondack Daily Enterprise* that McCarthy "went off his rocker" that evening and that Katy had the misfortune to be in his way.

"They weren't dating. They didn't know each other," Perretta said. "Apparently, he was looking for a victim, and he found her on her way back to the dorms."

Two days after Katy died, Perretta was on duty when Stephen Charles Williams visited the station and asked to speak to an officer handling the murder investigation. The 46-year-old Williams, whose nickname was "Whiskey," was a familiar face to Potsdam police, with an arrest record stretching back for more than a decade, mostly for offenses related to misdemeanor possession of marijuana.

Williams lived by himself in Madrid in a one-room cabin along the Grasse River. Until the previous week, he allowed McCarthy to stay in the upper part of a somewhat larger cabin that Williams owned nearby.

Williams said he wanted to share information about McCarthy.

"Sure, go ahead," Perretta said.

Not here, Williams insisted. "John, I want to talk to the district attorney with you," he said mysteriously.

"Okay, we can go over," Perretta said.

"I want a sandwich first."

Perretta bought Williams a sandwich and, accompanied by Patrolman Bartlett, the three traveled to Canton to meet with District Attorney Gardner.

At the meeting, Williams explained that he was convinced McCarthy murdered a 17-year-old girl who disappeared after staying with McCarthy at the Madrid cabin in 1984. Perretta remembered the girl, Mary Colb, because he arrested her and McCarthy that July after they broke into the Arlington Inn and stole food and beer.

Williams now wondered if Katy would still be alive if he had come forward sooner to tell the police about McCarthy and this missing girl. After the meeting, Perretta and Bartlett drove Williams back to his home, and Perretta assured him he would check out the story.

Three days later, on Saturday, September 6, Potsdam resident Bruce De-Shane was driving through Madrid at about 6:15 p.m. when he stopped to see Williams at his cabin. DeShane discovered his friend lying dead, face-up and soaked in blood, in a small depression in the ground. DeShane immediately contacted St. Lawrence County sheriff's deputies.

When authorities got to the scene, they initially thought it was a homicide due to slash marks on Williams' neck, a trail of blood, and the fact they could not find any weapon.

After an examination by coroner Phillip Brown, though, police came up with a different theory of how Williams died:

Sometime on Saturday morning, depressed over Katy's murder and feeling he could have prevented it, Williams stood outside and used a knife to slash his throat, deep enough to bleed but not enough to be fatal. Brown described them later as classic "hesitation marks."

Frustrated he did not have the willpower to stab himself to death, Williams tossed the knife into the river before walking back inside the cabin, dripping blood as he stared into a mirror. He then found a 7-Up soda bottle containing cedar oil, a poison used in disinfectants because its odor was strong enough to cover the stench of an outhouse. Williams gulped down the cedar oil and tossed the bottle, which rolled under a sofa. He went back outside, collapsed and died.

When the coroner examined the stomach contents during an autopsy, the smell of cedar oil was overwhelming. Brown told *The Post-Standard* that someone had to be pretty determined to die if they swallowed that vile liquid.

"It's an unusual case. There's no ifs, ands or buts about it," Brown said.

Williams left no suicide note. But his estranged wife, Roberta, did not dispute the coroner's ruling that Williams killed himself. Williams was "very depressed" after McCarthy was arrested, she said in an interview with the *Watertown Daily Times*.

Williams never knew he was wrong about Mary Colb. The teenager disappeared from Potsdam in 1984 because she got homesick and moved back with her mother. As Williams took his own life believing she was murdered, Colb was alive and well and living in Virginia.

On the afternoon of Sunday, September 7, flags hung at half-staff at Clarkson's Snell Hall, where more than 400 people showed up for a memorial service for Katy. Someone at the door handed out blue sheets printed with hymns. When people took their seats in the auditorium, a reporter later noted, it was eerily quiet, with none of the usual coughing or shuffling of feet. Even two overhead fans spun in silence.

The Rev. Hunt of the Catholic Newman Center spoke first, saying Potsdam was "saddened by death, maddened by its means, but gladdened by having this time together."

Michael Cooper, the university's dean of students, read a poem that Katy's friends wrote after her death:

Sweet Katy,
with your big blue eyes,
a smile always on your face.
In every one of our hearts,
you quickly found a place.

Your mouth was always going,
you had so much to say.
Our happy-go-lucky, beautiful friend,
you always brightened up our day.

You were the life of any party,
made us laugh until we cried.
So honest and sincere,
you couldn't hurt us if you tried.

Sweet Katy, so caring,
and sharing and giving.

You gave meaning to the words,
loving and living.

But the Lord has called an angel home,
and tears we shed each night,
You're still alive in all of us,
you've only left our sight.

Clarkson President Clark told the mourners Katy should be remembered as a "young woman with strengths and weaknesses and potential. ... Focus on the way she lived, not the way she died." He read from Thornton Wilder's "Our Town," comparing Potsdam to the idyllic small town in that play. Clark encouraged Katy's friends to "notice how good every day is," and to overcome evil with love.

Lois Vaccariello, a member of the faculty at Potsdam State's Crane School of Music, sang "On Eagle's Wings." Father Hunt concluded the service by saying, "Katy is in God's hands. We are in God's hands. Let us go in peace."

Joe Hawelka Sr. and his son, Joe Jr., made the trip from Verona Beach to attend the service, although neither took part. Years later, Katy's mother would not remember why she didn't go, although Terry recalled being upset by then that Clarkson officials had not shared with the family that the guards had witnessed the attack but didn't do anything to stop it.

"I'm thinking at that point that maybe they were a little more culpable than they led us to believe," she said.

To Katy's mother, the gulf between Syracuse and Potsdam seemed like a million miles in the days after Katy's murder. Most of what she was learning came from reading newspapers and watching TV newscasts; authorities weren't sharing much with the family, at least not with Terry. Her biggest fear was that she would pick up the paper one day and read that McCarthy wormed his way out of a life sentence with an insanity defense or plea bargain.

About two weeks after Katy's funeral, Terry went back to see neighbor Isabel McConnell, this time for advice on finding an attorney to advise the family on its rights. McConnell offered to set up a meeting with her nephew

Christopher Wiles and his law partner Joseph E. Fahey, one of Syracuse's most prominent defense attorneys. McConnell thought Fahey would know as well as anyone how to navigate the criminal justice system.

Setting up the meeting with the attorneys marked a turning point for Terry. After days of mourning, she decided that she would not succumb to the grief that made her want to crawl into a hole and die. She wasn't sure exactly how she would do it, but she knew she owed it to Katy to stand up to Brian McCarthy and to anyone else who stood in the way of justice.

Chapter 15

Joseph Fahey

IN March 1986, attorney Joseph Fahey stood in an Auburn, New York, courtroom and listened with disappointment as a jury found his young client, Thomas Bianco, guilty of the murder of an 18-year-old woman. Fahey was part of a legal team that argued at the trial that someone else kidnapped, raped and killed Julie Monson.

Before deputies led the body-shop mechanic away, Fahey assured Bianco that the lawyers would continue the fight, without charge, until they got him out of prison. Fahey would continue a seven-year legal battle that ultimately succeeded in persuading a judge to overturn the conviction.

One of his friends used to kid Fahey that he was a "true believer," the kind of attorney who embraced the role of defender of those without a lot of money or connections. Fahey's first job after earning a law degree in 1975 was working as a low-paid public defender for a legal aid society in Syracuse. "My clients were, as Clarence Darrow once said, the 'damned and the despised,'" Fahey once told the Syracuse *Herald American*.

In 1979, Fahey entered private practice by partnering with Christopher Wiles, whose expertise in real estate, probate and corporate law complemented Fahey's primary focus on criminal defense. Among others who partnered at various times with Fahey and Wiles was attorney Thomas Lynch, who handled personal injury cases.

Fahey became an expert on the "insanity defense," and, in more than one case, had argued that a client was not guilty because of mental disease or defect. When New York passed legislation in 1984 that shifted the burden of proof for insanity from the prosecution to the defense, Fahey challenged the law in court but lost in a widely publicized case involving a father who smothered to death his 4-year-old son with a pillow.

On the face of it, some might see a criminal defender such as Fahey as an unlikely ally for a grieving mother in a murder case. However, Terry Connelly was quickly won over by the 37-year-old Fahey's folksy manner and legal savvy as they met at the office of Wiles, Fahey & Lynch on the 10thfloor of the State Tower Building in downtown Syracuse. When Fahey spoke, he talked so sympathetically that Terry felt almost like he had known Katy personally.

Fahey explained he had been following the almost daily news coverage of the Potsdam rape and murder. "I'm so sorry about what happened to Katy," Fahey told Terry. "If there's any way we can help—in any way—we will do that."

Over the next hour, Wiles and Fahey listened as Terry talked about Katy's bright mind, cheerful personality and generous spirit, about her dream to work in business and her decision to study it at Clarkson, about the call Terry received that her daughter was in the hospital, and about the painful decision to remove life support.

Terry said she was looking now for legal help in monitoring the criminal case and representing the family's interest in making sure Katy's killer was properly punished. As far as she was concerned, there would be no justice if McCarthy received anything less than the maximum sentence of 25 years to life in prison.

Terry asked Fahey if McCarthy's lawyer might argue his client was crazy.

Fahey said he didn't know, but he was ready to find out.

"I need to know more about the case," he said. "Once I have a better sense of what the case is, I can tell you whether this insanity defense you have on your mind is going to be a factor. I need to go to Potsdam."

Terry was won over by Fahey's determination to find answers without delay. She did not doubt from that moment on that she wanted Wiles, Fahey & Lynch working for her.

By mid-September, Terry had returned to employment at a Syracuse company selling mortgages. Her assignments included visiting real estate agencies to talk about services offered to clients. But Terry would get in her car, start driving and suddenly realize she had no idea where she was or where she was going. She soon quit the job.

"People had mortgages for their houses, and those are pretty important things, and they needed someone who could concentrate," Terry said. "And I just couldn't concentrate. Everything was off-balance."

After the funeral, Joe Hawelka Jr. moved back in with his father in Verona Beach. After a couple of days at home, he was eager to return to Oneida High School, deciding that being with friends and resuming classes was better than mourning alone.

His sister Carey, after missing the first week of school, returned to Henninger, but everything seemed different. "I became very, very private my senior year," she said. "I would be walking the halls, like just thinking people were waiting for me to crack. So, I didn't talk about it and I didn't let anybody in." Fortunately, her teachers were understanding and let her slide on the schoolwork, knowing Carey always had been a good student.

Joe Hawelka Sr. went back to his Oneida dental practice, although his heart wasn't in it. Terry invited him to accompany her to a meeting with Fahey and Wiles. But while he was okay with what she was doing, he had no interest in talking to lawyers.

Terry saw a big change in her ex-husband after Katy's death. He suffered from anger, depression, and an unreasonable feeling of guilt that he should have done more to protect Katy. On the other hand, Terry felt like her mother did when a priest paid a visit to Alice Ryan's home not long after Katy was murdered.

The priest told her, "You shouldn't blame yourself, Alice. It's nothing you've ever done."

"Well, that's good to know. Thank you, Father."

Later, she told Terry it was an odd assumption for the priest to make.

"I didn't blame myself," her mother said. "I felt horrible I lost my granddaughter, but I didn't think it was my fault,"

Terry would never blame herself, nor would she ever try to fathom how God allowed bad things to happen to good people. She thought to herself: *If I ever start asking why this happened to Katy, I'll drive myself crazy, because there is never going to be an answer to that.*

Terry signed up Joe Jr. and Carey for grief counseling for teens. But at the first meeting, a girl started talking about her grandmother passing away after a long battle with cancer. It was a sad loss, but the grief wasn't the same as losing your teen sister to murder. Carey and Joe Jr. never went back. As Carey told her brother afterward, "There is no way they can comprehend what we have gone through."

Betsy returned to Florida and threw herself into her work as a newspaper graphic artist, trying to block out any thoughts of the murder. Betsy shunned therapy or counseling, and she even stopped going to church, unable to see the intersection between her Catholic faith and the horror of what happened to Katy.

At home, Joe Jr. didn't talk to his father much about Katy, although the two were always on the same page. It was almost telepathic. But there was nothing either one could say to make the pain go away. They were both hurting, each in his own way.

"In retrospect," Joe Jr. said later, "it seems we all kind of retreated to our corners. I don't remember feeling alienated from my parents, but I remember there was my grief that I had to deal with myself."

Katy's family members were not the only ones suffering after Katy's murder.

In a letter to the editor in the Syracuse *Herald-Journal*, Jim Damiano lamented that he "lost more than a best friend. I lost a part of myself. ... To all of Katy's friends: There is a little bit of Katy left in all of us. Let's follow her example and enjoy our lives and live them to the fullest. To Katy's family: Be thankful to have been blessed with such a fine person for 19 years. She loved all of you very much. I know she is in a much better place than here. She deserves it."

Nanci Parks, sometimes after a day of classes at St. John Fisher, drove herself from her home in Pittsford to the gravesite in Cazenovia, where she would sit and talk to her former Clarkson roommate.

"You should be at my college, and you're not," Parks would say through the tears. "This is not right. We should be together instead of me sitting at your friggin' grave."

Shortly after Katy's murder, Potsdam Police Officer John Kaplan was driving to a training academy in Albany, New York, when his mind flashed back to the horrific scene at Walker Arena. His hands began to shake so much that he had to park the car until he pulled himself together.

"I think that's when it finally all hit me, and I didn't feel safe to drive," Kaplan said. "It had only been a short period afterward, and it was me realizing kind of what I had been involved in and the true tragedy of what it was."

In late September 1986, Fahey and law partner Lynch drove north to Potsdam, swinging past the Clarkson campus to see the crime scene and retracing Katy's steps the night she was murdered. They also visited the Raymond Street police station in hopes of talking to someone about the case.

Investigator Perretta greeted them warmly. Like Kaplan and others in the police department, Perretta was both angry and deeply shaken by Katy's murder, and he was eager for McCarthy to pay the price. If there was a way Perretta could help the family, he would do so.

As he answered the attorneys' questions, Perretta frequently refreshed his memory by referring to his notes or to documents in the thick case file, which included transcripts of McCarthy's interviews with police, witness statements, crime scene photos, the autopsy report, and an inventory of items found at Walker Arena and elsewhere.

After a while, Fahey asked, "Could we get a copy of the file?"

It was still an open case, Perretta said, so he was not allowed to do that. Fahey understood.

The meeting continued for about an hour. As the two attorneys got up to leave, Perretta excused himself, leaving the file on a table. After a minute or two passed, Fahey and Lynch looked at each other, eyed the file, then decided that Perretta left it there for a reason. The two attorneys spent the next hour thumbing through and taking notes.

Fahey read with particular interest the first of two statements McCarthy gave to police a few hours after his arrest. Because McCarthy had the presence of mind to quickly fabricate a story about himself being the victim of an attack, it seemed to Fahey that McCarthy's attorney would have a hard time arguing that his client was mentally incompetent or legally insane at the time Katy was murdered.

Fahey also zeroed in on sworn statements from the two Clarkson University security guards, Shanty and Avadikian. By reading their accounts, McCarthy's confession, and other police records, Fahey pieced together a possible timeline of what happened on the morning of August 29, 1986:

At 3:25 a.m., Avadikian was inside Walker Arena when he heard noises, presumably when McCarthy began assaulting Katy. Avadikian radioed Shanty.

At 3:30 a.m., Shanty arrived at the southeast corner to see a partially naked couple engaged in what he thought was consensual sex. Instead of telling them to stop, Shanty drove away.

At 3:35 a.m., Shanty drove back to the scene with Avadikian in tow to find McCarthy still on top of Katy. Unsure of what action to take, the two guards decided to drive away and consider their options.

At 3:40 a.m., the guards made yet another stop at the southeast corner, this time to discover McCarthy was gone and Katy unconscious and critically injured. It was 10 minutes since the time Shanty first saw the attack.

At 3:41 a.m., Avadikian ran inside the arena and called the police.

"This is horrible," Fahey told Lynch as he studied the guards' statements. "They could have saved her."

After returning to Syracuse, Fahey set up another meeting with Terry. He shared the information the attorneys gathered in Potsdam, and his own view that McCarthy was unlikely to succeed with an insanity defense.

For the first time, Fahey suggested that Terry and Joe Sr. had a good case for monetary damages against McCarthy for wrongful death and against Clarkson and its two security guards for gross negligence. Fahey explained that a lawsuit would be more than about money. Just the filing of it would encourage Clarkson to take steps to improve campus security, and it might even prompt other universities to do the same.

Terry had to think about it and talk to Katy's father.

At Clarkson, not everyone was viewing Katy's murder as a wake-up call. While some students sought escorts back to campus at night and began keeping dorm rooms always locked, others shrugged off the danger. Patrolman Kaplan was working a night shift in mid-September when he spotted a young woman walking alone past the same spot where Katy was attacked.

"Don't you realize there was a rape-murder here a couple of weeks ago?" Kaplan asked.

"So?" she answered. "I need to get back to the dorm."

Some students were openly hostile to the idea that Clarkson needed to beef up security, fearing a police state where they would get in trouble for every minor infraction.

An editor at the Clarkson *Integrator* student newspaper, in an opinion piece, ridiculed parents and others who were urging the university to hire a full-blown security force and to "install stadium lights every 50 yards." He wrote that Katy's death "was not due to a lack of security on the Clarkson campus" but instead because she "put herself in a vulnerable situation" by walking alone at night. He insisted he wasn't blaming the victim, just pointing out that the costly increase in security wasn't necessary if students used common sense.

Clarkson officials, still viewing Katy's murder as an aberration, insisted it was doing everything it should do to keep students safe and to punish bad behavior.

However, that commitment to safety was again called into question after the evening of Friday, September 12, when about 150 people turned out for an unsanctioned "toga party" in one of Clarkson's dorms. Alcohol flowed, despite a dormitory ban on booze since the fall of 1985 when the state raised the drinking age to 21.

The party might have been overlooked except for an incident involving an 18-year-old female student. The freshman consumed two mixed drinks in her dorm room at about 7:30 p.m., then three more while visiting another room. Afterward, she returned to her room, wrapped herself in a sheet, and showed up at the toga party, where she drank some more. She eventually vomited into a garbage can, passed out, woke up long enough to throw up some more, then passed out again before waking up naked at 4 a.m. in another room with an 18-year-old male student on top of her engaged in sex.

She told him to stop, pushed him off her, and said, "I'm going." After he gave her a shirt to wear, she walked back to her dormitory.

Later that day, after discussing the matter with friends and meeting with Clarkson Dean of Students Cooper, the woman filed a complaint with

Potsdam village police, who arrested the male student on a charge of rape. Clarkson suspended the young man and fired the resident assistant who was on duty when the toga party occurred. President Clark announced that a disciplinary panel would hold hearings to consider punishments for anyone who participated in the party.

Feeling the bitter taste of negative publicity for the second time in a month, and facing increasing pressure to step up safety, Clarkson announced it was installing more outdoor lighting and setting up a radio connection with the village police so that its guards no longer needed to use a phone to report an incident. Clark appointed a committee to study security and to issue a preliminary report by October 15.

In response to concerns of parents and alumni, Clarkson set up forums in three cities, including Syracuse, to discuss university security and related issues.

Katy's mother received an invitation to the Syracuse meeting, which was scheduled for 5:30 p.m. on Wednesday, October 1, at the 200-seat auditorium at the Everson Museum of Art. She brought along attorney Wiles, who kept notes and later produced a one-page summary for his client's files.

Clark led a presentation dominated by statistics and other data to bolster his view that Clarkson was an exceptionally safe campus. He insisted once again that the university was blameless for the attack on Katy.

Unimpressed, Wiles wrote that Clark "talks a smooth line." Clark reminded him of someone who acted like "nothing so awful could happen where such a person as himself was involved or in charge."

Clark complained that newspaper accounts about Clarkson security were "wholly inaccurate," Wiles recalled, although the university president didn't say exactly what reporters got wrong. "He continued to defend the actions of the 'night watchmen' and stated that the Potsdam Police Chief was behind the actions of the College 100%," Wiles wrote. "Clarkson University has always depended on the Potsdam Village Police for protection and security." Clark noted that a student was attacked at Potsdam State a few weeks earlier, despite the campus having a much larger security force of 12.

The best way for students to be safe, he said, was to follow campus rules and not put themselves at risk. The way Clark saw it, Wiles said, paraphrasing the university president, "walking alone at 3:30 a.m. is putting yourself at risk."

As she quietly listened to Clark speak, Terry seethed. It was understandable that Clarkson would try to defend its campus security. But, to her, it was unconscionable it would do so by blaming the victim.

Not long after the meeting, Terry returned to the law office to sign papers authorizing the firm to prepare a lawsuit against McCarthy, Clarkson University and the two security guards.

As Fahey would remember it later, "She was ready for war."

In the North Country, other battle lines were being drawn, as the attack on Katy and other incidents continued to roil the community.

Chapter 16

Crossfire

On Thursday, October 9, 1986, more than 150 people participated in a "Take Back the Night" march in Potsdam, lighting candles and vowing to "reclaim the streets" that no longer seemed safe following the murder of Katy. Participants also cited two other recent sexual assaults locally and the October 2 arrest in Canada of a Clarkson staff member accused of soliciting teen girls to make pornographic films.

Sophia Theadore, a freshman at St. Lawrence University in Canton, told marchers that "we'll proclaim to rapists and pornographers that this night is ours. Tonight, with every breath and every step, we must assert our rights."

The event began on the steps of Clarkson's Snell Hall with remarks by religious leaders, women's activists, and college and university officials, including Clarkson President Clark, who stated that Katy was not Brian McCarthy's only victim.

"In the wake of Katy's death," Clark said, "there's left behind a family torn by anguish, the university shattered by a tragic event, and a community outraged by violence. That Katy's assailant seemed bent first on murder and second on rape only reminds us that rape is a crime of violence."

It was not clear from newspaper accounts why Clark was so certain Katy's killer had his mind set on murder before he sexually assaulted her. But the university president's statement aligned with Clarkson's legal strategy later that argued that Katy was fatally injured by the time the first guard saw the attack.

In other remarks before the march, David Howison, dean of student affairs at St. Lawrence University, took a moment to commend Clark and other Clarkson officials for the way the university responded to the assault on Katy. In an echo of comments by Clarkson, Howison reminded marchers that being cautious was a person's best defense against rape.

Afterward, the marchers chanted, "yes means yes, no means no" as they snaked their way on a one-mile route through Potsdam neighborhoods and into the downtown business district. Organizers had earlier announced plans to take the march past Walker Arena, retracing Katy's final steps, but they ended up back at Snell Hall without that dramatic detour.

On October 14, McCarthy returned to a courtroom, once again wearing a bulletproof vest, to enter a plea of not guilty to an indictment handed down by a St. Lawrence County grand jury.

The panel, after considering the evidence presented by District Attorney Gardner, indicted McCarthy on three counts of murder. Each count painted a different scenario. The first alleged that McCarthy intentionally killed Katy. The second accused him of strangling her during a rape. The third count said he strangled her, but only while *attempting* to rape her. To experienced courtroom observers, offering three murder scenarios —and choosing not to indict on a separate charge of rape—suggested that prosecutors lacked forensic evidence to prove McCarthy sexually penetrated Katy.

Conviction on any one of the murder counts carried an identical maximum sentence of 25 years to life in prison.

At his arraignment in St. Lawrence County Court in Canton, McCarthy spoke only to plead "not guilty" and to answer "Yes, sir, I do" when asked by Judge Eugene L. Nicandri if he understood his rights.

Defense attorney Nash informed the court he intended to "present psychiatric evidence at any trial," keeping open the possibility of the insanity defense. Nicandri ordered McCarthy to submit to an examination by Dr. David Butler, chief psychologist for the St. Lawrence Mental Health Clinic in Potsdam, to help to determine if the defendant may have suffered from mental disease or defect at the time of the slaying. The judge said Nash and Gardner could observe the exam but not take part.

In court, Nash also revealed he would be filing a request with the Appellate Division of New York State Supreme Court. Afterward, he declined to tell reporters anything about the filing, saying that doing so "would defeat the purpose of making the motions."

Three weeks later, Nash's cryptic comment became clear when he asked the appeals court to move the proceedings 175 miles away to Saratoga County in eastern New York state. Nash claimed that media publicity made it impossible for his client to get a fair trial in St. Lawrence County. As evidence, Nash provided sworn statements by several area residents, including a college instructor in criminal justice, a retired state police investigator and a bank vice president. Pierrepont Town Supervisor William Ford wrote that "the pulse of the people in my opinion is that, because of the alleged brutality and the continual media coverage, Mr. McCarthy would not receive a fair trial in St. Lawrence County." Ford acknowledged personally knowing the McCarthy family.

Nash, in his court filing, also sought to move the proceedings on the basis that Gardner committed "potential prosecutorial misconduct" by stating he would not consider a plea bargain in the case.

In his response in court papers, Gardner said media coverage "was reasonable and appropriate given the nature of the crime." He also denied any misconduct; Gardner insisted that what he said to Nash was that it would not be "productive to discuss the matter until the Court was contacted concerning its willingness to accept the sentencing condition put forth by counsel."

This was not the first high-profile clash between Nash and Gardner, who ran against each other for district attorney in 1983. At the time, Nash was a Republican from Canton with three years of experience as an assistant district attorney. Gardner, a Democrat, was a Gouverneur attorney who lived in the nearby town of Rossie.

Early in the campaign, Gardner quickly put Nash on the defensive with a series of allegations painting him as responsible for alleged failings of the district attorney's office. Late in the campaign, Nash began slinging mud of his own by accusing Gardner of false and misleading campaign advertisements. He also claimed his Democratic opponent was an incompetent attorney who had recently arranged for a client to plead guilty to felony charges because Gardner wanted to campaign instead of being tied up in a trial.

Gardner came away with a stunning victory, winning in a vote of 18,442 to 11,973 in a county with Republican-dominated election rolls. He subsequently fired Nash, who returned to private practice, joining the list of attorneys available to represent indigent clients, which was how he ended up as McCarthy's attorney.

Now adversaries in the prosecution of McCarthy, Nash won the first round by persuading Potsdam Village Justice Rogers to close portions of the preliminary hearing. Gardner won the second when the Appellate Division rejected, without comment, Nash's request to move the trial to Saratoga County.

The news media then had a victory. On November 15, New York State Supreme Court Justice Michael W. Duskas ruled in favor of the *Watertown Daily Times* in the newspaper's request to obtain a transcript of the September 5 preliminary hearing and to view McCarthy's confession to police. Duskas said Rogers had lacked sufficient findings to support her closure of the hearing, and he ordered the Potsdam judge to release a transcript "and also to provide access to any exhibits admitted into evidence that are under (her) . . . custody and control."

When it got a copy of the hearing transcript, the *Times* discovered that McCarthy never confessed to raping Katy, contrary to what various news media had reported.

At the preliminary hearing, Nash asked Potsdam Police Lieutenant Terry McKendree if McCarthy admitted during police questioning that he "consummated a rape."

"Completed the rape?" McKendree said. "I don't believe he testified to that."

Did McKendree ever hear McCarthy admit he strangled Katy?

"I did not hear him say that he strangled her, no."

"Were you in the room all the time, Terry?"

"Yes, I was," McKendree said.

After it obtained a transcript of McCarthy's second interview with police, the newspaper provided its fullest account yet of the horrors that Katy suffered. The *Times* highlighted McCarthy's admission that he shoved Katy's face into the arena wall, tried to rape her, and "just went nuts. I went crazy" and tried to "shake her insides out."

Not surprisingly, Fahey asked the *Times* for a copy of the confession, which he wanted in hand to help with the preparation of the lawsuit. However, the Watertown newspaper declined, saying the court ruling only authorized disclosure to the *Times*. District Attorney Gardner, for the same reason, also refused to make a copy for Terry's attorney.

Fahey contacted Justice Duskas' office to ask him to revise his order so that Gardner would have permission to give him a copy. An assistant in Duskas' office directed Fahey to request it from state Supreme Court Justice Domenic Viscardi, who sent Fahey back to Duskas.

"I'm beginning to think that this must be some sort of north-country winter sport," a frustrated Fahey said in a note to Terry.

Fahey then wrote directly to Duskas with a plea that was heavier on emotion than legalese.

"As Your Honor can understand," the attorney said, "my clients have suffered an extremely painful and tragic loss and are interested in knowing all the facts surrounding the incident that led to their daughter's death."

Duskas wrote up an order allowing Gardner to give Fahey a copy of the confession.

On November 12, defense attorney Nash filed a motion in county court, demanding that prosecutors turn over any evidence that Katy "had sexual intercourse with a boyfriend or boyfriends within a 48-hour period of the alleged time of death." How Katy's sexual history, if any, was relevant to this case, Nash's motion did not say. (Today, rape shield laws in New York prohibit inquiring about a victim's sexual past unless the defense showed it had a direct bearing on the defendant's guilt or innocence.) District Attorney Gardner responded to Nash's request by saying that prosecutors were "not aware of any evidence or information that the victim had sexual intercourse with any person other than the defendant at any time prior to the commission of the crime."

In another aggressive move, Nash filed a motion raising the possibility that it was doctors, not McCarthy, who killed Katy. The attorney asked for copies of Katy's medical records from Canton-Potsdam Hospital and from

House of the Good Samaritan in Watertown to determine if she was defini-
tively brain-dead at the time her family agreed to remove life support. A
non-medical expert reading the autopsy report, Nash said, would wonder
whether doctors performed tests on Katy's midbrain, pons or medulla to
determine if she lacked brain function. If not, Nash added, "disconnect-
ing of the life-support system may have been premature and due to gross
negligence or intentional wrong-doing of the doctors." Nash asked Judge
Nicandri to review grand jury minutes to determine whether prosecutors
presented proper medical testimony to this issue and, if not, to "take the
appropriate action."

Meanwhile, Nicandri permitted McCarthy and his attorney to listen to
tape recordings of the defendant's statements to police and to go over all
photographs from the investigation that the district attorney's office had in
its possession. The ruling was not publicized at the time, and Katy's family
would not learn until much later that McCarthy was permitted to sit in a
conference room with Nash on December 8, 1986, and view graphic photos
showing the victim lying battered and bloodied outside Walker Arena and in
the hospital. McCarthy also was permitted to view photos of Katy's naked
body on the autopsy table.

Years later, the images would haunt Nash, who in 2009 would describe
them to WWNY-TV in Watertown "as the worst crime scene photographs
that I've looked at as far as violence and brutality." In the TV report, Nash
did not describe McCarthy's reaction to seeing the photos. Nash would
later turn down a request to be interviewed about the case, citing client
confidentiality.

On December 22, Nash asked Nicandri to throw out McCarthy's statements to police or, in the alternative, schedule a suppression hearing on
whether to exclude them from the trial.

The motion included a five-page affidavit by McCarthy in which he
claimed he gave statements to police while "I was under the influence of alcohol and certain controlled substances which affected my ability to think
clearly." McCarthy also accused police of mistreating him by taking his
clothes, then placing him in a cold jail cell without a shirt or underwear.
Only after he gave his second statement, McCarthy said, did he receive the
replacement clothing dropped off by his mother. He said the police also

failed to feed him until the afternoon, when they gave him coffee and a single English muffin.

During his time in the police station, McCarthy said, he repeatedly asked Police Chief Matott and others for permission to make a telephone call, but he was not allowed to do so. He said he agreed to talk to the police because of "certain promises" to him—he didn't say what—and after "I was threatened by various personnel there (at the police station) which made me afraid."

McCarthy further stated that authorities delayed arraigning him for several hours in "order to allow the police to continue to interrogate me and take involuntary statements from me."

On January 29, 1987, Judge Nicandri ruled against most of the defense motions. He said that prosecutors had presented sufficient medical information to the grand jury on the cause of Katy's death to support an indictment. As for the defense motion to suppress McCarthy's statements to police, Nicandri said he would schedule a hearing in mid-March to hear evidence before issuing a ruling on the request.

Fahey would not wait that long to bring the family's lawsuit to court.

Chapter 17

$550 Million

JOE Hawelka Sr. walked into the law office of Wiles, Fahey & Lynch for the first time in January 1987 to review papers that would permit the law firm to file a suit on behalf of himself and ex-wife Terry as co-administrators of Katy's estate.

Katy's father, who had not been part of any discussions with the law firm, had told Terry he would go along with suing McCarthy, Clarkson University and the two security guards. But when he read over the papers, Joe Sr. wasn't comfortable with the demand for $700 million in damages— an amount Fahey would soon amend to $550 million.

"How did you pick *that* dollar figure?" Joe Sr. asked the attorney.

It was a shocking amount, Fahey conceded, but he thought the figure was necessary to get the university's full attention and to emphasize the suffering by Katy and her family due to behavior of the defendants.

"Let me ask you this," Fahey said to Katy's father. "If you had $700 million and you could buy her back, would you?"

"Of course, yes, I would."

"Then it's reasonable."

Joe Sr. signed the paperwork.

On February 4, Fahey filed the suit in New York State Supreme Court in Syracuse. After the law firm amended the amount, the legal action sought $250 million from McCarthy, $150 million from the two guards, and $150 million from the university in a combination of compensatory and punitive damages.

In his cell at the St. Lawrence County Jail, McCarthy was served papers notifying him that he was being sued for assault, negligence and wrongful death. The lawsuit alleged he caused Katy's death after he "either knowingly, intentionally or willfully choked, punched and kicked the decedent about her head, neck and body and repeatedly banged her face into the walls of Walker Arena." The attack caused multiple injuries to Katy, as well as "pain and suffering and extreme emotional trauma and terror."

The portion of the lawsuit against Clarkson University and guards Shanty and Avadikian accused them of "gross negligence and/or reckless conduct." It claimed that the guards were negligent for not preventing or stopping the attack, and that the university was negligent for hiring two men inexperienced in security and not providing them with proper training.

Furthermore, the lawsuit stated that Clarkson knew students were using the path behind Walker Arena but failed to provide adequate lighting or to ensure the area was "kept free of trespassers and other persons not enrolled at Clarkson or otherwise licensed to be there."

The filing of a lawsuit should have come as no surprise to Clarkson officials. In November, Fahey had filed a notice of claim to preserve the family's right to sue the Potsdam Volunteer Rescue Squad. Fahey ultimately decided not to proceed with a suit against the rescue squad after obtaining records showing there was nothing the ambulance crew did that caused Katy's death.

"It was no secret that there was a consideration of a lawsuit against somebody, and Clarkson was one of the somebodies," Potsdam attorney Verner M. Ingram Jr. told the Clarkson *Integrator* after the suit was filed against McCarthy and the university.

Clarkson reacted with a carefully worded denial of negligence and a vow to fight the lawsuit. It was clear in its statement that the demand for a total of $300 million from Clarkson and the two security guards rattled the university, just as Fahey hoped.

"Neither the amounts claimed nor the charges stated constitute any evidence whatsoever of merit in this suit," university spokesman Taylor said. "Clarkson will defend itself with all possible vigor. . . . We are confident that when all the facts are brought to light, judgment will be rendered in Clarkson's favor."

In reporting on the lawsuit, some in the news media pointed out that the filing was contrary to Joe Sr.'s assurance in September that the family didn't blame Clarkson. Fahey explained to the Syracuse *Herald-Journal* that Katy's father hadn't known all the circumstances at the time. It was only later, Fahey said, that the family learned Katy "may very well have walked away with only minor injuries" had the security guards stopped the attack.

While compensating the family for medical and funeral costs and other expenses, Fahey said, a significant jury award also would send a message to Clarkson and other universities that there was a high price to pay for failing to provide proper security.

Several months earlier, a similar lawsuit was filed by Howard and Constance Clery, who sought $25 million from Lehigh University in Pennsylvania after their daughter, Jeanne, was raped and strangled in a campus dormitory on April 5, 1986. The Clerys would subsequently embark on a campaign to force colleges to beef up security and to disclose statistics about campus crime. In an interview around this time with the *Chronicle of Higher Education*, the Clerys singled out the murder of Katy Hawelka as one of the more glaring examples of how a university's security was substandard.

On March 23, 1987, lawyers for Clarkson University and its insurance carrier, Great American Insurance, asked state Supreme Court Justice Norman Mordue to dismiss the portions of the lawsuit against the university and its guards. (Two sets of lawyers responded because Clarkson's liability policy with Great American only covered compensatory damages; the university hired the Syracuse law firm of Hiscock & Barclay to fight any punitive damages.)

In court papers, the defendants claimed that any losses the family sustained were caused by McCarthy and by Katy herself, saying she engaged in what they referred to as "culpable conduct." They did not specify what conduct they meant, although it sounded a lot like President Clark's statement that students walking alone at 3:30 a.m. put themselves at risk.

Fahey wasn't troubled by the defendant's legal strategy, which he saw as somewhat scattershot and lacking in any factual basis. "They threw an awful lot against the wall to see what would stick," he said.

By mid-March, McCarthy had yet to respond to the lawsuit. However, he would soon have plenty to say at the suppression hearing in St. Lawrence County criminal court, where the defense strategy would be reflected in this memorable headline in the *Watertown Daily Times*: "McCarthy: I Was Drunk, Stoned."

Chapter 18

Alternate Realities

ON March 24, 1987, Brian McCarthy arrived at the St. Lawrence County Courthouse, ready to sit through an uncomfortable hearing during which his attorney was going to paint his past behavior in the worst possible light. To persuade the judge to suppress McCarthy's confession to police, Charles Nash aimed to show that McCarthy was too incapacitated by alcohol and illegal drugs to intelligently waive his right to remain silent. This meant calling friends and others to testify about McCarthy's belligerent and erratic conduct in the hours before Katy was attacked.

Before the hearing, Nash and McCarthy met inside the judge's chambers with Nicandri and prosecutors. Nash asked his client to state, for the record, that he had listened to the tapes of his statements to police and would stipulate that transcripts were accurate.

"The advantage to you," Nash said to McCarthy, "is that the press would not hear what's on those tapes and (it) would not be printed in the newspapers. . . . Do you understand that?"

"I do. I do understand, and I agree," McCarthy said.

Nash didn't mention that the media had already reported on the transcript of the confession, or that keeping a tape from being played in court wouldn't stop them from doing so again. But it would keep anyone in attendance, including his family, from hearing McCarthy's damning admissions in his own voice.

In any case, Katy's family members would not have heard it since none of them attended the hearing.

FROM LEFT: St. Lawrence County District Attorney Charles Gardner, Potsdam Village Justice Kathleen Martin Rogers, St. Lawrence County Court Judge Eugene Nicandri and Potsdam Village Police Chief Clinton Matott. (WSYR-TV, Channel 9/The Post-Standard/New York Power Authority/The Post-Standard photos.)

The proceedings began at about 9:30 a.m. in the Canton, New York, courtroom with prosecutors calling Potsdam Police Chief Matott and others from his department. Patrolman Bartlett told how he and Officer Kaplan confronted McCarthy under stairs outside Walker Arena at about 3:45 a.m. on Friday, August 29, 1986. Others testified about evidence collected at the scene and the hospital, and about their interactions with McCarthy. The officers said they saw nothing to indicate the defendant was drunk or stoned, and several testified they did nothing to violate McCarthy's rights.

District Attorney Gardner rested his case.

"Mr. Nash?" Judge Nicandri said.

"Call Joe Lopez," Nash announced, deciding that his first witness would be McCarthy's friend who had spent much of August 28 with the defendant.

After raising his hand and swearing to tell the truth, Lopez took a seat on the witness stand.

"Mr. Lopez, will you state your full name and address, please?" Nash asked.

"Yes, it is Joe Louis Revas Lopez, 8 Garvin Avenue, Massena, New York."

"Mr. Lopez, do you know Brian McCarthy?"

"Yes, I met him."

Nash asked Lopez to recall the events of Thursday, August 28.

At about 2 p.m. that day, Lopez said, he and his wife visited the defendant in Madrid, where McCarthy was staying at a camp owned by a mutual friend, the late Stephen Charles Williams. Nash asked Lopez why he went to see McCarthy.

"Well, we talked for a while, and I had a job for him clearing some land in North Lawrence, some property I have out there."

At about 2:30 p.m., the three got into Lopez's red 1986 Mercury Topaz and headed for the property. Lopez wanted to show McCarthy what work was needed. Once there, another friend—Lopez only knew him as "Randy"—showed up with some beer, which he shared with McCarthy as they talked about a car Randy wanted to sell for $150.

McCarthy had $150, but he owed the money to a young man in Potsdam, Lopez recalled. McCarthy said he would "call that person up to find if he (McCarthy) could hold the money a little longer so he could buy the car."

The four left around 3:30 p.m., dropped off Lopez's wife in Massena, then went back to the Madrid camp so McCarthy could locate a phone number for the person he wanted to call.

After that, they stopped by the Madrid Hotel, where they each had a beer. McCarthy used a phone to call his friend in Potsdam.

"He couldn't seem to get ahold of his friend or cousin, whoever it was, so we proceeded to go back to North Lawrence," Lopez testified.

"Were they drinking beer in the car?" Nash asked, referring to McCarthy and Randy.

"No, they weren't."

After dropping Randy off, Lopez and McCarthy stopped at Chateau's in Winthrop around 8:30 p.m. "I believe we had a couple of hamburgers," Lopez said. "I had a glass of Coke. I think he (McCarthy) might have had a glass of Coke, too."

McCarthy soon got into a dispute with another customer, who accused him of stealing money left on the bar.

"Mr. McCarthy almost had a fight with him . . . and I had to step between the two of them and just break it up," Lopez said.

The bar owner ordered McCarthy to leave. Lopez turned to McCarthy and said, "Come on, let's go. I'll take you home." As they went out the door, the owner threw a pack of cigarettes that McCarthy had left behind. Lopez retrieved it off the floor.

Lopez was prepared to drive McCarthy back to Madrid. But when they got into the car, McCarthy demanded that Lopez detour to Potsdam about 13 miles away.

"No way," Lopez said. "I'll take you back home where you were."

"No," McCarthy insisted, "you're going to take me to Potsdam. I'm going to see a friend of mine."

As Lopez turned onto a road leading to Madrid, McCarthy opened the door and jumped out. Lopez stopped the car and stepped outside, where he tried to persuade McCarthy to let him take him home. Lopez didn't testify as to why he didn't want to take McCarthy to Potsdam.

When the argument almost turned to blows, Lopez said he had enough.

"Forget it. That's it. I've had enough of this baloney," Lopez said, before getting back into his car and driving away.

About 200 feet down the road, Lopez made a U-turn, not wanting to leave McCarthy along the darkened highway. Lopez rolled down the window. "Come on, get in the car," he said.

McCarthy got back in.

"You're going to take me to Potsdam. Take me to Potsdam," McCarthy demanded.

"No. I'm taking you home."

McCarthy opened the door and climbed back out again.

Lopez gave up.

"Well, I'll tell you what. Goodbye," Lopez said, and he drove away, this time for good, leaving McCarthy standing along the road.

Nash asked Lopez if he recalled how many beers he saw McCarthy drink that day.

"He might have had three, you know," Lopez said.

"Okay, Mr. Lopez," Nash said. "Did Mr. McCarthy consume anything else in your presence other than alcoholic beverages?"

"No."

"Any controlled substances?"

"No."

"Any marijuana?"

"No."

No matter how hard he tried, Nash could not get his witness to acknowledge he saw McCarthy drunk or using any illegal substances at all on August 28. In cross-examination, Gardner emphasized this point with a little math.

"So, during that six and a half hours, you saw him (McCarthy) consume three beers, you believe?" Gardner asked Lopez.

"Possibly three."

"Or less?"

"Or more, might have been four," Lopez said.

"And ingested nothing else, except two hamburgers and Coke, is that true, as far as you know?" Gardner asked.

"Well, as far as I know, yeah, that's all we had to eat."

When he turned to his next witnesses, Nash continued recreating a time-line of McCarthy's actions on August 28. The defense attorney called Robert J. Warren Jr., the Morristown man who picked up the defendant hitchhik-ing to Potsdam a little after 10 p.m.

"Can you tell us what, if anything, you observed about Mr. McCarthy when he was in your vehicle?" Nash asked.

"Well, my personal opinion he was, he was drunk and maybe high on something," Warren said.

"Okay, can you give the court some basis for that opinion?"

Warren said McCarthy was partly in the road, nearly causing Warren to hit him with his pickup truck. Also, during the ride to Potsdam, the defendant mentioned a violent argument he had with someone at Chateau's bar.

"He (said he) went outside or something, and he shot him in the leg, and, ah, just the way he was talking was—everything was slurred and just —" Warren paused in his testimony and backtracked a bit. "I don't think he was so much drunk. My own personal opinion: I think he was spaced out."

Nash also called to the witness stand Dick Hayes, another of McCarthy's friends. Hayes told the court that the defendant showed up at his Main Street apartment in Potsdam at around 11 p.m., holding a beer or two and acting "really hyper."

"What do you mean by 'hyper'?" Nash asked.

"He was talking really, really loud," Hayes said. "His eyes were really big. I got a dog from him, you know. He really liked the dog. The dog was out there, licking his face and biting his tongue and stuff."

During the visit, he said, McCarthy mentioned that he was carrying a gun.

"He was going to bring it out," Hayes said of the weapon, "and I just told him definitely, 'No, don't do that.'"

"Did he tell you he had anything else?" Nash asked Hayes.

"Yes, he did say he had some marijuana."

"Okay. Did he offer to bring that out?"

"Yes."

"What did you say?" Nash asked.

"I said, 'No, thanks. Keep everything to yourself.'"

Hayes said they talked about lots of things, including that McCarthy "bought a car" and that he had a girlfriend who was "cool." (McCarthy reportedly had been living recently at the Madrid cabin with a 17-year-old girl, who left that week for her first year of college.)

Hayes said he and McCarthy got into a playful wrestling match, which Hayes said "we used to do once in a while, which was no big deal. We didn't get carried away or anything." McCarthy left the apartment after visiting for about a half-hour, and Hayes said he never again saw him that night.

Nash called to the witness stand Potsdam State student Thomas Rupert, who testified that he and a friend were walking across the Clarkson Inn parking lot around midnight when McCarthy approached them and claimed he was a police officer.

"He put his hand behind his back and said he had a gun, and he was going to blow us away if we did anything," Rupert said.

Pressed by Nash whether McCarthy appeared intoxicated, Rupert said he didn't get close enough to smell any alcohol. But Rupert said he did see McCarthy drink a beer after they walked together afterward to Maxfield's restaurant on Market Street.

Following a recess, Judge Nicandri resumed the proceedings a little after 3 p.m.

"Mr. Nash?" he asked.

The defense attorney stood up and announced his next witness.

"Call Mr. McCarthy."

Looming over the marble-lined witness stand in the St. Lawrence County courtroom is a giant mural of the mythical figure of Justitia. Also known as

Lady Justice, she is a symbol of the right of every defendant to a fair trial. After McCarthy seated himself on the stand, he had a much better view, though, of an inscription on the rear wall displaying an alternate definition of justice: "He threatens the innocent who spares the guilty."

The *Watertown Daily Times* would note it was the first time in recent memory that someone accused of murder took the witness stand in St. Lawrence County.

A defendant testifying at a preliminary hearing is considered a risky strategy. Should the case go to trial, the prosecution could use what McCarthy said at the hearing to cast doubt on his credibility if he took the stand again and gave a differing version of events. Nash decided this was a risk worth taking, now that his other witnesses largely had failed to corroborate that McCarthy had been consuming mass quantities of drugs and alcohol before the attack.

After taking an oath swearing to tell the truth, McCarthy offered his own version of events on August 28 and 29. While Lopez testified that he showed up at McCarthy's residence at about 2 p.m. and that neither one consumed drugs during the day, McCarthy recalled it was closer to 11 a.m. And not only did he smoke marijuana in Lopez's presence, McCarthy said, they did so together.

"He asked me about some pot I had, and I showed him probably five or six different bags that I had," McCarthy said. "He asked me if I had any good pot, and I showed it to him, and he said, 'Let's smoke it,' and we did, approximately fifteen dollars' worth."

"For us uninitiated individuals," Nash asked drily, "will you tell us what fifteen dollars' worth of good pot quantity-wise is?"

"About seven and a half grams," McCarthy answered. That was enough for up to 14 marijuana joints, depending on how someone rolled it.

After smoking pot, McCarthy said, he accompanied Lopez and Lopez's wife to a small store in Massena. They bought a 12-pack of beer, possibly Busch, and then drove near Winthrop, where they stopped at a store and purchased another 12-pack, plus cheese curd and pepperoni. McCarthy said he and Lopez consumed both 12-packs, except for one or two cans that Lopez's wife drank. McCarthy didn't specify how many of the cans each of the men drank.

At about 2:30 p.m., McCarthy said, the three arrived at the North Lawrence property owned by Lopez, where the two men smoked more marijuana and discussed clearing the land. While there, Lopez's friend Randy offered to sell the car he was driving "because he said he had another one on the way," McCarthy said.

The four then headed back to Massena, where they dropped off Lopez's wife. The three men then headed to the Madrid camp where McCarthy was staying.

"What did you do there?" Nash asked.

"Smoked some pot, and we left to go to the hotel in Madrid."

"Tell the court what you did at the hotel."

"Played three, maybe four, maybe five games of pool and drank some beer, made some friends there at the bar, and then we left because Randy was complaining he wanted to go home," McCarthy testified.

"Do you know how many beers that was that you consumed?" Nash asked.

"Six, maybe five. Bought some shots, too."

It was dark by the time they left the hotel. After they dropped Randy off at his car in North Lawrence, McCarthy and Lopez drove to Chateau's. McCarthy said both of them ordered beers with their hamburgers. McCarthy confirmed he got into a dispute with another customer.

"A guy accused me of stealing three dollars off of the bar," McCarthy said, "and I just got a little bit upset at him, because he accused me of stealing it. I told him what I thought of him, and Joe just said, 'Come on, let's go.' He said, 'We don't need this,' or something to that effect."

When Lopez refused to take him to Potsdam, McCarthy said, he decided to hitchhike there on his own.

"I just sat down beside the road," he said. "Couldn't stand up very good. I kept wandering. I thought I was going to get hit because I kept wandering out in the middle of the road. I just stuck my thumb out, and two or three cars went by, and then somebody picked me up and brought me to Potsdam. I don't remember where they dropped me off."

In Potsdam, McCarthy said, he got something to eat, possibly another hamburger, at Morgan's Ice House, a bar next to Aubuchon Hardware on Market Street. McCarthy said he stopped there "because I knew the cook and wanted to see what his food was like." While at the bar, McCarthy said, he sold an ounce of marijuana to someone named Nick. McCarthy completed the transaction at the man's upstairs apartment, where they smoked some pot.

McCarthy said he then decided to see how his dog was doing at his friend Dick Hayes' apartment on Main Street.

"Do you recall anything that happened there?" Nash asked.

"Yeah, he inquired about any pot, if it was dry," McCarthy said. "I told him that I had a little bit. I pulled out just a little bit, under an ounce, and he asked me if I wanted to sell any of it. I told him, 'No, not really, but I'll smoke it with you,' and we smoked more than half of it."

In recalling what happened after that, McCarthy's testimony turned fuzzy. He said he visited an upstairs apartment where a woman was living. McCarthy said he did so because he was curious to see that part of the building.

"I just remember the place was a mess," McCarthy said, "and I don't remember coming back down. I don't remember where I went to, but the next thing I remember is having a yelling match in the Clarkson Inn parking lot."

McCarthy described the confrontation with two Potsdam State students as ending amicably, with one of them accompanying him to Maxfield's restaurant. "I told him that I was feeling my oats, you know, that I was just a little riled up. I wanted to buy him a beer and apologize for what I said to him because I called him names and stuff."

While at Maxfield's, McCarthy added, he drank beer and sat on the back porch, where he and the student also smoked marijuana.

Nash jumped ahead in his timeline to McCarthy's conversation with state police Senior Investigator Manor that took place in Chief Matott's office several hours after the attack on Katy.

McCarthy testified that Manor asked, "How are things going?"

"They aren't going very good at all right now."

McCarthy said Manor then told him, "You look awful nervous" or "You look tired" or something along those lines. "I can't remember exactly the words. I don't know. The whole thing is kind of blurry."

Manor offered him a cigarette. McCarthy took two. As they talked, Mc-Carthy recalled, Manor "said something to the effect of, 'Look, we know that you're not telling the truth, and if you cooperate with us, we can probably get you (a lighter prison sentence of) one to three, and get you some help.'"

"What did you say?" Nash asked.

"I just asked him—I said, 'Is this really going to be truthful or are you just giving me a BS story?'"

"And what did he say?"

"He really didn't say anything," McCarthy recalled. "He just looked at me and said, 'Well, we'll see.'"

After that, McCarthy said, Manor asked if he was ready to change his statement to give a truthful one.

"I just told him, 'Yeah,' and he went out in the other room and got Chief Matott and Lieutenant McKendree, and they come in, and they fumbled around with tapes, and they tested them—"

Nash interrupted. "Subsequently, a statement was recorded?" he asked.

"Um, they seemed to," McCarthy said before returning to his description of the recording process. "They took the tapes out, and they played with them, and then they put them in, and then they tested them, and then they rewound them, and then they started the statement."

Nash said he had no more questions of the defendant. The district attorney said he had nothing to add.

Although McCarthy's testimony went on for more than an hour, it left many unanswered questions. Precisely how much alcohol and pot did McCarthy consume that day? Was he so insistent about getting to Potsdam because he needed to obtain money from someone so he could buy Randy's car? What did McCarthy do after leaving Maxfield's but before he showed up outside Walker Arena? Nash also did not ask McCarthy about claims in the defendant's affidavit that police denied him a phone call, food and proper clothing, and that they improperly delayed arraignment.

Earlier, however, Chief Matott testified he did not recall if McCarthy asked to make a phone call. The chief said he did offer McCarthy coffee in the morning, but the defendant turned it down. Matott said he allowed

McCarthy's mother to bring him clothing. As for the arraignment, officers took a long time to schedule it because they were busy that day, filling out the paperwork and handling other police business.

Manor, testifying for the prosecution, didn't recall promising McCarthy that he would receive no more than one to three years if he confessed. Manor said he might have told McCarthy that he needed psychiatric counseling, but he didn't remember offering to help him get it.

Manor did remember the defendant admitting to him the attack on Katy.

"One remark was that he had pushed her face against the wall, and another remark something about kicking her, but I didn't pursue that with him at that time."

Following McCarthy's testimony, Nicandri adjourned the hearing. He announced it would resume in a few weeks when Potsdam Village Justice Rogers would be available to answer questions about the delays in arraigning McCarthy.

When she took the stand on May 14, 1987, Justice Rogers acknowledged that she repeatedly telephoned police on the day of McCarthy's arrest to find out when he would be ready to be arraigned. Rogers said she did this only because she wanted to make sure that police knew how to reach her, not because she thought police were stonewalling.

Following her testimony, Nicandri announced, "The hearing is closed," although he gave Nash until May 29 to file a motion to reopen the hearing.

In his chambers, the judge told Nash and Gardner that he expected to decide by the end of June whether to suppress the confession. In the meantime, he wanted to know if there were going to be any plea bargain discussions.

Gardner said the prosecution had offered to allow McCarthy to plead guilty to any one of the three murder counts in satisfaction of all charges. However, the district attorney said McCarthy would have to make that decision within 10 days after Nicandri ruled on the admissibility of the confession.

Gardner added he had discussed a possible plea bargain with Joseph Fahey, the attorney for Katy's parents, and "they have no objection to that."

A few weeks earlier, Terry Connelly and Fahey had met with Gardner in Canton. The way Terry recalled it, the meeting didn't go well. She was put off by Gardner's somewhat cold, all-business legal approach that contrasted with Fahey's friendly and compassionate demeanor. She recalled Gardner talking with Fahey for several minutes before the district attorney finally turned to her and expressed condolences for Katy's death.

Terry told Gardner she opposed any deals with McCarthy. She wanted a trial, a conviction, and the maximum life sentence, and she thought prosecutors should push for all of those things. That way, the public—and any future parole board—would know exactly what McCarthy did.

However, Gardner thought that a plea bargain made sense in this case. While McCarthy could choose a murder count where he wouldn't have to admit raping Katy, the potential sentence was just the same as if he did. The other reason to offer a plea bargain: It would avoid the risk that a jury might vote to acquit.

The district attorney assured Terry that a judge would require McCarthy to tell the truth when the defendant entered a guilty plea.

"When he sits in the courtroom in front of the judge," Gardner said, "in order to plead guilty, he will have to admit what he did and take responsibility for it."

With such an assurance, Terry said she would support a plea bargain.

Another factor in her decision to support the prosecution's approach was knowing that, even if the case didn't go to trial, she had a civil lawsuit to get at the truth.

By late spring 1987, Fahey had begun the process of sharing documents and trading legal motions with the attorneys for Clarkson and its insurance company. However, a key figure on the university campus would not be in Potsdam to see the outcome of the civil or criminal cases.

Chapter 19

Clark and Clarkson

CLARKSON President Allan H. Clark departed for a vacation in Europe in late May 1987, a day after learning that the university's science faculty was circulating a letter calling for his resignation. Not willing to postpone the trip, Clark decided he would deal with that crisis when he got back.

Unbeknownst to him at the time, the 51-year-old Clark's troubles were far worse than some disgruntled professors. The executive board for Clarkson's trustees had met April 14 and decided to seek his resignation—but it held off the announcement so the news wouldn't overshadow the May commencement.

It was a dramatic and swift fall for Clark. The Princeton-educated mathematician who loved to quote literature became Clarkson's president with much fanfare less than two years earlier, offering a vision of academic excellence packaged in a playful sense of humor. In his first year at the helm, Clark wagered 100 bagels against St. Lawrence University President Lawrence Gulick's 100 chocolate chip cookies over which school would win a men's hockey game. (Clark had to pay up after the Golden Knights' 6-5 overtime loss.)

But in 1986, Clark would confront multiple tragedies and scandals that would stir enormously negative news coverage. Any university would be shaken by a murder of one of its students on campus. As president, Clark also faced hostile questions about the actions of guards Shanty and Avadikian, doubts about the overall quality of campus security, and second-guessing about what some perceived as a lax attitude about public sex on campus. He additionally had to deal with the alleged rape following underage drinking at the dorm toga party, the arrest in Canada of an employee using university equipment to make pornographic tapes, and a report that a high school sophomore left a suicide note stating that a high-ranking Clarkson administrator sexually abused him.

Writing about Clark later, Clarkson historian Bradford B. Broughton concluded that, during Clark's time as the university's 13th president, "more seriously unfortunate events occurred than during the tenure of any previous Clarkson president." Broughton could not resist adding, "President Clark's two-year service as president of Clarkson could well add credence to people's belief that thirteen is an unlucky number."

Some of the damage to Clark's reputation appeared to be self-inflicted, such as the university's careless decision to publicly disclose Katy's name on the morning of the attack, even though she was a living victim of a sexual attack.

Katy's family initially expressed gratitude to Clarkson for its kindness and support, not wanting to blame the university for McCarthy's criminal actions. However, the family's attitude toward the university soured as it began to question whether the kindness had an ulterior motive, which was to keep the family from suing. Clark's subsequent comments suggesting Katy, not Clarkson, was partly to blame for the attack only made things worse.

Truth was, publicly and privately, Clark believed that neither the university nor the security guards were at fault in the murder. Clark sincerely felt horrible about what happened to Katy and about the anguish her murder was causing her family. But he also had compassion for the guards, whom he would recall being "extremely distraught and overwhelmed with the horror of what they had seen. One of them was so upset he required counseling."

While publicly defending Clarkson's security, Clark privately told university trustees they needed to spend more on safety, if for no other reason than to decrease potential liability should another student be attacked. However, the trustees balked at costly security upgrades at a time when revenues had declined due to falling enrollment. Many students also rebelled at another layer of policing. University employees, Clark found, didn't care one way or the other.

By spring, the university stirred more turmoil when it announced budget cuts and a 6.9 percent tuition increase. At that point, some faculty and administrators began to complain that they didn't have access to Clark to discuss this and other issues.

By April, the trustees had decided the university needed fresh leadership. Board of Trustees Chairman Bayard D. Clarkson planned right after the May 17 commencement to inform Clark that the trustees agreed to buy out his contract if he resigned. But the chairman, a descendent of the family that founded the university, was called out of town before he could talk privately with Clark. The trustees then decided to ask Clark for his resignation at a June 4 meeting, once he returned from his vacation.

However, in late May, news of Clark's pending ouster leaked to the press. When a university administrator found out, he placed a long-distance call to Clark, who cut short his vacation and returned to Potsdam on May 29 in hopes of changing the board's mind.

A board representative greeted Clark by handing him a letter from the trustees requesting his resignation. The trustees did offer to meet with Clark, but the letter made it clear the board's decision was final. Without meeting the board, Clark handed in his resignation. Clarkson appointed R. Thomas Williamson, vice president for external affairs, as acting president.

According to Clark, the letter never revealed the reasons why the trustees wanted him gone. However, trustee Oleg Pohotsky told the Clarkson *Integrator* that the board was unhappy "things were not going smoothly" under Clark's leadership, with Katy's murder and the negative publicity that followed at the top of its list.

In a statement the day after his resignation, Clark acknowledged that a "series of unfortunate events has made these last two years the most difficult period of my career."

Several months later, after he took a research job at Purdue University, he told *The Integrator* that, while he enjoyed his time at Clarkson, it was "a relief not to have the day-to-day pressures of it. But I still liked it when I did it. It was the most fun I had."

Referring to the board's decision to oust him without talking to him first, Clark added, "Every once in a while, you get hit below the belt. Better this than cancer."

A few years later, Katy's mother received a letter from Clark, saying that he planned to write a book about the murder and asking if he could interview the family.

After talking to Fahey, Terry declined, and she never heard about the book again.

Fahey was not surprised she did not want to do Clark any favors. "I mean, Terry is as Irish as they come," her attorney mused. "As I always say about Irish Alzheimer's: You only remember the grudges."

As the drama over Clark's ouster played out in Potsdam, Fahey was busy in Syracuse battling motions filed by Clarkson and its insurance company. The defendants' lawyers asked state Supreme Court Justice Mordue to toss the lawsuit—or, at the very least, dismiss specific claims against the university and the two security guards.

In one court filing, the defendants' lawyers suggested there was no factual basis to believe that Katy was conscious during the attack. "It is very well established that no recovery for pain and suffering will be allowed where the decedent did not regain consciousness," they wrote. "Accordingly, plaintiffs' claim for pain and suffering should be dismissed."

As evidence, they cited a statement in Katy's autopsy report. The assistant medical examiner had written: "From the moment of apparent assault to the time of her death, she never regained consciousness." However, it was clear to Fahey, and perhaps to anyone else who read the autopsy report, that Joven G. Kuan was only pointing out that Katy had become unconscious as the result of the attack, not necessarily from the instant it began. Moreover, in a July 1 reply, Fahey wrote that Brian McCarthy's confession to police established that Katy was conscious during the time McCarthy engaged in "the sustained brutal, vicious attack."

The lawyers for Clarkson and Great American Insurance also sought dismissal on the basis that Katy's parents weren't dependent on her for income and, therefore, suffered no financial injuries. In his reply, Fahey noted that the law was "well-settled" that representatives of the deceased have a right to recover medical costs, funeral expenses, and other financial damages from individuals responsible for a person's death. While Katy's parents were not financially dependent upon her at the time of her death, Fahey noted this did not mean they would not one day turn to her for voluntary assistance or support.

In a written decision on July 9, Mordue refused to dismiss any part of the lawsuit, rejecting without comment the arguments by Clarkson and the insurance company. The defendants appealed the ruling, even as both sides moved ahead with motions to discover evidence.

In response to the defendants' Demand for a Bill of Particulars, Fahey shared that the family had $4,228 in funeral expenses and more than $12,000 in medical costs. He turned over a list of Katy's past income, including $2,467 in 1985, when she worked for Peter's Groceries in Syracuse. She also worked for Christo's Restaurant in Syracuse in summer 1986, but Fahey didn't immediately have information on her earnings there.

In his court motions, Fahey demanded that Clarkson turn over personnel records of security guards Shanty and Avadikian, training materials, work orders regarding campus lighting, logs of calls to Potsdam police, and any reports by employees about the attack on Katy.

Fahey also demanded "copies of any and all tape recordings" and transcripts of interviews by Clarkson personnel with Avadikian and Shanty concerning their response to the assault outside Walker Arena. It was a fairly routine request to cover all the bases; Fahey did not know at that point that anyone at Clarkson conducted any such interviews.

On July 24, Clarkson attorneys revealed to Fahey that President Clark had indeed conducted taped interviews with Avadikian and Shanty. However, the university argued it was a rogue action by Clark, saying the "conversation was extraordinary and not made in the regular course of business, nor was it in the usual course of business procedure to have such conversations."

"Accordingly," the attorneys added, "the transcripts will not be disclosed."

The university lawyers later gave a different reason for refusing to turn over the tapes and transcripts, saying Clark conducted the interviews while preparing for potential litigation, which made the tapes exempt from disclosure in a subsequent lawsuit. In a letter to Fahey, Clarkson attorney Robert Barrer wrote, "I am sure that you will agree that documents created after the fact (with the exception of accident reports) are not properly discoverable or relevant to these proceedings."

Fahey, it turned out, didn't agree. If the university was so determined to withhold the tapes and transcripts, he thought, there must be something in them helpful to his case.

In a court filing, Fahey noted that a discussion between the university president and employees about their job duties was, by definition, part of the regular course of business.

"Moreover," Fahey wrote, "while Plaintiffs have not been made privy to the contents of the tape recordings, they (the recordings) presumably concern some discussion of what the Defendants failed to do during the course of their duties, and as such, would constitute their regular course of business."

As for the university's subsequent claim that the interviews were prepared for potential legal action, Fahey noted "no litigation was pending or contemplated" by Katy's parents until well after Clark interviewed the guards on September 2, 1986.

For most of the summer of 1987, criminal proceedings involving McCarthy grounded to a halt while both sides awaited Judge Nicandri's decision whether prosecutors could use his confession against him at trial. On Tuesday, August 4, Nicandri ruled they could.

In a nine-page decision, the judge said that McCarthy had given a "knowing and intelligent waiver" of his rights before Potsdam police questioned him. Nicandri also rejected the defense claim that police delayed McCarthy's arraignment to pressure him to confess. As for the allegation that state police Senior Investigator Manor promised McCarthy he'd get "one to three" if he confessed, "the Court gives no credence to such claim," Nicandri wrote.

In one minor victory for the defense, Nicardi ruled that any remarks that McCarthy made privately to Manor could not be used by prosecutors at a trial. District Attorney Gardner told reporters he wasn't bothered by that restriction because he never planned to ask Manor to testify about what he discussed while alone with McCarthy.

By allowing the confession to be used, the judge all but eliminated the possibility that defense attorney Nash could successfully argue at a trial that McCarthy didn't kill Katy or that it occurred accidentally. Nash's only viable options now were to prepare an insanity defense or to plead guilty and hope the judge would give McCarthy less than the maximum sentence for doing so. Nash would leave it up to McCarthy to choose the next step.

The prosecution had given the defense 10 days to make a decision. For eight days, Gardner heard nothing.

Then on the ninth, at about 9:30 a.m., Gardner was working in his office when Nash rushed in. McCarthy had made a decision, he said, and they needed to bring him before Judge Nicandri right away before he changed his mind.

"He's going to do it. Let's do it right now," Nash said.

Chapter 20

The Plea

THE courtroom in Canton was nearly empty of spectators when St. Lawrence County Court Judge Nicandri began proceedings just after 10 a.m. on August 13, 1987. The plea hearing had been called so quickly that there had been no time to alert news reporters, let alone wait for Katy Hawelka's family to drive from Syracuse to hear what McCarthy would say. However, the court transcript would note that his mother, Florence McCarthy, and two of his brothers did attend.

"I understand there's a change in the status of this case, Mr. Nash," the judge began.

"Yes, your honor," the defense attorney said. "I believe at this time, on behalf of Mr. McCarthy, I will offer to the court a plea of guilty to the third count of the indictment: murder in the second degree, based upon the theory of felony murder with the underlying felony being attempted rape."

In other words, McCarthy chose to plead guilty to the one count where he would not have to admit that he intentionally killed Katy or that he raped her.

That was okay with District Attorney Gardner, who had no objection if the judge accepted the plea in full satisfaction of the indictment. The maximum sentence would still be 25 to life, no matter which of the counts McCarthy chose.

After swearing in McCarthy, Nicandri asked if the defendant was making the plea voluntarily and without being under the influence of drugs or alcohol.

"Yes, I am."

"Now, Mr. McCarthy, are you satisfied with the services of your attorney in regard to this indictment?"

"Yes, I am."

"Now, have you had a full and adequate opportunity to discuss this plea with members of your family and with Mr. Nash before offering it to the court?"

"Yes, I have."

With those preliminary questions out of the way, Judge Nicandri turned to the morning of Friday, August 29, 1986. He asked if McCarthy came upon "a person maybe not known to you but subsequently known to be Katherine Hawelka."

"Yes."

"Where did you see her first?"

"Lying against a wall on the south side of Walker Arena."

"Then what happened?"

"I noticed that she had blood on her," McCarthy said, "and somebody had taken off her clothes, except for her sweater. And I thought about taking advantage of her. But, instead, I tried to pick her up."

"You mean physically pick her up?"

"Yes."

"When you say, Mr. McCarthy, that when you first saw her, she didn't have any pants on, is this correct?" Nicandri asked.

"That is correct."

McCarthy was still insisting, as he told police, that Katy already had blood on her. But some other details had changed, such as now claiming he tried to lift Katy in the air. His new version also contradicted his confession to the police that he removed her jeans and a boot.

The judge turned to the relevant elements of the crime.

"And you went to her for the purpose of having sexual relations with her?"

"No."

"What was your purpose in—when you said you went to take advantage of her?"

"No, I thought about taking advantage of her, but I didn't make any moves to, and I decided to help her," McCarthy said. "So, I tried to pick her up and put her over my shoulder, and I couldn't stand up that well. It seemed like she was fighting me. She didn't want any help. So, any person's natural reaction when somebody rejects your help is to say, 'The hell with them,' and that's what I said, and I threw her."

Nicandri asked, "You threw her against the wall of the arena?"

"Not with the *intention* of throwing her against the wall."

"Well, did you, in fact, throw her against the wall of the arena?"

"Yeah."

"Did, in fact, her head strike—and face strike—the cement wall of Walker Arena?"

"I guess so."

"Well, do you know?"

"Not for a fact, I don't," McCarthy said.

Nicandri was at an impasse. If McCarthy would not admit that he injured Katy and that he tried to rape her, the judge would have no choice but to reject the plea and schedule a trial.

"May I have just a minute, your honor?" Nash asked

"Yes."

Nash conferred quietly with McCarthy before addressing the court again.

"I think, Judge, it would be easier for Brian if he could start in his own words and tell you what happened as he walked by her that night."

"All right. Mr. McCarthy?" Nicandri said.

McCarthy said he "walked by her and noticed—like I said—she didn't have any pants on, and she had blood on her, and I thought about taking advantage of her. In fact, I wanted to, but I couldn't."

"When you say you couldn't," Nicandri asked, "are you talking about, you couldn't physically because of—"

"Yes, because of drugs and alcohol," McCarthy said.

"You're telling me that you were physically incapable of having sexual intercourse because of that?"

"Yes."

"Then what happened?"

"I did try to help her, but it made me mad because I couldn't do anything. In turn, I threw her."

"That's against the wall of the arena?"

"Yes."

Nicandri continued. "Mr. McCarthy, in one of the statements made to police, you indicated that you shook this girl, is that correct?"

"Yes, it is."

"And this was before or after you had thrown her into the wall of the Walker Arena?"

"I think it was before."

"Was she helpless at that time?" Nicandri asked.

"She seemed to be."

McCarthy was, by his refusal to state outright that he injured Katy while she was helpless, was getting even closer to placing his guilty plea in danger of being rejected.

Nicandri looked to the prosecution for help.

"Mr. Gardner, any questions you would like to pose to Mr. McCarthy?"

The district attorney, who was not allowed to question the defendant directly, suggested that the judge ask McCarthy if the victim offered any resistance, before or after he shook her and threw her against the arena wall.

Nicandri repeated Gardner's question.

"Just to—just it, (she) seemed to be rejecting, you know, of any help or touching her or whatever," McCarthy answered.

Gardner told the court he still didn't think McCarthy had sufficiently admitted to injuring the helpless Katy and trying to rape her. The DA suggested asking McCarthy if "he did, in fact, physically attempt to rape her" after shaking her and throwing her.

"You heard Mr. Gardner's question, Mr. McCarthy?" Nicandri asked.

"Yes, I did."

"Did you, in fact, attempt to rape her at that point?" the judge asked.

"Attempt to rape her?"

"Yes."

"Like I just said, I wanted to, but I couldn't. I couldn't physically."

This still wasn't good enough. Gardner pointed out that McCarthy's guilty plea wasn't sufficient if he only admitted that he "believed it in his mind" that he wanted to rape Katy without actually doing anything to make it happen.

"Whether he did or did not rape her isn't the point," Gardner said. "But I believe there had to be some evidence that he physically attempted to."

Nicandri gave it another try.

"Aside from what went on in your mind," he said to McCarthy, "did you attempt to have sexual intercourse with this individual which you found, or ran across, or came across at the back of the Walker Arena in the village of Potsdam?"

"I really don't know how to say it any plainer," McCarthy answered. "I thought about it. I wanted to."

"Did you try to?"

"I couldn't be aroused. I—"

"Did you *try* to?" the judge repeated, his patience clearly wearing thin.

Before McCarthy could answer, his attorney jumped in.

"May I inquire?" Nash asked.

"Yes," Nicandri said wearily.

"Brian," Nash began, "can you tell the court in your own words what, if anything, you did with your clothes? Did you take off any of your clothes?"

"I started to."

"What did you start to take off?"

"My pants."

"Tell the court what you did, in your own words," Nash said.

"I started taking off my pants, and I didn't—it didn't appeal to me. It didn't seem right."

Perhaps it was because McCarthy's mother and two brothers were in the room, or maybe it was just the defendant's loose grasp on the truth, but not even Nash could pry an admission from the defendant that he tried to rape Katy.

The judge called for a short recess.

When the proceedings resumed, Nash said he had spoken to McCarthy outside the courtroom. He said McCarthy was struggling "to verbalize what happened."

Nash turned to his client.

"Brian, you and I discussed this outside," Nash said. "The best you can, you have got to tell the court what acts believed to be of a sexual nature that happened that night. Just tell us what you did. I think, before we left, you told us what you did with your clothes, and tell us what you did after that."

McCarthy said, "I unbuttoned my pants, and I unzipped them. I wanted to have sex, so I laid down on top of her."

"Brian, was that at the point that you found, because of the alcohol and any other substances, that you were physically unable to have sexual intercourse?" Nash asked.

"I barely could stand up."

"What happened then?"

"I couldn't do anything. I noticed that I had blood on my sweatshirt, and it made me sick," McCarthy said. "Then, I got scared. I didn't know what to do."

Nicandri asked, "At this point, Mr. McCarthy, was this individual conscious when you were laying on top of her?"

"No."

Nash continued. "Brian, was she saying anything, or were there words coming out of her mouth, mumbling, do you recall?"

"I don't know if you'd call it words or what."

"Just tell us what you heard," Nash said.

"Sounded like somebody choking."

District Attorney Gardner reminded the court that the autopsy report showed Katy died from asphyxiation due to manual strangulation.

Nash asked McCarthy if he told police he shook the victim.

"Yes."

"After that, did you throw her head into the wall there at Walker Arena?"

"Not with the intention of throwing her. Just her head into the wall, but I did."

"Did you tell that to the police when you talked to Chief Matott and Mr. Manor?"

"Yes, I did."

With that, Nicandri decided he heard enough to accept McCarthy's guilty plea to second-degree murder committed during an attempted rape. It didn't matter if McCarthy was lying about other things, including his bizarre claim about finding Katy naked and bleeding.

The only question left that mattered: How many years should McCarthy spend in prison?

The judge set sentencing for Friday, September 11, 1987, giving the county's probation department time to prepare a presentencing report summarizing facts of the case, McCarthy's criminal history, recommendations from interested parties, and other relevant information.

Gardner told Nicandri that he heard from attorney Joseph Fahey, who wanted to make sure the probation department contacted Katy's family to add their input.

"My experience with Mr. Fahey is that he's a very busy man, so I would suggest they do it as quickly as they can, so they can get something back timely."

"All right," Nicandri said. "They will contact the probation department."

With that, Nicandri concluded the proceedings with a brusque, "That's all."

That afternoon, the news media scrambled to catch up with the sudden guilty plea. With no immediate transcript, reporters turned to Gardner and Nash to explain what happened.

Gardner emphasized that McCarthy was not promised a lesser sentence in exchange for his guilty plea. Although two counts were dropped, he said, McCarthy still faced the same potential sentence as if found guilty of all three—a minimum of 15 years to life, a maximum of 25 years to life. "They all are the same crime. The judge has the same sentencing options available to him," Gardner told the *Watertown Daily Times*.

As for McCarthy not having to admit he raped Katy or intentionally killed her, Gardner suggested this was an acceptable concession by prosecutors. "I think it was easier for the defendant to rationalize the events by pleading to the third count of the indictment."

Asked why McCarthy pleaded guilty, Nash said his client knew he would have a tough time winning an acquittal once Judge Nicandri ruled his statements to police were admissible.

"Obviously, it had a lot to do with the proof available to the prosecution," Nash said in an interview with the Potsdam *Courier & Freeman*. "In this case, they had two confessions to go along with the circumstantial evidence.

If they hadn't had the two confessions, I don't know what Mr. McCarthy would have chosen to do. . . . I've seen them go both ways. There's the individual situation, the family's situation and the amount of evidence available to the prosecution."

Nash said McCarthy consulted with his family before deciding to plead guilty.

Asked by a reporter about the guilty plea, Potsdam Police Chief Matott said he was "very pleased with the outcome," calling the prosecution of McCarthy "kind of a technical case."

State Police Senior Investigator Manor, who leveraged his friendship with McCarthy's parents to persuade their son to confess, said he thought the plea would ease the burden the case had placed on the defendant's family. "I think it's a good thing for them," Manor told the *Times*. "They have gone through enough." The newspaper did not include any comment from Manor expressing similar sympathy for Katy's family.

Fahey said Katy's parents would ask Nicandri to give McCarthy the maximum sentence. "Katherine Hawelka was a lovely, intelligent, talented lady who had a lot to offer the world and now can't," Fahey told *The Post-Standard*. The attorney said Katy's parents were pleased that McCarthy pleaded guilty without a promise of a reduced sentence.

"I don't know that they could ask for anything more," he said.

Fahey saw the proceedings much less favorably on August 20 when he obtained a copy of the plea hearing transcript, which he copied and mailed to Katy's mother. In an accompanying letter, Fahey expressed frustration that McCarthy "was allowed to repeat this stupid story about coming upon Katy being already beaten and unclothed."

Fahey added, "It appears to me he (McCarthy) admitted the bare minimum facts to satisfy the requirements of a guilty plea; however, since all parties in the criminal action appear to be satisfied by that, there is little to do but let sentencing go forward."

Terry couldn't understand why McCarthy was allowed to plead guilty without explicitly admitting he killed Katy and attempted to rape her. "What happened to Gardner's promise that McCarthy would have to take responsibility and admit what he did?" she asked. She thought McCarthy's lies about finding Katy bleeding and naked were reason alone to give him the maximum sentence.

When the *Massena Observer* got a copy of the transcript and reported the details from the guilty plea, Gardner told the newspaper that he knew McCarthy was lying about someone else attacking Katy. But the district attorney saw no reason to challenge McCarthy's statements as long as the defendant made the necessary admissions in pleading guilty to murder.

Clarkson University officials declined to comment on McCarthy's guilty plea, citing the ongoing civil suit filed by Katy's parents.

By the time he received the transcript, Fahey had already filed a motion with Judge Nicandri, seeking permission for the family to speak at sentencing. Fahey knew the request was a long shot. In 1987, the New York State Legislature was years away from enacting legislation to statutorily permit the victims of a felony crime to give this kind of oral statement in court.

But in his application to Nicandri, Fahey asked for the court's discretion. He wrote that Katy's family members "much prefer that their views with respect to an appropriate sentence be made in open Court before the Defendant at the time of sentencing." He added that limiting the family's comments to the presentencing report would not capture the intensity of their loss.

On August 21, Nicandri rejected Fahey's request, framing the matter as one of judicial decorum. He said it was clear that the Legislature, in drawing up the criminal procedure law, wanted to avoid an opportunity to "becloud the judicial atmosphere and to unbalance the process of sentence imposition" by allowing victims to confront the defendant in court.

"The charged atmosphere at sentencing is fraught with the opportunity for someone bent on mischief or with interest in other civil or criminal matters to attempt to intimidate the Court, provoke the defendant or generally disrupt the sentencing proceeding," Nicandri wrote.

However, Nicandri added he was "sensitive to the interest, and in fact, the need of the victim's family to have input in regard to any disposition." He suggested the family share its views with the court by writing to the probation department.

Fahey didn't give up. He wrote again to Nicandri, this time with a copy of his proposed remarks, in hopes the judge would reconsider once he read that the family had no intention of disrupting the sentencing.

In his prepared remarks, Fahey contrasted Katy's promising life with McCarthy's history of unemployment, criminal convictions, and time spent in a Virginia prison. McCarthy was an "admitted narcotics abuser" with an immense capacity for violence, Fahey said, as reflected by "the ferocious nature of his attack upon Katy." The statement continued:

As one who has practiced criminal defense work extensively throughout my career, I can tell you quite candidly that there is not one redeeming feature about Mr. McCarthy that I could bring to your Honor's attention were I to be so unfortunately charged with that responsibility.

I have followed the progress of Mr. McCarthy's criminal court proceedings quite closely, and I expect that this morning Mr. McCarthy or his attorney will urge upon the Court that Mr. McCarthy's conduct is mitigated by his claim he was under the influence of drugs and alcohol at the time of this incident, and, therefore, his sentence should be less than the maximum allowed by law.

In considering the validity of this claim, I would point out to Your Honor that from the moment of apprehension at the scene, Mr. McCarthy had sufficient presence of mind to formulate a false, exculpatory version of his involvement in an effort to try and throw off suspicion from himself for the attack. He initially attempted to claim that he happened upon Katy being attacked and was himself a victim of an attack, and he was sufficiently convincing so that the Potsdam Police transported him to the Canton-Potsdam Hospital where he was found to be uninjured and released. He then modified this version during the early morning hours of August 29th to claim that Katy had already been beaten and stripped of her clothing at the time he encountered her physical injuries. He has persisted in maintaining this obvious fiction throughout his plea of guilty on August 13, 1987 before Your Honor.

Mr. McCarthy's ability to invent these claims at the time of his apprehension at the scene of the attack clearly suggests that he was in complete control of his faculties at the time he subjected Katy to this sustained,

vicious physical and sexual assault, and that he consciously strangled her during a murderous rage resulting from his sexual frustration.

Katy will never know what it is to be middle-aged. She will never experience the happiness of marriage. She will never know the joy of having children. She will never enjoy the pride and satisfaction of career achievement. . . . In short, one who has contributed nothing to this world callously and viciously took the life of one who contributed much and who was capable of so much more.

The statement concluded with Fahey's hope that McCarthy, "in the future, at any age," be denied parole to ensure he never hurt anyone else this way.

After receiving Fahey's letter, Nicandri declined again to let Fahey make a statement at sentencing.

On September 10, 1987, Fahey, Katy's parents, older sister Betsy, and grandparents Alice and Frank Ryan checked into hotel rooms in Canton so they wouldn't have to drive from Syracuse for sentencing the following morning.

Carey, now attending St. John Fisher College, and Joe Jr., a student at Oneida High School, did not make the trip. Katy's younger siblings had hoped to attend the sentencing, but their parents refused to allow it, believing the proceeding would prove to be too upsetting for the teenagers.

A few days earlier, a friend of Terry expressed sympathy that she would have to be in the same room with McCarthy.

"It's going to be such a tough thing," the friend said.

Terry responded that nothing about sentencing would be as awful as what Katy had endured the morning of August 29, 1986. Besides, Terry wanted to look McCarthy directly in the eye, force him to see a mother's tears, and make him leave for prison with the knowledge of how much people hated him for killing Katy.

"No, there is no way I wouldn't be there," Terry said.

Chapter 21

"The Burden of This Incident Forever"

By the time Katy's family entered the courtroom just before 9:30 a.m., Brian McCarthy was already seated at the defense table. Terry found a spot in the front of the public seating at an angle where she thought it likely that McCarthy would see her if he glanced back.

Joe Sr., Betsy, Terry's parents, and Joseph Fahey sat in the same row as Terry, while two dozen of Katy's friends sat directly behind them. It made Terry think of a wedding where the bride's friends and family sat on one side, the groom's on the other, except McCarthy didn't seem to have anyone there for him.

McCarthy, his hair neatly trimmed and his face sporting a thin mustache, wore a gray suit with a vest, a white shirt unbuttoned on top, and brown boots. If he was wearing a bulletproof vest, none of the reporters in the courtroom noted it.

About 15 uniformed and plain-clothed deputies kept watch just behind the defense table and around the courtroom. To enter, spectators had to pass through a metal detector and submit to pat-downs. When Joe Sr. entered the courtroom, a deputy stuck a hand in his breast pocket to check for a weapon.

Finally, as Judge Nicandri entered the courtroom, deputies locked the doors.

Before announcing a sentence, the judge noted that he had reviewed the St. Lawrence County Probation Department's report, including confidential portions of the defendant's mental health evaluations in 1982 and 1987, and a drug and alcohol evaluation in 1987. The judge also pointed to Mc-Carthy's extensive criminal history, beginning as a youthful offender and continuing as an adult in New York and Virginia.

Nicandri noted for the record that McCarthy murdered Katy while on probation from Virginia. This appeared to be the first time anyone had stated this publicly, although the judge did not add that the defendant had been allowed to roam the streets without probation supervision.

Nicandri took a moment to explain his August 13 decision to accept Mc-Carthy's guilty plea, despite the defendant failing to fully admit what he did. The judge explained that the court only needed to satisfy itself that McCarthy knew what he was doing during his plea and that he "acknowledged criminal conduct sufficient for the court to be satisfied beyond a reasonable doubt that he did, in fact, commit the crime to which he pled guilty."

In deciding on a sentence, the judge said, he had to weigh several factors, including the impact Katy's murder had on her parents. He noted that Joe Sr. "sustained a deterioration in health as a result of this incident" and that he has "an inability to properly conduct his general practice and finds a great deal of difficulty and impossibility to deal with the loss of his daughter." Katy's mother also "has had a difficult time in concentrating and has had to request a job change . . . and to undertake counseling for herself and other family members."

The judge pointed out that Katy's parents, their attorney Fahey, the Potsdam Police Department, the probation department, and numerous others asked for the court to give McCarthy the maximum sentence. Nicandri noted that one local priest asked the court for leniency.

A factor weighing against giving McCarthy a maximum sentence, Nicandri said, was a recent opinion of the U.S. Court of Appeals for the Second Circuit. The judges expressed concern that imposing the maximum when a defendant pleaded guilty might have a "chilling effect" in obtaining guilty pleas from others. The court feared the courts would be overwhelmed with trials if defendants knew there was no reward for pleading guilty.

Nicandri then submitted for the record, and read aloud in court, a letter written by McCarthy on September 1, 1987, and given to the probation department:

The past year of my life could be a close comparison within the confines of purgatory. I wish this upon no one person, regardless of the grudge I hold. I have done wrong and have not understood it or accepted it but have owned up to this severe tragedy. In my opinion the pure essence of injustice has been throughout the proceedings and nothing I could do to prevent it would have swayed the final outcome. There is no perfect person on the face of the earth and I don't consider myself special.

My Constitutional rights have been violated with lies in newspapers headlines, perjury from the chief of police officials for personal benefits in the areas of justification.

I feel real bad for what has happened and knowing the lord has forgiven me, it will never be forgiven or forgotten by myself. When I was born I was baptized a catholic, needless to explain the phrase, an eye for an eye, a tooth for a tooth. There is 25 years of my life or less, to serve as punishment for acts against my religious beliefs. In my final statement, I would give my life for the resurrection of the girl, without a second thought!

As Nicandri read the letter, McCarthy sat with his head bowed slightly, his hands folded in his lap. Terry saw in McCarthy's body language a sense of impatience and a feeling of irritation he had to endure this proceeding. In his letter read by the judge, she heard only self-pity and arrogance with no apologies or true remorse.

She hoped, if nothing else, that the letter would show the court why McCarthy deserved the maximum sentence.

When it was his turn to speak, District Attorney Gardner declined to make any sentencing recommendation, even though most prosecutors would in such a case.

"The police department did their job," Gardner told Nicandri. "It's my opinion the prosecutor did their job, and I'm confident the court will do its job. Thank you."

The district attorney later stated he didn't recommend a sentence because he didn't think it was appropriate for a prosecutor to tell a judge what he should do. On the other hand, defense attorney Nash had no qualms about making a recommendation. He asked Nicandri to impose less than the maximum sentence.

"I'm not naïve," Nash said. "I don't stand before the court here asking that you impose the minimum sentence possible (of 15 years to life). . . . I am asking that you think about a sentence that is somewhat less than the 25 years, and I think we're talking somewhere between 22 and 24 years as the minimum. This at least would hold out some hope for Mr. McCarthy during those 22, 23 or 24 years of obtaining rehabilitation within the prison system. And that only makes him eligible to go to a parole board. It doesn't in any way say he's going to be released, and that would be up to an independent parole board."

Nash continued, "I think the easy sentence in this case is 25 to life. I'm sure the court has considered that, has considered everything. I'm sure that anything less than that, although it may be unpopular, the court does have an obligation to Mr. McCarthy to balance that competing interest of the possibility of rehabilitation."

After Nash finished, Nicandri turned to the defendant.

"Mr. McCarthy, you have an opportunity to make a statement to the court if you wish at this time. You are not under an obligation to, but if you would like to make a statement to the court prior to sentencing, now would be the time."

McCarthy stood, looked at the floor, then at the judge. "No, Your Honor. I think everything has been said that needs to be said. That's all I have to say."

He spoke in a voice so low that Katy's family strained to hear it and had to ask reporters after sentencing to repeat what he said.

McCarthy remained standing next to his attorney as Nicandri proceeded with the sentence.

"Mr. McCarthy," the judge began, "whatever is imposed will not and cannot make whole the family and friends of Miss Hawelka. That relief is beyond the scope of this life. You will, for however long you do live, have the burden of this incident forever with you, as will I'm sure, anyone who was associated with Miss Hawelka."

With that, Nicandri announced, "It is the judgment of the court that you be sentenced to an indeterminant sentence of imprisonment which shall have a maximum term of the remaining period of your natural life, and the court hereby imposes a minimum period of imprisonment of 23 years."

Terry and Betsy began quietly weeping. Joe Sr. showed no visible emotion, but like his ex-wife and oldest daughter, he was stunned to hear the judge give McCarthy two years less than the maximum. With credit for time served in the county jail, McCarthy would be eligible for parole beginning in 2009 when he was a relatively young man of 46.

After Nicandri advised McCarthy of his right to appeal the sentence, the judge placed him into the custody of the sheriff for transportation to Clinton Correctional Facility in Dannemora, New York. The hearing ended at 10:08 a.m.

As two sheriff's deputies in civilian clothing escorted McCarthy out of the courtroom and back to jail, Terry kept hoping that he might glance back. But McCarthy kept his head bowed, looking away.

In the courthouse lobby, Terry and Joe Sr. referred reporters' questions to Fahey. "Justice is never served when she's gone and can't be brought back," their attorney said. "There's no justice in that." Fahey said the victim's family would forever suffer from "a vicious crime (that) was committed because Katy had the misfortune to run across a vicious, sick individual."

Several days after sentencing, Virginia officials received word of McCarthy's murder conviction and now had to decide what to do, since being convicted of a felony was a clear violation of his terms of probation.

Mark W. Long, a deputy chief with the Virginia Department of Corrections, Probation and Parole, summarized the situation in a September 23 letter to Judge James M. Lupkin, who had sentenced McCarthy in March 1985. Long noted that McCarthy was released on parole October 23, 1985, with a plan under which New York state officials would supervise the former inmate's probation indefinitely. However, that transfer of supervision was still "pending" 10 months later on August 29, 1986, when McCarthy murdered Katy. Long's letter offered no explanation or apology for a bureaucratic mixup that allowed McCarthy to roam free without supervision during a time when he was using drugs and being repeatedly arrested in the Potsdam area.

Brian McCarthy is escorted from the St. Lawrence County Courthouse in Canton, New York, by sheriff's personnel following his September 11, 1987, sentencing. (WSYR-TV, Channel 9 photo.)

Long told Judge Lupkin that "there doesn't seem to be any point" in charging McCarthy with violating his Virginia probation since he was off to prison for a long time. In an October 7 response, Lupkin agreed to close the case, writing that any attempt to bring McCarthy back to Virginia to finish his sentence "would be an exercise in futility."

The letters, found in court records in Richmond, Virginia, do not indicate whether state officials conducted any review to determine why the transfer supervision never occurred or whether steps were taken to prevent the deadly mistake from happening again. Three decades later, Virginia probation officials declined to release records related to McCarthy, saying this information was exempt from disclosure under the state's Freedom of Information Law.

After McCarthy's sentencing, Virginia officials weren't the only ones try-

Joseph Fahey, attorney for Katy Hawelka's family, speaks to reporters on September 11, 1987, immediately following the sentencing of Brian McCarthy. To Fahey's left are Katy's parents, Joseph Hawelka Sr. and Terry Connelly, and their oldest daughter, Betsy Hawelka. (WSYR-TV, Channel 9 photo.)

ing to brush aside the past. On October 5, the Clarkson student newspaper in an editorial headlined "Clarkson Moving Toward Future; Past Is Meaningless" expressed weariness with the "accusations, denials and rumors" that had consumed the campus since Katy's murder.

"The events of the past year cannot be blamed on anyone. These events have to be put behind us," the *Integrator* wrote. "It's time to look at the good things happening at Clarkson. Further controversy will only damage our community and our university. We must not dwell on the past. We must forge ahead and look to a better future."

In Syracuse, Katy's parents were forging ahead, but it was in civil court, where the lawsuit was already paying off in ways that had nothing to do with money.

Chapter 22

The Clarkson Tapes

A day after Brian McCarthy was sent to prison, Clarkson University announced that it had hired its first security director, Lori Trani-Gettelfinger. A nine-year veteran of the Princeton University security force, Trani-Gettelfinger's job would involve coordinating Clarkson's campus safety efforts, including plans to hire a fourth night watchman, add a training program for these employees, and organize other efforts. Dean of Students Cooper said these additions were "not heavily into enforcement, but more into increasing awareness," such as teaching students and staff how to look out for themselves. "Safety and security is everyone's responsibility," Cooper told the *Ogdensburg Journal*.

The university said its newly hired security director would begin her duties in November after ending her maternity leave at Princeton.

In Syracuse, Fahey thought the hiring of Trani-Gettelfinger and the timing of other steps announced by Clarkson had less to do with McCarthy's sentencing in St. Lawrence County Court and more to do with the proceedings in New York State Supreme Court. These moves sounded to him like steps that defendants in a lawsuit take to reduce punitive damages for negligence by showing "they ameliorated the conditions for it."

"I don't think they would have done any of that had we not brought the lawsuit," Fahey said.

At the time of the announcement, Fahey and Clarkson's attorneys were still battling over whether the university would turn over tapes and transcripts of interviews that President Clark conducted with security guards Shanty and Avadikian.

On October 26, 1987, state Supreme Court Justice Mordue, without comment, rejected Clarkson's arguments the documents were privileged material.

When Fahey finally got his hands on the transcripts in mid-December, he understood why Clarkson wanted to keep them secret. Fahey was certain a jury hearing the tapes or reading the transcripts would conclude that Clark had improperly attempted to steer the guards toward recollections favorable to the university.

Clark had interviewed each man separately on September 2, 1986, the same day as news reports that said Shanty and Avadikian saw the attack on Katy but never acted to stop it. The transcripts do not state in which order Clark interviewed the two guards, but it would have made sense to talk to Avadikian first since he was the one who heard the initial commotion outside Walker Arena.

"What was the first indication that something was wrong?" Clark asked Avadikian, referring to events on the morning of August 29, 1986.

While inside the arena guarding personal computers, Avadikian said, he heard a noise outside that "sounded like people yelling." He radioed Shanty to check it out, then left his post at the front of Walker Arena to check out the back of the building.

"By the time I had gotten to the end of the arena, nothing. I went down the middle of the ice rink. Don called on the radio and told me he saw two people out there in the grass. . . . He said he was kind of embarrassed because the male had his pants down."

Shanty then drove to the front of the arena and picked up Avadikian to "see if we can scare them off," Avadikian said.

"You are a temporary employee?" Clark asked.

Avadikian nodded.

"What were your instructions about the arena?"

"To make sure no one got in and no computers got out," Avadikian answered.

"Were you asked to patrol the outside of the arena in any way?"

"No. I was inside. There's a burglar alarm in the back, and all the rest of the doors are chained from the inside."

Clark did not press Avadikian to explain why, if his job didn't involve patrolling outside, why he joined Shanty in riding around the arena.

With Avadikian in the passenger seat, Shanty drove once again to the southeast corner of Walker Arena. In the car's headlights, Avadikian said, he could see that a man "was still on top of her, and there was no sign of struggle."

After Shanty drove away the second time, Avadikian said, the two pondered whether to call the police or to go back and tell the couple to move on.

"You said there was no indication to you when you first saw them that there was any criminal activity? No struggle?" Clark asked.

"If there had been a struggle, we'd have stopped it," Avadikian said.

"The general area is generally well-lit?" Clark asked.

"If it's not well-lit, it's lit," Avadikian said.

"If you were walking on the road, you could see where you are going? You could see people from some distance?"

"Yes," Avadikian said, then acknowledged that perhaps "there might have been a light out that night. It seemed a little darker than (at the nearby) physical plant."

In his interview with Clark, Shanty said he "didn't think too much" of what he assumed was a couple having consensual sex because he saw this public activity previously on campus.

"Has it happened before in that precise location?" Clark asked.

"Behind the arena, there was an act of sex. That was last year."

"What happened in that case?"

"Just scared them off," Shanty said.

"Do you have any specific instructions on how to deal with this problem?"

"No. The general policy is to get them to move on, at least."

In the case of a "serious" incident, Shanty said, he was instructed to call the police.

"You were not instructed to try to solve problems yourself?" Clark asked. "If students are fighting or if there is a theft in progress, it's not your duty to try to stop it?"

"No."

"You're not trained as a security officer?" Clark asked.

"No. Fire/watchman is my job title," Shanty said.

Shanty told Clark it was "pure luck that we found them as quick as we did" in the early morning darkness.

"It was well-lit?" Clark asked.

According to the transcript, Shanty answered, "I would say it's well-lit —unless you put a light in that corner." Which doesn't make sense unless what he actually said—or meant to say—was, "I *wouldn't* say it's well-lit —unless you put a light in that corner," meaning that the only way he'd consider it "well-lit" is if the university added lighting.

"My opinion is that it's reasonably well-lit," Clark said. "A poor choice if not wanting to be discovered."

The opinion of Clark aside, the transcripts gave Fahey further reasons to believe that poor lighting around Walker Arena hampered the guards in recognizing that Katy needed help. Fahey also saw in the transcripts further proof that the university had failed to properly train the men on what to do when they saw a crime, and that Avadikian and Shanty didn't always follow what instructions they did receive.

In January 1988, the lawsuit was split into two parts when Justice Mordue declared a default judgment against McCarthy and severed that part of the case from the action against Clarkson University and the two security guards. Because McCarthy failed to respond to papers that Fahey served on him at Attica Correctional Facility, the only question now was how much damages the convicted killer should pay Katy's estate.

The case against Clarkson would go on the back burner while Judge Mordue scheduled an "inquest" for March 29, 1988, to hear the family's $250 million claim against McCarthy. Unlike a regular trial, it would be a one-sided proceeding with Fahey presenting all the evidence.

As the inquest got underway in the Onondaga County Courthouse in Syracuse, Katy's parents sat at the plaintiff's table next to Fahey's sister, attorney Mary Fahey. She agreed to be a "second chair" to assist her brother with legal matters during the inquest.

The only activity at the defense table was an untouched pitcher of water, its ice slowly melting.

After picking a jury of four women and two men, with two alternates, Joseph Fahey warned the panel that this case "has no light moments."

"It centers on the violent and terrifying death of a young girl," he said. "We know what Katy endured. We understand what . . . (her parents) lost. And we're going to punish Brian McCarthy for what he's done and say to the world, 'Never again.'"

Fahey said evidence would show that McCarthy beat, kicked, raped, and strangled Katy after ambushing her as she walked from downtown Potsdam toward her residence on the Clarkson University campus shortly after 3 a.m. on Friday, August 29, 1986.

Terry took the witness stand first. She described her second-oldest daughter as an "A" student in high school who saved money from part-time jobs to help pay for her education at Clarkson University. Katy had a "super" relationship with her brother and two sisters, Terry said, and the girl could be generous to a fault. Katy came home from college for the Christmas break in 1985 lacking enough cash to buy presents. So, when she received $50 from her grandfather, she spent all of it on gifts for others.

"That was Kate," Terry said, her voice breaking.

Joe Sr. was more stoic on the witness stand, recalling with almost clinical detachment his recollections of seeing Katy at the hospital, her face so bruised and swollen he initially failed to recognize her. When Fahey showed him a school photo of Katy, her father observed, "That was when she was alive and vibrant."

Katy's father identified several exhibits documenting a paper trail of medical futility, including a four-page bill from Canton-Potsdam Hospital for $1,019.80, an 11-page bill for $8,923.23 from House of the Good Samaritan, a $611.95 bill from Anesthesia Associates and a $405 bill from North Country Orthopedic.

Fahey also presented the jury a copy of the autopsy report from the Jefferson County medical examiner and the incident report from the Potsdam Volunteer Rescue Squad. Based on these records and McCarthy's statements to police, Onondaga County Medical Examiner Erik Mitchell testified that Katy likely was conscious throughout most of the attack.

Robert Seidenberg, a psychiatrist and an expert on rape trauma, took the witness stand to say that Katy suffered a horrifying "combination of helplessness, being overpowered and overwhelmed, and a feeling of a lack of any indication of anyone coming to her help" until McCarthy choked her into unconsciousness. Seidenberg added, "It was like being attacked by a wild animal out of the blue."

Syracuse University professor Kenneth Reagles, an expert on vocational rehabilitation, testified that Katy would have enjoyed a lucrative career with lifetime earnings of at least $1.08 million, not adjusted for inflation.

As the inquest stretched into a second day, Clarkson University student Todd Kilburn testified about walking Katy back to campus. Potsdam police dispatcher Paul Howard recalled sending officers to the scene. Village patrolman Dale Culver described seeing Katy's face "badly beaten and bruised and covered with blood." Investigator John Perretta testified about finding blood on McCarthy's boots that matched Katy's type.

As the officers testified, Fahey introduced 22 police photos as exhibits, being careful to display them in such a way Katy's parents would not see the graphic images.

Near the end of the inquest, Fahey played for the jury one of the two audio recordings of McCarthy's confession. Earlier, Fahey advised Katy's parents they didn't have to be in the courtroom to hear the unsettling interrogation. Joe Sr. and Terry insisted on being present.

For 23 minutes, Katy's parents listened with the jurors as they heard McCarthy describe how he pushed Katy "right into the wall, hard, with her face." His voice echoed through the courtroom as he described how "I dropped her head real hard, and it hit the side of her face," how "I saw blood start coming out of her face," and later how he tried to "shake her insides out" before trying to rape her.

Terry dabbed tears from her eyes as the tape played. At times, she and Joe Sr. buried their heads in their hands.

After the recording ended, Fahey showed the jury a photograph that Perretta took at Canton-Potsdam Hospital shortly after the attack in which McCarthy directed an obscene gesture at the investigator. "Look at his middle finger," Fahey said as he slapped the photo onto the rail in front of jurors. "That is the kind of remorse Brian McCarthy showed. That is how much sorrow he was able to summon."

Joseph Fahey, attorney for Katy Hawelka's family, shows a photo to the jury during an inquest on March 29 and 30, 1988, in New York State Supreme Court in Syracuse to determine monetary damages against Brian McCarthy. (WSYR-TV, Channel 9 photo.)

In his final remarks, Fahey told the jury that evidence showed Katy was awake for an extended period after the attack began, during which time her killer inflicted injuries over 16 areas of her body.

"She was conscious, trying to talk," the attorney said. "She experienced it. She tried to talk to him before he choked the life out of her."

While McCarthy denied to police that he raped Katy, Fahey said the statements by the security guards and the physical trauma she suffered proved otherwise. Fahey's final exhibit was a copy of Katy's death certificate listing the cause of death as asphyxiation due to strangulation, with the notation: "Deceased was raped and assaulted."

Fahey summed up the case by telling the jury, "I have tried ever since to find a word to describe what she experienced. I settled on 'horror,' but even that doesn't do it anymore. No one—no one—should die that way."

The jury did not deliberate long before reaching a verdict. As the jurors

Terry Connelly reaches over to hold ex-husband Joe Hawelka Sr.'s hand as a jury foreman in New York State Supreme Court announces a judgment against Brian McCarthy on March 30, 1988. (WSYR-TV, Channel 9 photo.)

filed back into the courtroom, Terry reached over and held Joe Sr.'s folded hands to await the decision.

The jury awarded $1 million to compensate the parents for lost wages, medical costs and other expenses, $500,000 for Katy's pain and suffering, and $2 million in punitive damages. The total was $3.5 million.

Outside the courtroom, Fahey told reporters he was happy with a $3.5 million verdict, even though it was substantially less than the $250 million sought. "I don't know of anybody walking around who doesn't think of $2 million (in punitive damages) as a lot of money."

Joe Sr. said he hoped McCarthy would "spend a long, long while in prison." While unlikely the parents would collect a penny from him while he was behind bars, Katy's father said the financial judgment would follow McCarthy, ensuring "he will never enjoy one bit of life."

Joe Sr. quietly added, "About the only thing I can say is there was a point made here today, but it won't bring Katy back."

Terry insisted that the inquest—in fact, the whole lawsuit—was not primarily about money. "I think we got accomplished what we set out to accomplish, to have Katy's story told. That was our main purpose, to have Katy's story told," she said. "In previous court proceedings, Katy was kind of lost in the shuffle."

Reporters asked Terry why she and Joe Sr. also were suing Clarkson when, in September 1986, the family stated that it didn't believe there was any fault on the part of the university or the village of Potsdam. At the time, Terry explained, the family felt grateful to Clarkson "because, during the three days we were in the hospital, university representatives were there constantly, reassuring us that the security guards did a good job. The president of the school kept describing they had done everything possible. They even talked about a security guard holding her head and helping her breathe. They never talked about the drive-bys."

While the inquest didn't involve Clarkson, the $3.5 million award sent a sobering message to the university how its part of the lawsuit might turn out. "Let's be realistic," Fahey told reporters. "The facts of this case don't change."

Just before the inquest, Clarkson University trustees had appointed a new president, Richard H. Gallagher, who had been provost and vice president for academic affairs at Worcester Polytechnic Institute in Massachusetts. Former President Clark took the occasion to write to the Clarkson *Integrator*, urging the new president to make it a priority to establish a campus police force.

In his letter, Clark also took one more dig at the board that forced his resignation.

"At Clarkson," Clark wrote, "adequate campus security is a cause with many rebels: trustees resent the expense, students dislike the surveillance, faculty see no benefit for themselves. . . . The University must recognize that the murder . . . shattered forever the illusion that Clarkson is immune to student crime. Aside from the risk to students, the University itself is assuming unacceptable risk in not moving swiftly to establish a campus police force. Anything less may be construed as negligence."

Clarkson and its new president had no public response to Clark's letter.

Meanwhile, Clarkson's lawyers seemed convinced they could settle the lawsuit if they came up with the right dollar figure. Fahey met at one point with a junior lawyer for Clarkson's insurance company, who scoffed at the $300 million the family was seeking. The lawyer suggested they could settle this right then and there with a "generous" settlement that would include paying Fahey's law firm for its legal work.

Fahey told him to slow down.

"You don't know what this lawsuit is about," Fahey said. "This lawsuit is not about money. It's about the way she (Katy) was portrayed, and additional steps you're going to have to take to ensure it doesn't happen again."

The family would never settle, Fahey said, unless—in addition to a proper dollar amount—it also got a public apology from Clarkson for blaming Katy for what happened, a statement acknowledging the university was negligent, and a promise from Clarkson to improve security.

The insurance attorney said the university would never give in to these demands.

However, on the eve of the case going to trial, Clarkson blinked.

Chapter 23

Settlement

O N the morning of Friday, September 15, 1988, Justice Mordue was ready to oversee jury selection in Syracuse when Joseph Fahey and the Clarkson lawyers informed him they had settled the lawsuit. Both sides worked late the previous evening to hammer out a deal that would include a cash payout, a promise from Clarkson to upgrade security, and an end to a court action that brought nearly 18 months of negative publicity for the university.

Under the settlement, both sides agreed not to reveal the amount Clarkson was paying Katy's estate. Not even Mordue would know the amount when he approved the settlement after questioning Katy's parents to confirm they believed it to be fair and reasonable.

The terms of the settlement included a three-page statement by Clarkson that was remarkable in its tone of contrition.

"Immediately following this incident," the statement said, "it may have appeared to some that Clarkson University believed Katherine Hawelka somehow contributed to her tragic death. Any impression of this sort is incorrect and senseless. Clarkson does not believe that Katherine Hawelka in any way contributed to this situation. While a crime of this magnitude had never occurred on the Campus, Clarkson acknowledges its responsibility to Ms. Hawelka and her family and deeply regrets the loss that has befallen them."

The statement did not mention that one reason "it may have appeared to some" that Clarkson blamed Katy was because the university did precisely that in court papers.

Clarkson's statement added that the university had "undertaken a thorough review of its responsibilities to Ms. Hawelka and has taken steps to evaluate and improve campus safety programs to ensure that such a tragic occurrence will never be repeated."

While not quite the full-throated apology and admission of negligence that Katy's parents demanded, the statement omitted the typical claim by a defendant after it settles that it did so without admitting any wrongdoing.

However, Clarkson attorney Charles Manheim insisted to *The Post-Standard* that the university had not admitted liability. As a technical matter, that may be true, although Fahey would see Clarkson's admission of "responsibility" as, in effect, the same thing.

"Let's just say I'd consider that a distinction without a difference, okay?" Fahey said. "That's just word parsing and perhaps a fig leaf that they can hold up to their trustees, their donors, and people who might be contemplating going to the university. Because they hated the publicity. They loathed it."

As for the amount in the settlement, Fahey told the *Herald-Journal* the family asked to keep it confidential because they "don't want what happened to their daughter to be remembered in the public mind as a matter of dollars and cents."

Much of Clarkson's statement emphasized improvements it made to campus security in the previous two years, including the addition of a department with a trained staff of six "proctors" hired to patrol the campus and to encourage students to practice safety. The university also installed more outdoor lighting, created a direct radio link to village police, instituted a nighttime bus service to downtown, and installed a locked gate to keep students from taking the shortcut behind Walker Arena at night.

"Clarkson will be a safer campus," Terry Connelly told reporters. "I hope we can keep one more family from going through what we've gone through. . . . What we were looking for from the university was to accept responsibility and to do more consciousness-raising, so this would not happen again. What came out of this was an awareness of crime on campus."

While the settlement ended Terry's fight with Clarkson, she decided there was more work to be done. She joined the board of Victims of Crime Advocacy League of New York (VOCAL), a victim-rights group that Methodist minister Howard Velzy formed after his daughter, Linda, was murdered in 1977 while a freshman at the State University of New York at Oneonta.

During an interview with Syracuse ABC affiliate WIXT-TV (now WSYR, Channel 9), Terry held up a brochure from VOCAL as she argued that the criminal justice system provided only "justice for the criminals."

"The victims don't have rights," Terry said. "One of the things VOCAL has pushed is a victim's notification so that when a criminal does come up for parole, the victim's family is notified." As for the possibility that McCarthy would seek parole in 2009, she said, "My recommendation would be to keep him there, to never let him walk the streets again. Because I would feel, in my heart, he would probably do it again."

The news report ended with a shot of Terry's car and a VOCAL bumper sticker on the back that read, "JUSTICE FOR ALL. EVEN THE VIC-TIM."

Terry also joined forces with Howard and Connie Clery, the couple who sued Lehigh University following the 1986 campus murder of their daughter, Jeanne. The Pennsylvania university reportedly agreed to settle with the Clerys for $2 million and to take steps to improve campus safety. Terry first met the Clerys when she traveled to New York City to participate in a forum at Columbia University, where panelists offered advice to students on campus safety.

Terry saw remarkable similarities between her own family's experience and that of the Clerys, including how it took a tragedy to get Lehigh to offer proper security.

"It was the same kind of thing as us—they sent their daughter to a small campus and thought she was safe," Terry said.

In spring 1989, Terry and the Clerys visited Albany to lobby New York lawmakers to pass legislation requiring colleges and universities to collect campus crime statistics and to make this information available to prospective students.

George Sussman, executive director of the Association of Colleges and Universities in New York State, told *The Associated Press* that his group opposed forcing colleges to disclose crime statistics. He said colleges don't need warning labels like the ones the U.S. surgeon general required on packs of Winstons and Camels.

"Colleges are not like cigarettes," Sussman said. "Most people don't die from them."

"Tell that to Katherine Hawelka's parents," countered the Syracuse *Herald-Journal* in an editorial supporting the legislation.

Clarkson spokeswoman Karen St. Hilaire told the *Watertown Daily Times* that the university had already begun to track incidents of crime on campus. But the university had no plans to share the information with outsiders. "At this point, we keep those statistics for our own use," she said. "We have not in the past reported crimes, but with our new security, we have started to keep track of them."

If others wanted to know about a crime at Clarkson, St. Hilaire added, they should contact the Potsdam Police Department, which continued to patrol the campus and to investigate incidents there. In any case, she added, "We don't have a big problem. . . . Clarkson has always been a pretty safe campus. Safety has not been a major issue."

In testimony in Albany, Katy's mother saw things differently:

It has been over two years, and I still don't know why this happened to my child. I do feel that if the guards had intervened sooner, Katy might still be with us. I'm grateful that McCarthy was apprehended and is serving a 23-years-to-life prison term. I pray he will never walk the streets again.

The security at Clarkson has been vastly improved. I hope and pray that another family will not have to endure the pain and suffering we have had to go through. Unfortunately, this is probably unrealistic. As long as colleges and universities do not take seriously their responsibility to their students' safety, it will happen again.

I also feel the students have to become more aware of the dangers on our campuses. I know Katy's sister and brother, who are now in college, are more aware, as are her friends and theirs. I am just very sad that this awareness had to be at the expense of our Katy.

Howard Clery offered a much darker assessment of Clarkson security. In testimony to the state Senate Higher Education Committee, he singled out the university for a pattern of incidents "that describe the depravity of that campus." He went on to list what the *Watertown Daily Times* described as a "litany of allegations" from 1986: Katy's murder and rape, the alleged rape at a toga party, underage drinking, a staff member's use of university equipment to make porn, and three employees accused of sexually assaulting minors. Clery said Clarkson also had a lax attitude toward public sex, citing the inaction by security guards in stopping the attack on Katy.

"It is very interesting that, despite all this, Clarkson still refuses to share any information," Clery told lawmakers.

In Potsdam, St. Hilaire responded by saying Clery's "depravity" comment was so outrageous it wasn't worthy of a response. She told the *Times* that Katy's murder was the only such crime on campus in Clarkson's long history. As for the staff member arrested for soliciting girls to make porn in Canada, St. Hilaire noted he had resigned from the university. The other alleged incidents either didn't occur in 1986 or were unproven, she said. (A St. Lawrence County grand jury declined to indict the Clarkson student accused of raping a freshman.)

Following Clery's testimony, the Higher Education Committee voted to support the "Campus Security Act." However, the full Legislature failed to pass it into law.

Not long afterward, the U.S. Congress went over the heads of state lawmakers, passing similar legislation known as the "Student Right to Know and Campus Security Act." President George H.W. Bush signed it into law on November 8, 1990. In the years since, the federal law has required American colleges and universities to, among other things, distribute a public report annually listing their campus crime statistics and describing safety measures.

Over time, the statute would evolve into the "Jeanne Clery Disclosure of Campus Security Policy and Campus Crime Statistics Act," also known simply as the Clery Act.

Years later, compliance with the Clery Act became one of the responsibilities of John Kaplan, the Potsdam police officer who dragged McCarthy from under the stairs outside Walker Arena. After serving for a time as Potsdam's chief of police, Kaplan headed the police forces for SUNY Potsdam and SUNY Canton. In 2019, Boise State University appointed him as associate vice president for public safety.

In his frequent talks to students about the need to be alert to crime, Kaplan often tells of his own experiences of August 29, 1986, and the searing memory of seeing the battered body of young Katy Hawelka lying on the grass outside Walker Arena.

"There's no way in the world, in my life, that I can hear the word 'Clery' —and I talk about it every week in one way or another—without also thinking about Katy," Kaplan said.

By the time the Clery Act passed, Terry had already begun to pull back from the public limelight. The anger that fueled her activism began to fade, leaving only a hollow heartache.

"At some point, it was just too hard to focus on it all the time and to put all that energy into him," Terry said about McCarthy. "Nothing we can do is going to bring Katy back. McCarthy is in prison, and that's the best result we can have."

After leaving Katy's bedroom largely untouched for several years, Terry stored or gave away most of her slain daughter's remaining possessions. Just about the only personal items that Terry kept in Katy's room were a Henninger High School pennant pinned to a closet wall and a sorority jacket from high school.

Terry decided the best way to honor Katy's love of life was to find it again for herself, to embrace time with family and friends, and even to celebrate the holidays. Terry also knew others still needed her to be a daughter or mother, or, eventually, a grandmother.

In the back of Terry's mind, though, she kept a countdown clock set to hit zero in 2009 when McCarthy would become eligible for parole. McCarthy would learn then that, when he murdered Katy in a dark corner outside Walker Arena, he could not have chosen a victim whose mother would be more determined than Terry Connelly that he would never again see the light of day.

Chapter 24

2009

O N a frigid morning in February 2009, Joe Hawelka Jr. showed up at New York State's parole office in Syracuse to give his first impact statement opposing Brian McCarthy's release from prison. Katy's brother would compare the process to someone ripping a bandage off a wound that never completely healed.

Joe Jr. had nearly 23 years to prepare for this day when he would walk into the Senator John L. Hughes State Office Building and take a seat for a meeting with a parole commissioner. He was eager to tell the parole board why it should never release McCarthy, who was then serving time at Mid-State Correctional Facility in Marcy, New York.

Still, after so many years tamping down the awful memories and trying to remember only the good times with Katy, Joe Jr. suddenly was back in 1986. Once again, he could hear his mother's anguished scream during the early-morning call from the police. He was back at the Watertown hospital, waiting for doctors to remove Katy's life support. He was again picking out a casket because his dad couldn't bear to do it.

"I almost forgot about the circumstances of her demise, but that first parole hearing brought it all back," Joe Jr. said.

The Division of Parole allowed Katy's next of kin to present family impact statements a few weeks before McCarthy's first parole hearing, set for March 31, 2009, at Mid-State prison.

"The purpose of the meeting is to give you the opportunity to discuss the impact the crime has had on you and your family," a parole official wrote. "It is also an opportunity to ask whatever questions you may have about parole. To ensure the accuracy of the statement, a court stenographer will be present to make a record of the meeting. A written transcript will be provided to the Parole Panel when they interview the inmate at the correctional facility. You will be notified of the Board's decision."

The board also informed the family that it could expect to have about an hour to share its thoughts with a parole commissioner.

Joe Jr. arrived at the parole office just before 10 a.m., accompanied by his mother, Terry, and by attorney Mary Fahey, who had taken over as legal advocate for the family. Her brother, Joseph Fahey, was elected as an Onondaga County Court judge in 1996, and since then was no longer permitted by judicial ethics to weigh in on McCarthy's fate.

Mary Fahey was a former associate counsel for the Wall Street firm of Stroock, Stroock & Levan. She later worked for the Onondaga County District Attorney's Office before taking a job as a law clerk for Stewart F. Hancock Jr., a judge of the New York Court of Appeals. After that, she joined the Onondaga County Law Department in Syracuse. No one was prouder of Mary Fahey's success than her brother Joseph. He was fond of pointing out that she once wrote a law-review article about the Constitution's double-jeopardy clause that was cited by United States Supreme Court Justice John Paul Stevens.

Terry did not know Mary Fahey very well in 1988 when the attorney was "second chair" during the inquest that led to the $3.5 million judgment against McCarthy. But very quickly in 2009, Terry grew close to her, enjoying the attorney's sense of humor and marveling at her legal knowledge, relentless enthusiasm, and kindness.

"She came in, and immediately I got the feeling she knew Katy," Terry said. "She was just very, very caring."

Security was tight in the lobby of the state office building when Terry, Joe Jr. and Mary Fahey signed in. Joe Jr. noticed several ex-cons signing in to meet their parole officers.

Before passing through a metal detector, visitors had to empty their pockets. Joe Jr. pulled out a Leatherman five-way metal tool he forgot he was carrying. The device included a knife, screwdriver, and pliers.

"Oh, dear," the elderly guard said when he saw the tool. "I think you're in trouble. Are you on parole?"

"No, I'm not on parole. I'm meeting with the parole board. Victim impact," Joe Jr. said.

The guard smiled as he held up the tool. "Okay. But I'm going to hang onto this." Joe Jr. could have it back when he left.

The guard gave them directions to the parole office, and soon the three were sitting in a windowless room where Parole Commissioner G. Kevin Ludlow and a stenographer were waiting. Ludlow, a longtime attorney from the Utica area who was appointed to the parole board in 2002, greeted them warmly.

For the first time in years, Terry recited to a stranger her memories of Katy's murder and the enduring grief that followed for family and friends. Terry told Ludlow she feared no community would be safe if the parole board allowed McCarthy to go free.

When it was Joe Jr.'s turn to speak, he read portions of a written statement.

"I miss my sister terribly," he said, "and not a day goes by without me thinking about her. It took a long time for me to think of the good times with Katy, as opposed to the way she died."

Joe Jr. contrasted the lives of the two people who crossed paths outside Walker Arena on August 29, 1986. Katy had accomplished so much in her 19 years and had a bright future with "unlimited potential." On the other hand, Joe Jr. said, McCarthy "was a true burden on society with numerous arrests" and a long history of using and dealing drugs.

"People like Mr. McCarthy have no place in society," he said, "and to ever grant parole would be like condoning these acts. . . . It is my job to oppose (McCarthy's) parole for the rest of my life, and it is McCarthy's job to serve life."

After they finished their impact statements, Ludlow took several minutes to answer the family's questions and to explain what would happen next.

When McCarthy appears before the board, Ludlow said, two or three commissioners will question him, then decide later whether to grant him parole. Typically, these hearings occur face to face in a prison conference room, although commissioners had begun interviewing some inmates remotely using a video conferencing link.

The public is not allowed to attend the hearings. But the parole board later releases transcripts, often with huge chunks deleted to protect the privacy of inmates and others.

The commissioners typically schedule two-dozen or more hearings during a prison visit, meaning each inmate might only get 10 to 15 minutes to make his case. As inmates wait their turn outside the conference room, the commissioners begin in alphabetical order with those newly eligible for parole. After that, they interview inmates previously denied parole, followed by those given a new review after going to court.

The inmate sits in a chair about six to 10 feet from commissioners, who face him from behind a table. Next to the commissioners are boxes packed with file folders with information about the inmates they will be seeing. A stenographer and prison staff are also present.

Commissioners typically question an inmate about his past criminal activity, his disciplinary record in prison, his educational accomplishments while serving time, his future goals, and where he plans to live after his release.

Members of a parole panel hope to hear some words of remorse, although commissioners never ask for them. As former commissioner James Ferguson once testified to state lawmakers, "If you asked someone, 'Do you have remorse?', you would have to be an exceptionally dull individual to not say, 'Yes, I have remorse.'"

Once the inmate leaves the room, the commissioners usually decide on the spot whether to grant parole. A 2-1 vote in favor means the inmate will be released. If just two commissioners are present, a 1-1 split decision means the inmate's appearance is "null" and the board will need to schedule another hearing right away. Those denied parole are placed on a "hold" for up to two years before they are eligible for their next hearing.

The commissioners, in their rulings, are required to explain their decision. First and foremost, they will reject parole if they believe an inmate might commit a crime again. An inmate with a recent history of bad behavior in prison also has a tough time winning parole. Some are denied parole for no other reason than the board believes doing so will "deprecate the seriousness of his crime as to undermine respect for the law."

Some notorious New York inmates, such as John Lennon assassin Mark David Chapman, have remained incarcerated, despite repeated parole hearings and a history of good behavior in prison. "The panel has determined that your release would be incompatible with the welfare and safety of society," one panel of commissioners explained in denying Chapman's release.

Commissioner Ludlow commended Terry and Joe Jr. for taking the time to present impact statements, which the commissioners heavily weigh in their decisions. He pointed out that only a handful of the parole cases he saw included such impact statements, which he chalked up to many victims also being criminals.

"I've drawn the inference that that is because the crime in this state is pretty much driven by illegal drugs and the effects of illegal drugs," Ludlow said, "and as a result, you don't have one drug head coming in to give a statement against another drug head. It doesn't happen."

Although he was meeting with Katy's family, Ludlow noted, he might not be one of the commissioners deciding whether to release McCarthy. The board assigned commissioners to cases on a somewhat random basis to try to minimize unofficial pressure. Even the commissioners did not know of assignments until shortly before the hearings took place.

Katy's family would have to take a leap of faith that the commissioners deciding McCarthy's fate took the time to read the transcripts of their statements.

Mary Fahey later told the family in an email that she was happy with the meeting. "Commissioner Ludlow was great, especially on questions about parole appearances (I certainly learned a few things, since I have never been in charge of facilitating victim impact hearings). Terry and Joe showed great courage, but also made very effective statements. This is a difficult climb, but you are all doing great. I am so proud of you all, and grateful to get to be a part of this effort."

In February 2009, Katy's sisters, Betsy and Carey, also gave impact statements separately, but their efforts to oppose McCarthy's parole had begun months earlier.

On December 8, the family launched an online petition asking the public to sign their names in opposition to McCarthy's release and to share their thoughts with the parole board. This campaign at **gopetition.com** noted

FROM LEFT: Attorney Mary Fahey and New York parole Commissioner G. Kevin Ludlow in undated photographs, and Brian McCarthy in a prison mug shot in 2007. (Fahey family/G. Kevin Ludlow/New York State Department of Corrections and Community Supervision photos.)

the "heinous nature of the murder of Katherine Hawelka, as well as the fact that he (McCarthy) had recently been paroled and was using drugs and alcohol at the time of the attack."

By the end of 2008, the petition had collected more than 700 signatures, many from people living in other states. One commented that McCarthy should consider himself fortunate he committed his crime in New York, where he didn't have to face the death penalty. "Please do NOT allow this murderer to go free," the person wrote. "He should never be permitted to see freedom again! He took a life after torturing her. Parole should have NEVER been an option! If he was here in the South, he wouldn't be anywhere near free, he'd be on death row!"

Meanwhile, Katy's family launched a blog at **4katy.blogspot.com** with a link to the petition, newspaper clippings about Katy's murder, and a section for visitors to post comments.

As the family began to shed two decades of privacy to make their battle public, one voice was noticeably absent.

For years after his daughter's murder, Joe Hawelka Sr. struggled to maintain his Oneida County dental practice. He was often sick, which Terry thought at the time was from the effects of stress and grief.

Then in the summer of 1994, he called Carey, not long after she had received her bachelor's degree in communications from St. John Fisher College and found a job in public relations in Ohio. He told her that doctors had diagnosed him with non-Hodgkin lymphoma, a form of cancer. He was telling her this now because she was planning to get married that October. He wanted to give her time to find someone else to walk her down the aisle because he wasn't sure he'd be healthy enough.

Somehow, though, after chemotherapy at University Hospital in Syracuse, a sickly Joe Sr. had the strength to walk his youngest daughter to the altar when she became Carey Patton at the Cathedral of the Immaculate Conception in Syracuse. The following March, he would do the same for his oldest daughter when she became Betsy McInerney in a wedding at Holy Family Church in the Syracuse suburb of Fairmount. (As if that weren't enough wedding bells in the family, Terry got married to Doug Taber, owner of a General Motors dealership in Cato, New York.)

Joe Sr. went into remission, and he was able to continue working, although he retired from his dental practice and took a part-time job in Utica reviewing dental claims for an insurance company.

Meanwhile, Terry's father, Frank Ryan, died September 27, 2001, at 93 years old. Her mother, Alice, passed away on January 2, 2006, at age 91. They were laid to rest at St. James Cemetery, Cazenovia, in a plot not far from Katy's.

Then on Friday, August 10, 2007, Joe Sr. lost his battle with cancer, passing away at age 67 at his home in Verona Beach. He was buried in St. John's Cemetery in North Bay, New York. He had dictated his own obituary. In it, after listing survivors, he wrote without elaboration: "A daughter, Katy Hawelka, died in 1986."

In 2009, as the news media began requesting interviews about the petition drive, Joe Jr. tried to figure out what his father would have wanted them to do.

"Would Dad be okay with this?" Joe Jr. asked Uncle Bill Hawelka about putting Katy's murder back in the spotlight.

"Absolutely," his uncle said. "Anything we can do to keep him (McCarthy) in."

What would become a media blitz began January 12, 2009, when Channel 9 in Syracuse interviewed Terry, Betsy, and Joe Jr. for a report on McCarthy's upcoming parole hearing. Sitting on a sofa in Terry's living room, a framed photo of Katy on an end table behind them, they recalled the lasting devastation that McCarthy wrought on the family.

FROM LEFT: Joe Hawelka Jr., Terry Taber, and Betsy McInerney are interviewed in 2009 at Terry's home in Syracuse. (WSYR-TV, Channel 9, photo.)

"Our lives changed the minute that he attacked her," Betsy said, her voice quaking. "Time stopped. Our family as we knew it. Our lives as we knew it. It was drastic."

At his guilty plea and sentencing, Betsy noted, McCarthy "never addressed us as a family. Never any remorse. Never any 'I'm sorry.' You know, he took the easy way out with a plea deal. And I want to make sure he doesn't take the easy way out with parole."

Joe Jr. added, "There wasn't much I could do for Katy the few days she did survive. But I can do this for her."

Terry told Channel 9 her goal in speaking out was not only to keep McCarthy behind bars. "I just want to keep Katy alive in everybody's hearts, and I don't want her to be forgotten."

At the time of the interview, the family's petition had collected more than 800 signatures. Within two weeks, it had grown to 2,300.

On January 28, the *Watertown Daily Times* revisited Katy's murder in a story under the headline, "Online drive aims to keep killer locked up." The article focused on the family's fears for residents of the North Country and elsewhere if McCarthy were released.

"He's dangerous," Terry said. "We want to keep him in prison. He's not the guy you want to have on the streets."

Carey emphasized in an interview that McCarthy was a stranger to Katy. "This was a random act. My sister didn't know Brian McCarthy. He was on parole when he brutally murdered her."

On Sunday morning, February 15, *The Post-Standard* pulled together an exceptionally detailed feature story that took up much of the front page and an entire page inside. The article did more than focus on the family's campaign to deny parole. Through interviews and court documents, it retraced events before and after August 29, 1986, including McCarthy's troubled history, the failure of guards to stop the attack, the family's decision to remove Katy from life support, McCarthy's guilty plea, and his less-than-the-maximum sentence.

One legacy of Katy's passing, the family told the newspaper, was that it brought them closer. Afterward, they never said goodbye to each other without also saying, "I love you."

"That's her continuing to hold us together," Joe Jr. said of Katy.

Among those interviewed by the Syracuse newspaper was Eugene Nicandri, the St. Lawrence County Court judge who sentenced McCarthy. Now retired from the bench, he said that the brutal nature of Katy's murder had stuck with him. "I don't see how a family could ever get past something like this," he said. Nicandri said he was relieved when McCarthy pleaded guilty and spared the family a trial.

Brian McCarthy did not respond to *The Post-Standard*'s request for an interview. The newspaper said some of McCarthy's family members declined to talk about the case or couldn't be reached for comment. Donald Shanty and Kim Avadikian, the two security guards who witnessed the attack, also did not return the newspaper's messages, holding onto a public silence that would continue in the following years.

The morning that *The Post-Standard* article was published, Joe Jr. woke at about 4 o'clock and drove for a half-hour around Syracuse until he found a gas station selling the paper. Afterward, he called Betsy and Carey and read the article to them, then watched over the next few hours as the number of petition signatures steadily climbed to more than 3,000.

As the day of the parole hearing approached, current Clarkson President Anthony G. Collins, a faculty member on campus when Katy was murdered, wrote to the parole board to say the university would feel less safe if McCarthy were released.

"August 29, 1986, was the darkest day in the 113-year history of Clarkson University," Collins said. "Clarkson submits that justice and the physical safety, and emotional wellbeing of our campus community, require that Mr. McCarthy be denied parole and that he serve the rest of his natural life in prison."

Katy's family was pleased with all this public opposition to McCarthy's parole. However, because letters to the board are confidential, Katy's family had no idea how many might be arguing for his release.

In the past, prison rights activists often supported the release of murderers who served the minimum time on life sentences. Sometimes, corrections officers have spoken up for an inmate who was a model prisoner, earned a college degree, embraced religion, mentored younger prisoners, and otherwise made it clear he was no longer a threat if paroled.

But after obtaining a copy of McCarthy's prison record, Mary Fahey didn't think it likely any corrections officer would be going to bat for him.

Chapter 25

Inmate 87D0088

B RIAN McCarthy had been an inmate at Attica Correctional Facility for barely a month when he had his first documented disciplinary action: a write-up on November 2, 1987, for fighting and refusing to obey a direct order. Prison disciplinary records available from that era didn't offer many details, including punishments. But they did show a continued pattern of violence by McCarthy and a resistance to doing what he was told to do.

On January 20, 1988, he received a disciplinary ticket for repeatedly kicking and punching another inmate. Eight days later, he was cited for refusing to obey an officer's order to be silent; McCarthy reportedly called the officer a "scumbag" and said, "Fuck you! Lock me up!"

On March 14, McCarthy received a ticket for "refusing to lock-in." He had to be escorted back to his cell by two officers.

On May 29, officers searching McCarthy's mattress found a shank, a sharp weapon fashioned from materials found inside the prison. Three months later, on August 15, McCarthy attacked another inmate, smashing the victim's head into a wall in an assault that Mary Fahey found chillingly similar to the attack on Katy Hawelka.

"The inmate has not been a model prisoner," Mary Fahey wrote to the parole board in February 2009. "His conduct during incarceration demonstrates that he is extremely dangerous—he had engaged in violence, hid weapons, obeys direct orders only when it suits him, and is devious and manipulative. . . . He goes to any length to get what he wants, including bullying, harassing, and attempting to extort corrections officers. This has necessitated a series of transfers during his incarceration that is nothing short of remarkable."

McCarthy entered the New York state prison system on September 18, 1987, at Clinton Correctional Facility in Dannemora. Assigned inmate number 87D0088, he would remain there until corrections officers transported him on September 30 to Downstate Correctional Facility in Fishkill, a reception center for new inmates.

There, prisoners were fingerprinted, fitted for forest green prison clothes, had their mug shot taken, and required to participate in a battery of exams. On an IQ test, McCarthy scored 112, or "high average." Prison records noted he had obtained his high school equivalency diploma in 1985 during his brief stay in a Virginia prison.

On October 15, McCarthy was sent to Attica, the maximum-security prison in western New York that is infamous for a riot in 1971 in which 43 people died, including 33 inmates. As with other state prisons, Attica inmates found guilty of minor offenses could lose privileges for several days. Major offenders might find themselves isolated for 23 hours a day in the Special Housing Unit, also known as the SHU or "The Box."

After six violations in his first year at Attica, McCarthy kept his record clean until June 16, 1989, when he again was ticketed for fighting with an inmate.

On October 14, 1989, officers caught him smuggling cornmeal, which inmates often used to make alcohol. Prison records from this point onward list disciplinary actions. For this cornmeal offense, McCarthy lost phone privileges and was confined to his cell for 10 days in a punishment known as "keeplock." His offense was classified as a mid-level Tier II violation under a three-tier system in which Tier I was a minor infraction and Tier III was considered the most severe.

On January 8, 1990, records show, McCarthy refused to obey a direct order by staying in bed and not doing his assigned job at the prison. For that Tier II violation, he lost phone privileges and received keeplock for 20 days.

On November 6, 1990, McCarthy refused to follow orders by an officer locking in prisoners. "Start with another fucking cell!" McCarthy yelled. For that Tier II violation, he got five days of keeplock and a loss of phone privileges. On top of that, for 20 days, he wasn't allowed to take part in recreation, special events and viewing of movies.

On May 6, 1991, officers found McCarthy guilty of possessing letters and legal materials belonging to another inmate. This was a violation of prison rules on unauthorized exchanges and contraband. This time, McCarthy received "counsel" about the Tier II offense.

On December 9, 1991, McCarthy called a corrections officer a "fucking asshole" and stated, "I'd love to kick your fucking ass" when the guard asked if he wanted to go to the yard or eat. McCarthy got 10 more days of keeplock and a loss of phone privileges for this Tier II violation.

Three months later, on February 24, 1992, McCarthy was transported back to the prison at Dannemora, a facility nicknamed "Little Siberia" because of its harsh northern winters and, according to some, a history of staff misconduct and brutality toward inmates. McCarthy settled into a trouble-free stay, with no offenses on his record at the prison.

While at Dannemora, he took steps to appeal his sentencing, winning approval from the state Supreme Court, Appellate Division, Third Department, for another assigned counsel. As this appeal was pending, McCarthy became concerned that another person was snooping through his court records.

"I have reason to believe someone is trying desperately to obtain records relative to my legal proceedings," McCarthy wrote on March 29, 1994, to the St. Lawrence County Clerk's Office. "Could it be possible to assure this does not happen without my authorization? I am at Clinton County, Dannemora prison and do not wish to have any of my records released to anyone."

His unusual and unenforceable demand ended up as part of the official court file, although it is unclear exactly who McCarthy feared was seeking to view the material. In any case, all documents in his court file not sealed by the judge remained open to public viewing.

McCarthy's trouble-free stint at Dannemora ended on September 10, 1995. Four days before his thirty-third birthday, McCarthy was in the prison yard at about 7:40 p.m. when a 20-year-old inmate attacked him, causing a superficial cut to the left side of McCarthy's neck. Officers failed to recover a weapon, and records don't show if prison officials determined why the inmate, who was serving time for attempted robbery, attacked McCarthy.

Immediately afterward, the prison placed McCarthy in involuntary protective custody, where he would remain until March 4, 1996, when the corrections department transferred him to the maximum-security Auburn Correctional Facility. McCarthy was now assigned to serve time in the small city of 31,000 where Katy's father grew up and where Joe Sr. still had family and friends.

Just four months after his arrival, on July 15, a frisk of McCarthy's cell turned up a shampoo bottle containing alcohol, which was a Tier III violation. For that, McCarthy received 15 days of keeplock and a loss of package, phone and commissary privileges.

On November 1, McCarthy received a Tier II ticket for refusing to leave a supervisor's office, and for bullying and threatening an officer. McCarthy was given 12 more days of keeplock with a loss of package, phone and commissary privileges.

McCarthy managed to stay out of further trouble until February 18, 1998, when an officer found him in possession of stolen LED lights, which he was using in a clock he owned. During a cell search that day, officers also discovered that McCarthy had illegally hooked into the facility's cable television system with the help of a civilian volunteer. McCarthy's punishment for this Tier III ticket was another 15 days of keeplock, and a loss of recreation, package, commissary and phone privileges for 30 days.

On October 19, 1999, McCarthy was sitting in his cell when several Auburn corrections officers and supervisors confronted him about items stolen from the prison mess hall. An officer had discovered a large cache of food—a 25-pound bag of flour, a five-pound bag of potatoes and a five-pound tub of peanut butter, among other items—hidden in the kitchen maintenance room where McCarthy had been working with two other inmates. The officers searched McCarthy's cell but found no contraband food. When they questioned him, he denied taking the food or knowing who did. The other inmates said the same thing.

Like the other two, McCarthy got another 30 days in keeplock for a Tier II violation. He appealed the ticket, but the senior officer who conducted the hearing expressed skepticism at McCarthy's claim he didn't know how the food got stolen.

"You have no idea how any of this . . . grocery store got in there?" the lieutenant asked.

"Come on, 50 pounds of flour?" McCarthy said. "I can get things from anybody, any civilian that I ask. I don't need to steal stuff. It's not—it's not on my report. I don't do that."

After the lieutenant rejected the appeal, McCarthy took his boldest step yet to reverse a punishment. On February 20, 2000, McCarthy in court filed an Article 78 petition against Auburn Prison Superintendent Hans Walker. McCarthy asked the court to overturn the guilty finding and to order the prison system to delete any reference to it from his records.

The case dragged on until November 2001, when the state Appellate Division decided the lawsuit was "moot," apparently because the prison removed the violation from McCarthy's record, since it wasn't present in the documents obtained by Mary Fahey.

By the time the court dismissed the case, McCarthy had left Auburn. Officials transferred him on May 10, 2000, to Wende Correctional Facility, noting in records that the move was necessary due to his "unsuitable behavior."

At Wende on September 19, 2000, McCarthy was caught bringing food items into the mess hall and exchanging apparel with another inmate. He was given "counsel" and received no punishment for the Tier II violations.

His next ticket occurred on April 17, 2002, for creating a "disturbance" by refusing an order to stop talking. He was given seven days of keeplock with no phone privileges or the use of his television. A prison official affirmed the Tier II punishment after McCarthy appealed.

On November 17, 2002, he got another Tier II ticket for refusing to stand up for a count. "Who the fuck do you think you are talking to?!" McCarthy shouted at an officer. "I don't give a fuck what time it is! Would you talk to your mother like that?!" For harassment and violating a direct order, McCarthy was given 30 days of keeplock with a loss of phone and television. A senior officer, once again, upheld the punishment.

On November 5, 2003, a few months before his mother passed away, McCarthy was transferred to Cape Vincent Correctional Facility because it was his "area of preference." At just 98 miles from Potsdam, Cape Vincent brought his incarceration much closer to his hometown.

On November 9, 2004, Cape Vincent officers caught McCarthy attempting to smuggle a letter he had written to a woman by mailing it to someone else, and asking that person to forward it. For that Tier III offense, he received his most extended punishment—66 days in the Special Housing Unit. McCarthy appealed again but lost. He served the time in the SHU at Elmira Correctional Facility, where the prison system transferred him due to "unsuitable behavior."

On October 31, 2005, McCarthy was on the move again, this time to the general population at Orleans Correctional Facility. Although prison records don't show him committing any offenses at Orleans, he was transferred December 12, 2007, to Livingston Correctional Facility with this notation: "Unsuit—separ. from inmates."

At Livingston, McCarthy became embroiled in his worst trouble yet in prison. On December 9, 2008, his state-issued razor went missing, a significant offense because prisoners often use contraband blades as weapons. For that Tier III offense, officers gave McCarthy two more months in the SHU with a loss of privileges until February 9, 2009. The prison affirmed the punishment on appeal.

Because of this violation, the corrections department canceled McCarthy's transfer to Gowanda Correctional Facility. He planned to participate in its Sex Offender Program, or SOP, so he would have this therapy on his record when he appeared before the parole board. McCarthy was instead sent to Fishkill Correctional Facility to serve his two months in its SHU.

Once he completed that, he was transferred on February 12 to Mid-State Correctional Facility to await his first parole hearing at the end of March.

In her letter to the parole board, Mary Fahey said that McCarthy's sexual assault and murder of Katy was enough reason to keep him locked up. His disciplinary record in prison showed he remained violent and lacked the temperament to be supervised.

"In short," she wrote, "this inmate should never be paroled. He has done nothing to earn it. He is not, in any way, rehabilitated. It is in the interest of the state, and the community, to incarcerate him for life."

Privately, Mary Fahey told Katy's family she thought it was a "slam dunk" that the commissioners would reject McCarthy's parole this first time. But she reminded them that the commissioners had surprised people in the past; the board had full discretion to release anyone eligible for parole, including serial killers and mass murderers.

As the date of the parole hearing approached, Terry Taber began to wonder what her daughter's killer might have to say after 22 years of public silence. Would he finally be truthful about what happened on the morning of the attack? Would he now reveal anything about Katy's final conscious moments? Would he, at long last, apologize to her family, and express sincere remorse for taking another life?

Based on what she knew about McCarthy, Terry wasn't holding her breath.

Chapter 26

The First Parole Hearing

I T was already afternoon on Tuesday, March 31, 2009, by the time Mc-Carthy got his turn before the parole board, which convened early that day at Mid-State Correctional Facility. He took a seat in front of three commissioners on a panel headed by Debra Loomis, a former supervisor for child protective services in Washington County, New York. The other commissioners were Thomas Grant, who joined the board after working as executive assistant to the chairman of the Division of Parole, and Lisa Elovich, a former administrative law judge for the state Office of Children and Family Services.

G. Kevin Ludlow, the commissioner who had taken the impact statements from Terry and Joe Jr., was not assigned to this hearing.

McCarthy had gained a few pounds and his hair had thinned, but at 46, he still looked a lot like the suspect seen in news photos following his arrest. But commissioners always checked, just to be sure.

"Are you Brian McCarthy?" Loomis asked.

"Yes, ma'am."

"This is your initial appearance before the panel. You're serving 23 to life for murder-second, and you pled guilty to that, right?" she asked.

"Yes," McCarthy said.

"Okay. Now that involved an incident back in August of '86. It looks like, around the Clarkson campus, the record indicates that you physically assaulted and strangled a young female student. And then there's also information regarding an attempted rape at the time, right?"

"Yes, ma'am."

"Okay. Now, what do you want to tell us about all this?" Loomis asked.

"I was young then, and I was involved in drugs," McCarthy answered. "I admit it was a very heinous crime. It was a long time ago, and I no longer live that lifestyle of drugs. I want to express how remorseful I am for the act that I committed."

Loomis noted from the record that McCarthy declined to give an oral statement at sentencing.

"Is there anything different now that you wanted to say, as opposed to back then in that statement?"

"There is," McCarthy said, "and I would also like to add to how remorseful I am, knowing that I was involved in drugs. I had no alternative other than to think that way. Through the programs that I have participated in, I realize that I can't have drugs in my life at all."

In case the commissioners missed it the first time, McCarthy wanted them to know that he was remorseful and that he would never use drugs again.

"Okay," Loomis said. "And back then, you were making statements like your constitutional rights had been violated, that the police officers had lied pretty much about things, right?"

"Yes, ma'am."

"Do you think any differently about that now?"

"Yes, I do." McCarthy didn't go on to explain how or why he now thought differently, and none of the commissioners asked.

"Now, there was an attempted rape at the time?" Loomis asked.

"Yes, there was."

"Okay. Had you admitted to that back then?"

"Yes, I did."

"You did?" Loomis asked.

"Yes, ma'am."

This was where McCarthy might have scored points for honesty by explaining to the parole board that he had trouble in 1987 acknowledging in court that he tried to rape Katy. Instead, in 2009, McCarthy chose to be technically correct that he admitted to the attempted rape, since it was an element in his guilty plea to murder.

Loomis moved on.

"All right," she said. "And how did you have contact with this girl? How was it that you came across her that day?"

"She was on the campus, on the Clarkson campus, and she was going home, and I was going across the campus to meet some friends. And it was —I was inebriated, and I was involved in drugs, and she was inebriated. And she asked me if I wanted to participate in having sex, and I tried, and I couldn't. And she got mad and spit in my face, and that made me angry."

Loomis seemed taken aback by McCarthy's decision to paint his murder of Katy as a consensual sexual encounter gone bad. Never in McCarthy's admissions to the police in 1986 or to a judge in 1987 had he suggested he was anything more than a stranger to Katy. Besides, he had also just admitted that he tried to rape Katy.

"Did you know her at all?" the commissioner asked.

"I had met her a few times."

"Okay. But you didn't have any kind of a relationship with her? You didn't date her or anything like that?" Loomis asked.

"No."

Commissioner Grant jumped in, clearly perplexed.

"Where had you met her?" he asked.

"Excuse me?"

"Where did you meet her before?" Grant repeated.

"On campus."

"In what context?"

"I think we were in a bar, I believe, and we were shooting pool. And I met her one time when we went to—there was a hockey game," McCarthy said.

Loomis asked, "But you weren't going to school at the time, right?"

"No."

"Okay, so you weren't a student there?" she asked.

"No."

Grant returned to McCarthy's claim about knowing Katy.

"You didn't accompany her to the hockey game or accompany her to the bar, did you?"

"I did to the hockey game," McCarthy replied.

"You had a date with her at the hockey game?" he asked.

"Well, not really a date. We had seats together, and we went together, and we saw the hockey game. We were interested in the same teams."

"Who acquired the seats? How did the seats end up being next to each other?"

"I knew people that worked at the college, and they told me there were seats available, so we could utilize them," McCarthy said.

"So, you say—how did she get into that seat? You asked her to sit in that seat?"

"Yes."

"So, you did know her before?" Grant asked.

"Through someone else, but not personally. But it was only a happenstance that we did have the seats together," McCarthy said.

Grant was puzzled.

"Well, explain that to me," he said, "because I don't understand."

"The two tickets were—well, actually there were four tickets and two of the people didn't show up," McCarthy said. "Two of the tickets were given to me, and I went to one of my friends that was at the college campus, that was going to Clarkson, and he had asked me if I wanted to go to the game. And I assumed that he was asking me to go. He handed me both tickets."

When he asked the friend what to do with the second ticket, McCarthy said, the friend suggested taking Katy or one of the other women.

"So, I said, 'Okay, fine.' That's how I met her."

"So, she wanted to go to the game? She didn't necessarily want to go to the game with you, right?" Grant asked.

"Exactly. She was just interested in the hockey game and not interested in me."

McCarthy's story about sharing a hockey ticket with Katy makes no sense just on a procedural level. As a student at Clarkson, Katy got into hockey games at Walker Arena just by using her student ID; she did not require a ticket from McCarthy or anyone else. Clarkson roommate Nanci Parks Gage attended every home game with Katy—and never was McCarthy part of their group.

For McCarthy to now claim that Katy asked for sex with him outside Walker Arena at 3:30 a.m., Gage said, "makes my blood boil."

At the parole hearing, the commissioners turned to McCarthy's history of crime before the attack on Katy.

"And this wasn't the first time you've been in trouble, right?" Loomis asked.

"No, ma'am."

"Okay. You had quite a bit of trouble, it looks like, in New York state as well as Virginia. Did you live in Virginia for a while?"

"Yes, ma'am."

"Okay. Did you have family down there?"

"No. I worked down there for a roofing company."

"Okay. So, how come you got in so much trouble down there before this happened?" Loomis asked.

"I was involved in drugs."

"It looks like it's larcenous in nature for the most part, right?"

"Yes."

Loomis asked McCarthy if he had family support when he returned to the Potsdam area after serving time in a Virginia prison in 1985.

"Very little, but I—I tried to do most of it myself. Because I was kind of a troublemaker. I didn't want to get other people involved, so I was trying to do things my own way."

"And you think if you hadn't been under the influence of drugs, this never would have happened?" she asked.

"I know that it wouldn't have happened."

Loomis turned to McCarthy's disciplinary record in prison, including his most recent ticket at Livingston Correctional.

"I believe that was the loss of property. That's when somebody stole my state razor," McCarthy explained.

And his 2004 ticket for violating prison rules by sending a note to one person through correspondence to a second?

"I wrote to a religious volunteer that came to the facility, and it wasn't directly written to her. My mother had passed away just around that time, and I was going through some pretty hard times. I wrote to her (the volunteer) through the deacon, and asked to thank her because the thing—the support through the, through the retreat that she had given me."

"Okay," Loomis said. "Now, upon your release, where would you go?"

McCarthy said he planned to move in with a woman who became his girlfriend while he was in prison. He planned to find employment in one of his areas of expertise, having completed training in radio and television repair, auto repair, and food services.

He also prepared for release by participating in therapy programs for those with a history of drug abuse and violence.

"And you're recommended for the Sex Offender Program, but you don't have it here," Loomis noted.

"I've been chasing that for quite a few years, and they told me that I will be re-evaluated in June."

"All right," Loomis said. "Do you think you need that program before you go home?"

"I mean, I—I don't know," McCarthy said, apparently realizing that if he were being re-evaluated in June, it meant he had been denied parole. "I'm willing to participate in the program if I'm released, and I'm willing to participate in the program if I'm in here."

Loomis asked McCarthy if he had anything else to say about his release plans.

"I don't know what the community thinks of me," McCarthy said. "I know I'm not the same person. My release plans: I would really like to go back to school, whether I do it through the computer, which I am computer literate. It's available to me. I would like to get a decent paying job. I know the economy isn't too good right now. I would also like to have the opportunity to repay society for some of the bad thoughts they've had about me and maybe get back into their good graces."

McCarthy continued, "I've tried to maintain a positive attitude under the—under the guidelines of the program, and I've tried to utilize some of the tools given to me through the programs. I can't resort to violence. I can't have any type of involvement with drugs in my life, ever. And I've really tried hard. I've been looking forward to this day for a long time."

Loomis returned to the morning that McCarthy attacked Katy and how he initially told police someone struck him from behind.

"Were you hit in the head by her, or by somebody else?"

"I don't know. I have no idea."

"What do you remember after that?"

"The ambulance ride."

"And do you know if you were picked up on the ground next to her at that point or—"

"I don't know. I don't know," McCarthy said. "I was in the ambulance, and they immobilized me for whatever reason, I don't know."

Commissioner Grant asked what else he remembered about that morning.

"It's—it's, I mean, sometimes I think I see flashlights, but I don't know for sure. I can't state that for a fact. But it's something I thought hard about over the years, whether you can bring that memory to fact, or whether you're possibly making it up. I don't—it's not something that I can state."

In other words, according to McCarthy, even he didn't know if he always believed what came out of his mouth.

He did not handle the next question any better.

"What's the last memory of the incident that you have that you're pretty certain actually happened?" Grant asked.

"Striking Kathy Walker." If any of the commissioners noticed that McCarthy got his victim's name wrong, none indicated so to him.

"What did you strike her with?" Grant asked.

"My hand."

"Your hand. And that's the last thing you remember, until the ambulance ride?"

"Yes."

Loomis asked McCarthy if he had anything further for the board to consider.

"I hope that I've made a good impression, and I thank you for your time."

Grant then asked McCarthy about his "unusual sentence" of 23 years to life, which was slightly shorter than the typical 25 to life for a murder conviction.

"Any thoughts about what that meant to you?" Grant asked. "Or do you have any sense as to why you were given that particular sentence?"

"No."

"None at all?" Grant asked.

"I know that—I know that it's not a standard sentence. It's an unusual sentence, but I don't know what the significance of getting 23 to life is," McCarthy said.

After commissioners Grant and Elovich said they had no more questions, Loomis told McCarthy, "We'll consider everything we have here today, and we'll give you a written decision in a few days."

"Thank you," McCarthy said before officers escorted him out of the room and brought in the next inmate.

Three days later, on Friday, April 3, Carey Patton called the parole department's Victim Impact Unit to learn the decision. After hanging up the phone, she was quick to share the news with the rest of the family. Betsy posted the decision on the blog at 1:29 p.m.: "DENIED PAROLE!" she typed out in large letters that danced across the screen. "Hold for 24 months. Next appearance: April 2, 2011."

In their 3-0 decision, the commissioners made it clear McCarthy did himself no favors with his answers. His testimony, Loomis wrote, "demonstrated limited insight into your violent, heinous act and your remorse was superficial at best and geared toward ingratiating yourself with the panel. All factors considered, the panel concludes that your release at this time is incompatible with the welfare and safety of the community."

By adding two more years before he was again eligible to seek parole, McCarthy effectively would receive that 25-to-life sentence he had avoided by pleading guilty.

Interviewed afterward by *The Post-Standard*, Joe Hawelka Jr. admitted the past few months had been stressful. "I didn't realize the sense of relief we would all feel," he said. "We're finally going to get a good night's sleep."

However, relief transformed to anger in late April, when the Division of Parole sent the family a copy of the hearing transcript. Joe Jr. was furious that McCarthy would try to win parole by "soiling the memory of my sister" in making up a story accusing Katy of spitting in his face because he couldn't perform sexually. Katy's brother thought it also was telling that McCarthy thought so little about his victim that he couldn't get her name right.

Terry Taber saw her fears come true that the parole board would be left wondering why McCarthy got less than the maximum sentence. After reading the transcript, she concluded that McCarthy hoped to leave the panel with the mistaken impression that the judge had gone easy on him because what he did wasn't bad enough to warrant a full 25 to life.

Terry and others in the family saw one positive from the transcript: Mc-Carthy's misleading statements and outright fabrications gave them new issues to point out at their next impact statements in 2011.

In May 2009, about a month after he was denied parole, McCarthy was transferred to Oneida Correctional Facility to begin participation in its Sex Offender Program.

McCarthy, though, wasn't waiting for another parole hearing to try to get released.

That summer, he filed a motion in St. Lawrence County Court to toss out his 1987 guilty plea. He claimed his indictment was "defective" because it had included three murder counts, which he said violated his rights against double jeopardy. He further alleged that his attorney, Charles Nash, failed to prepare a proper defense, never kept him informed of its progress, and didn't negotiate a satisfactory plea.

McCarthy's other claims included alleged misconduct by Judge Nicandri, who, McCarthy said, had failed to remain fair and impartial "due to the publicity of the victim's family, as well as motions made to this judge regarding the defendant and the impact statement." As evidence of improper influence, McCarthy included a report on how attorney Joseph Fahey asked to present an oral statement at sentencing.

In fall 2009, the St. Lawrence County District Attorney's Office responded to McCarthy's motion by saying it was too late for him to raise these issues, which would have been proper to do on appeal shortly after sentencing. The DA's office said it didn't find any records showing McCarthy went ahead with filing an appeal, despite obtaining an attorney to do so.

As for McCarthy's allegations, the DA's office rejected them all. It said the grand jury correctly charged McCarthy with three murder counts offering varying theories of how he killed Katy. The grand jury had left it up to the trial court to determine from the evidence which one best applied.

As for the quality of the work by McCarthy's attorney, the DA's office appended numerous documents from court records showing Nash gave an aggressive defense, including seeking a change of venue and fighting to suppress his client's confession. It also said Nash argued "eloquently" at sentencing for McCarthy to receive less than 25 to life.

Prosecutors noted that Fahey's request to speak at sentencing didn't violate McCarthy's rights since the judge refused to allow it, "thus protecting the Defendant from the prejudice that would have been engendered by such a statement."

In another odd twist to the murder case, McCarthy's latest court motion would be decided by Kathleen Martin Rogers, now a Surrogate Court judge who was also handling some criminal court cases in St. Lawrence County. As a Potsdam village justice, she had sentenced McCarthy for petty crimes in the early 1980s, arraigned him on a murder charge in 1986, and testified at his 1987 suppression hearing. It would have been hard to find an active judge more familiar with McCarthy or his criminal record.

On November 9, 2009, Rogers rejected McCarthy's request to throw out his conviction, agreeing with prosecutors that he should have raised these issues on direct appeal two decades earlier. She also noted she saw nothing in the record to support any of his allegations.

McCarthy would remain at Oneida until April 10, 2010, when the prison system transferred him to the nearby Marcy Correctional Facility. There, housed in an open cubicle instead of behind bars in a cell, he began to shape a new strategy to win parole.

Chapter 27

2011

IN early 2011, Betsy McInerney was still angry over the fact that, at the initial parole hearing, Brian McCarthy referred to her sister as "Kathy Walker," which she saw as evidence that he had never given much thought to Katy. Almost as upsetting to Betsy was the fact the commissioners either didn't notice the gaffe or chose not to correct him. Betsy made a point when she returned to the Syracuse parole office for her second impact statement to spell out K-A-T-Y H-A-W-E-L-K-A slowly for the stenographer.

She also handed over a picture of Katy for McCarthy's parole file. Not unlike her mother's decision to share a photo with the ICU nurses in Watertown, Betsy wanted the board to see Katy as a vibrant young woman, not just a deceased victim of a long-ago brutal crime.

"They didn't have a picture of her," Betsy said. "They're just looking at piles of folders on their desk, or however they review these things. I want them to see it was a life. It was a person, not just someone's name on paper."

For McCarthy's second parole hearing, Katy's family reshaped their approach in other ways, too. This time they didn't do media interviews. The news articles in 2009 had accomplished the family's goal of stirring broad community opposition to McCarthy's parole and had built up the petition, which now had 5,772 signatures; Carey Patton took the time to print them out, double-spaced, and include them with her impact statement. Terry Taber and Joe Hawelka Jr. also submitted new statements, pointing out McCarthy's lies and half-truths at the initial hearing in 2009.

Mary Fahey weighed in with another letter to the parole board in which she noted that her fresh check of McCarthy's prison record found no new infractions.

"Obviously, the inmate is hoping that by 'behaving', he will earn parole," Mary Fahey wrote. However, she saw "no reason to believe that the inmate has changed in any way in the last two years," adding that "his release is completely incompatible with the welfare and safety of the community."

On Tuesday, March 29, 2011, McCarthy's second parole hearing got underway at Marcy Correctional Facility with just two commissioners: Sally Thompson, a former New York City police officer who had investigated violent crimes as a detective in the department, and G. Kevin Ludlow, who had taken impact statements from Terry and Joe Jr. in 2009.

Because there was no third commissioner present, a split decision would require the parole board to immediately schedule another hearing for McCarthy.

"Good afternoon, Brian McCarthy?" Thompson asked.

"Yes, ma'am."

"I am Commissioner Thompson. Also, on the panel with me today is Commissioner Ludlow," she said. "You are here for a reappearance. Crime of conviction is murder-second, serving 23-to-life . . . and that is by plea, is that correct?"

"Yes, ma'am."

"The instant offense involved you raping and strangling the female victim, ultimately causing her death."

"Yes."

It was unclear if McCarthy meant to finally acknowledge he had raped Katy and killed her by strangulation, or if he just didn't correctly hear the question.

"Okay," Thompson said. "What happened here? How did you meet this victim?"

"I had known her through some friends at the college campus that I was at."

"Were you attending the college?"

"No, I was not."

"Okay."

"That was my hometown," McCarthy said of Potsdam, "and I knew a lot of people that go there."

McCarthy said these friends gave him hockey tickets to a Clarkson game. "I think I had six, and I gave them to several people to pass them around, and she was one of the ones that wanted some of the tickets. That was one of the first occasions that I had met her. Prior to that, I had seen her, but I didn't know who she was. We went to the hockey game, she had tickets and so did I, and that was it."

McCarthy tweaked some details, but he was sticking with his story from 2009 that he had once accompanied Katy to a hockey game after providing her a ticket.

"How did you ultimately end up committing this horrific crime?" Thompson asked.

"Some time later—this was a while after we had gone to the hockey game —I met her on a walkway, and she was pretty inebriated. I was out partying all night, too. I was involved in drugs and drinking at the time."

"What drugs were you involved in?"

"Marijuana, and I was drinking some beer. We had agreed to have sex, and when I couldn't perform—I was too inebriated, I guess. I don't know what the problem was—she got mad at me and laughed at me and spit in my face, and I got mad and retaliated, and I hit her—hit her bad enough to where it caused her death and, regrettably, she died two days later."

Thompson had read from McCarthy's parole file that the cause of death was asphyxiation due to strangulation.

"No," McCarthy insisted, "that (her death) was because the way she hit the ground, because the way she fell it was asphyxiation."

It wasn't true that Katy died from an awkward fall, but neither commissioner challenged McCarthy's claim.

"And what happened after that? She was taken to the hospital?" Thompson asked.

"Yes. The officers were there at the scene and ultimately charged me with rape, and then three days later, they charged me with murder."

Thompson noted, though, that McCarthy now seemed to be saying the sexual contact with Katy was consensual.

"I thought it was at the time, but since then I have looked at it, because I have taken this program that they had at Oneida," referring to months of therapy in Oneida Correctional Facility's Sex Offender Program. "I look at it, and I asked myself, *What was the catalyst to that? Was it really consensual if she angered me to the point where I assaulted her?*

"I was not thinking properly. I look at that time because I did take the anger out on her. But who was the one that initiated it? I think we both did because we knew each other prior, but we didn't know each other that well. You understand what I mean? It was kind of like at first, 'No, that didn't happen,' but maybe now in retrospect, now that I look at the program and the tools that they gave me to look at, what I actually did."

It was hard to make sense out of what McCarthy was saying, but Thompson let him continue.

"You have no idea how much remorse I have for what I did," McCarthy said. "You cannot imagine the things that I have gone through. But to think at the time that that was something that I couldn't do. Maybe I did. Maybe I did have that thought because of something that originated when I was a child. I don't know. How do I go from larcenist behavior to taking a person's life?"

The commissioners didn't pursue McCarthy's offhand remark that something in his childhood might have spurred his violent behavior.

"I see your history is basically larceny," Thompson said.

"There is nothing in there that is assault or violence," McCarthy said, referring to his criminal record before the attack on Katy. "And how does someone go from pretty good upbringing (to then going) through larcenist behavior, acting like an idiot, to taking a person's life? That is pretty hard to explain."

Commissioner Ludlow joined the questioning.

"You just hit her once, is that your best recollection?"

"Yes," McCarthy answered.

"Did you have a weapon at that time, sir?" Ludlow asked.

"No, I did not."

"Did you have a club?"

"No, I did not."

"What did you hit her with, your fist?" Ludlow asked.

"My hand."

"Okay. She presumably fell to the floor at that time?"

"It was outside and next to a building. And the best that I can remember is, she hit the floor, and her head hit the wall—and that is where they claim the asphyxiation happened because it was so close. It was almost perpendicular to the wall but her shoulders on the grass. It was a pretty direct fall against the wall."

Thompson asked, "This happened outside?"

"Yes," McCarthy said.

"Even the sexual contact?"

"Yes."

"That was outside?"

"Yes.

"Sad situation," Thompson said.

"Very sad."

"How old was the victim at the time?" she asked.

"Nineteen."

"Nineteen," she repeated. "How old were you?"

"Twenty-three. I just turned 23," replied McCarthy, who, in truth, was days away from his twenty-fourth birthday at the time he killed Katy.

"You say you were under the influence of drugs and alcohol at the time?

"Yes, ma'am."

"And you did participate in the sex offender counseling?"

"Yes, I did," McCarthy said. "I have tried to pursue programs to help me understand, as well as taking the recommended programs to try to figure out—I am not saying that I am trying to overemphasize to the point where I am trying to please somebody else. But I need some answers for myself, because I don't exactly understand. Even though I have a lot more tools to try to figure out what I did, I still need to answer a few more as to my own questions as to my actions."

McCarthy said that, if granted parole, he planned to move into the up-state New York home of his longtime girlfriend, who was now his fiancée, and to look for a job in air conditioning or electrical repair.

"Commissioner Ludlow, any other questions?" Thompson asked.

Ludlow had none but said, "This is a terrible tragedy, no matter how you look at it from whatever perspective."

"It is very hard to live with, too," McCarthy said, apparently referring to himself.

Thompson asked if McCarthy had anything else to say.

"I want to thank you for your time, and I hope that you seriously consider my eligible release," McCarthy said. "I thought a long time of the opportunity to come in here and speak to the parole board members about what I have done, and what I plan to do, my goals—not just for myself but for possibly the people that are hurt or the people that have been hurt because of something that is not directly related to them, my own family, to the victim's family, Kim Avadikian. I hope to some day progress and help other people avoid the stuff that I have caused, such a traumatic act and heinous crime."

McCarthy didn't explain why he was worried about hurting Avadikian, the Clarkson guard working at Walker Arena the morning of the attack.

"If you could speak to the victim's survivors, what would you say to them?" Ludlow asked McCarthy.

"I don't know if l could do that."

"Hypothetically."

"I would ask for their apology in accepting of what I hope to look at—what they look at—as remorse."

Ludlow corrected McCarthy. "I think you would ask them to accept *your* apology."

"Yes, I am a lot nervous." McCarthy said.

"Just to clarify the record," Ludlow said.

McCarthy added, "Yes. I would also contribute to Kim Avadikian. I would spend the rest of my life educating people and set up a goal for a financial grant in her name so she can be remembered as someone who tried to do something good."

It was now clear that McCarthy, when he mentioned Avadikian, actually was referring to Katy. For the second time in two hearings, he got his victim's name wrong.

Ignoring the gaffe, Ludlow asked, "Did you have a relationship with her prior to the night in question?"

"It is kind of hard to define 'relationship.' I did know her, and there was an intimate relationship with her prior to the night in question," McCarthy said. "But it was not something that was an everyday thing or week thing or month. Like I said, I had only known her a short time."

"Did you look for college girls to socialize with?"

"No, I didn't need to. There was enough girls that were interested in me as a person because of my status in the community and my family. I came from a very good family," McCarthy said. "My mother's maiden name is Snell, which is a very, very big name up there."

"In what way?" Ludlow asked.

"Part of the college is donated by my great-aunt, in her name. There are other outstanding establishments in that area. Snell Locks in the St. Lawrence Seaway, that was a relative. There is also some reputable people that are associated with the family farm that I worked on, businesses. There are establishments up there. I didn't have any problem with going out with girls or having any associations. It was pretty stable."

Thompson asked, "So, why not walk away from this (assault on Katy) if you had no problem finding girls, or girlfriends was not a problem? Why not leave?"

"I think the anger and beer and drugs that I was involved in just came out as an angry vent, take it out on whoever is in front of me. I am not saying that is right. That is not an answer that is acceptable. Sometimes the truth is not something that you look for as an acceptable answer."

Without any further questions, Thompson concluded the hearing.

"Thank you very much," she said to McCarthy. "We'll review your case and let you know in a couple of days."

"Thank you," he said.

Three days after the hearing, Betsy posted the panel's decision on the family blog. "Good News! NY State Dept Parole Board has again DENIED parole for Brian McCarthy in his second appearance. Thanks to everyone for their continued support!!"

In their 2-0 decision, the commissioners cited the "heinous nature" of the crime and McCarthy's "propensity for callous . . . disregard for the sanctity for human life" as reasons for denying his parole. "Note is also made of your positive programming, disciplinary record, and parole packet," Thompson wrote. "However, all relevant factors considered, discretionary release is inappropriate at this time, for the Panel to hold otherwise would so deprecate the seriousness of the crime as to undermine respect for the law."

The board placed McCarthy's release on hold until April 2013, when commissioners would operate under a new state agency with a revised method for assessment, which some prison rights groups hoped would make it easier for inmates to win parole.

Chapter 28

2013

MOMENTS after leaving a parole office in Buffalo, New York, in 2013, Carey Patton sat in the parking lot and wept. She had driven to Buffalo because it was the closest location to her home in Cleveland to present her latest impact statement opposing McCarthy's parole. Now in tears, Carey called her brother in Syracuse.

When Joe Hawelka Jr. asked what was wrong, Carey repeated what a commissioner had just told her: "Well, you have to prepare yourself for the fact he's going to be let out one day."

Until then, Carey had never let herself consider the possibility that the parole board would release McCarthy. Now, someone who made such decisions was telling her that, no, there was a good chance he would enjoy life again outside prison walls.

As he was taught by his father, Joe Jr. saw himself as someone who was supposed to protect his mother and his sisters from being hurt. But just like what happened to Katy in 1986, there were some things a brother couldn't stop.

"I was in Syracuse. My sister, who lives in Cleveland, was in Buffalo in the middle of winter. She calls me, crying hysterically, and I felt helpless again," he said.

Joe Jr. would conclude after several impact statements that the process was something that each of them had to endure in his or her own way. In 2013, he invited his wife to accompany him when he gave his statement. After seeing how emotionally difficult this was for her, he decided he would not put her through it again.

"It's a highly personal endeavor," he said quietly. "I just try to get through it."

In 2013, a new state agency collected their impact statements: The New York State Department of Corrections and Community Supervision, formed from the merger of the Division of Parole and the Department of Correctional Services. The goal, according to state officials, was to streamline the operations while putting the primary focus not on incarceration but on the "reentry" of inmates into communities.

By 2013, the panels had begun using the Correctional Offender Management Profiling for Alternative Sanctions program, or COMPAS, to help decide whether to release inmates. COMPAS is a computerized assessment tool that analyzes data—including an inmate's prison disciplinary record and history of drug abuse—to score him on his likelihood of success if granted parole. Advocates for COMPAS had argued it would help commissioners make decisions based on facts rather than whim or emotion. However, panels could still take into account other factors, including the severity of the crime, impact statements, and community sentiment.

And by the time of McCarthy's third hearing, a large part of the general public had spoken loud and clear. The number of petition signatures opposing his parole stood at 5,851.

"Are you Brian McCarthy?" Commissioner Lisa Elovich asked as the hearing got underway at Marcy Correctional Facility on Wednesday, April 17, 2013.

"Yes, ma'am."

"I am Commissioner Elovich. This is Commissioner Sharkey."

Edward Sharkey previously was a district attorney in Cattaraugus County. McCarthy was already familiar with Elovich, who sat at McCarthy's first panel that denied him parole in 2009.

After noting she wasn't bound by any previous vote, Elovich said she had taken the time to read McCarthy's 1987 sentencing transcript and other documents related to the murder of Katy, and she would make them a factor in her decision.

McCarthy responded, "I have been working hard to be prepared for rehabilitation."

"Let's talk about the reasons that you are here. Very, very horrible crime," she said before summarizing the events of August 29, 1986, when police found "you brutally killed a 19-year-old, second-year college student who was going to class, Katy Hawelka." Elovich said that the attack left Katy with "fractured fingers, numerous bruises all over her body, fractured larynx, broken nose," and caused her death through strangulation.

"As you put it during the last board interview," she added, "when this first happened, you denied that you did this. You said you were also a victim of the attack, is that right, in your first statement?"

"In the sense, it was correct," McCarthy said.

Without asking in what "sense" he could consider himself a victim, Elovich pointed out that, "when that (claim of being attacked) didn't work," McCarthy admitted to police that he struck Katy—but insisted someone else attacked her before he did.

Now, in his application for parole, Elovich noted, he changed his story again, no longer trying to insist that someone else attacked her first.

"That is correct," McCarthy said. "I did own up to what I did, because of the severity, once I was not so drug-induced. And I am not blaming the horrific act—that the heinous crime that I committed—on drugs. But I also noted, in the beginning, was deception in my mind knowing what I did, thinking that I did not do what I did, I was not the same type of person."

Elovich reminded McCarthy of his testimony in 2011. "You said to Commissioner Ludlow during the last parole board interview—I read in the transcript—that you only struck Katy once and that she fell and hit her head." She told McCarthy this claim was "kind of a slap in the face" to the truth, which was that Katy suffered massive injuries over much of her body.

"How could that possibly happen in one punch?" she asked.

"In a rage, in the process of a blackout," McCarthy answered.

"You are saying it could have been one punch?"

"It could have been more than one punch, more than one incident."

"From you?"

"From me," McCarthy said, adding, "It is pretty sad to know that I was capable of something like that."

While McCarthy finally was admitting that he might have repeatedly punched Katy, he also was suggesting he had a "blackout" and couldn't remember the details.

Elovich turned to McCarthy's participation in the 10-month Sex Offender Program at Oneida Correctional Facility. She said she read in his parole file that he claims he was sexually abused by a "family friend" when he was a child.

"It explains some education of the rage that I kept in," McCarthy said. "The counselors that I have had at different facilities, and also programs, had given me the insight. And obviously, I have gotten older and a little bit wiser. I understand some of the things that were induced were because I was molested."

This appears to be the first time that McCarthy had stated for a public record that he was sexually abused as a child. Such a claim, if true, would not be shocking to anyone in the criminal justice field. Studies have found that being sexually abused while growing up is often a factor in someone becoming a killer. However, not all killers were victims of child abuse. And with McCarthy's history of telling lies and half-truths, the commissioners had to weigh whether he made up this story to win sympathy and to shift some of the blame off of himself.

"What was the most important thing that you learned about yourself in that program?" Elovich asked, referring to the Oneida SOP.

"The root of what I caused, knowing that I hurt so many people, in the acknowledgment that (what) I did was so far-reaching, I had no idea. I couldn't even conceive the destruction that I caused," McCarthy said.

Elovich noted Katy's murder had caused great fear on the Clarkson campus, especially among female students.

"There is tremendous opposition to your release," she said.

"I am aware of that."

"I know that you also have people supporting your release. I did read your packet, and you have people in your community that would like to see you come home, and you have letters of support in the file, which we'll consider as well."

"Thank you."

Elovich said she also reviewed McCarthy's COMPAS risk assessment, which she noted outlined what steps he needed to take if released on parole.

"Okay," he said.

"What do you think your greatest need is in terms of conditions under supervision?"

McCarthy said his COMPAS scores, as well as two psychological evaluations, "say I am not aggressive behavior" and place him at a low chance for recidivism.

"The supervision that I will be mandated to have is going to be a plus for me. After 27 years of incarceration, it gives me a little bit different outlook than what is available out there today. It is not the same society that I came from. I know I am going to be looked at kind of odd, but I am also going to try to seek help."

If released, McCarthy said, he would live with his fiancée and look to start his own business, possibly in air conditioning or refrigeration.

After Commissioner Sharkey said he had no questions, Elovich asked McCarthy if there was anything else the panel should know.

McCarthy said he was "uneasy" about one aspect of his COMPAS assessment, which was "saying I am going to need drug rehabilitation."

"I have not done drugs in 27 years," he said. "I didn't think there was any need for further rehabilitation based on what I voluntarily participated in facility needs, ASAT (Alcohol and Substance Abuse Treatment), ART (Aggression Replacement Training), learning the violence, acknowledgment of the Sex Offender Program."

Elovich explained that COMPAS reached its conclusions based, in part, on whether he abused alcohol and drugs before he arrived in the highly structured confines of prison. The assessment was pointing to the need for drug testing and monitoring of him to prevent relapse if released on parole.

"The COMPAS risk assessment is . . . certainly not exact science. It is based on a lot of factors that are not tangible as well," she said. "The actual risk scores that they give, we'll give it the weight that it deserves as we do with every other factor that we are considering."

McCarthy said he was already a changed man. When he's participated in prison programs, he said, the "light goes on" and "at least I did start to correct that error." One thing he learned was that "the intent of raping this woman, it is just as bad as raping her."

"All right, sir. We have a lot to consider here," Elovich said. "Thank you for coming in."

"Thank you," McCarthy said.

Three days later, commissioners decided 2-0 to deny him parole. In its decision, the panel praised McCarthy's successful participation in prison programs, his letters of support, and his release plans. "More compelling, however," Elovich wrote, "is the extreme violence you exhibited in the instant offense and callous disregard for the life of a young female college student, who you brutally killed. This heinous crime was a continuation and severe escalation of a pattern of illegal conduct. There is significant community opposition to your release, as your actions have not only affected the family of Katy Hawelka but also affected and still affects an entire community."

The panel set McCarthy's next parole hearing for April 2015.

By the third time around, McCarthy's parole hearing process began to feel to Katy's family like the movie "Groundhog Day," except it was a two-year cycle of events that kept repeating, each time slightly different, with each new denial resetting the clock.

"I'd like to think it hurts a little bit less each time," Joe Jr. said. "But then you wait two years and you go through the hearing again, and it kind of dredges it all up. I don't like what it does to my mother. I don't like what it does to my sisters."

He added, "You put on a strong front, and you go in there and say your piece to the parole board and pray to God everybody's paying attention, and they don't let this jackass out of jail. It's pretty cut and dried when you think about the black and white of it. But, again, it kind of reopens the wound every two years to some extent."

In New York, Katy's family members weren't the only relatives of victims who chafed at this two-year cycle of parole hearings. Several other families lobbied state legislators in 2015 to change the law so that inmates who served their minimum sentences wouldn't automatically get a parole hearing every two years.

Among them was the family of Lorraine Miranda, a 24-year-old disabled woman whose fiancé, Chris Patterson, mutilated and fatally strangled her on December 5, 1988, in their Staten Island apartment. Her family's experience of opposing his parole every two years since 2003 inspired state legislation known as "Lorraine's Law," which would give parole boards the option of putting an inmate's parole on hold for up to five years.

Also lobbying for the legislation were parents of 4-year-old Derrick Robie, whose neighbor, 13-year-old Eric Smith, lured the boy into the woods near their homes in Steuben County and beat him to death on August 2, 1993. Dale and Dori Robie had spoken out against Smith's parole every two years since 2002. "We're just trying to live normal lives. We didn't invite any of this, and every two years our jobs get put on hold, our family gets put on hold, and everything gets ripped out through your gut again, and public opinion gets stirred up again," Dori Robie told the Hornell *Evening Tribune*. "Two years is not enough time between those turbulent interruptions."

In June 2015, the Republican-led state Senate passed "Lorraine's Law," but the Democrat-controlled Assembly declined to schedule a vote on the legislation.

By then, the winds of parole reform were blowing hard in the other direction.

Advocates for prisoner rights had their own tales of injustice, such as the case of 55-year-old Craig Crimmins. In 2015, he was serving 20 years to life for the 1980 murder of Helen Hagnes Mintiks, a violinist found naked at the bottom of an air shaft at New York City's Metropolitan Opera House, where he worked as a stagehand.

In prison, Crimmins was a "humbled inmate" who worked in the commissary and earned an associate degree in substance-abuse counseling, according to a profile at *City Limits* (**citylimits.org**). Despite being an older inmate who was no longer seen as a threat, parole panels had repeatedly denied his application. "Every time they turn me down," Crimmins said, "it's always about the nature of the crime, nothing about who I am now or what I've done since then. I could have cured cancer, they wouldn't care."

Former parole Commissioner Robert Dennison told the website that parole board members know they risk losing their jobs if they make a controversial decision to let someone go. He noted that George Pataki, when he was the Republican governor of New York, didn't reappoint two parole board members after they decided in 2003 to release former radical Kathy Boudin, who was serving time for her role in a 1981 armored car robbery that resulted in the deaths of two police officers and a guard.

"So, everybody knows, if you like the job and you want to keep the job, you don't vote to release people who are going to wind up in the media the next day," Dennison said.

But under a Democratic governor, that might no longer be the case.

By 2015, prison rights groups were actively lobbying Governor Andrew Cuomo to replace commissioners appointed by Pataki. Criminal defense website *Simple Justice* (**blog.simplejustice.us**) complained that parole boards were sitting as "super judges, ignoring the decision of the sentencing judge and imposing a politically-motivated sentence of whatever length they deem proper." It said the COMPAS risk-assessment system, instead of being used by parole boards to more fairly judge whether an inmate should be released, "became just another bit of data to ignore."

Taking a somewhat middle stance was state Assemblyman Daniel J. O'Donnell, of Manhattan, who agreed that some inmates, such as John Lennon's killer, remained a threat and deserved to stay in prison for the rest of their lives. "One of the problems is the family of the defendant hears '20' and the family of the victim hears 'life,'" O'Donnell noted about sentencing in a case of 20 years to life. "The other problem, and it's a problem with the media, is that they don't seem to understand how the system works."

Joe Hawelka Jr. argued it was prison rights activists who most often fail to understand how parole is supposed to work. It angered him whenever he heard someone complain that the parole board was, in effect, "resentencing" an inmate if it made him serve time past his initial parole eligibility date.

"Does anyone really want to argue the fact McCarthy was sentenced to 23 to *life*?" Katy's brother said. "It wasn't '23 and then we'll throw the life on there to appease people.' I don't know why someone thinks 23 is the hard number and all he has to serve. This sentence was 23 to life. 'Life' meaning, you try to be good in prison and take your chances."

After reading the 2013 transcript, Terry Taber thought McCarthy had presented himself better than at the first two hearings. For most of that, she credited his fianceé, who McCarthy acknowledged helped to prepare him for the parole hearing.

Terry was happy to read, though, that the commissioners had recognized there was overwhelming community opposition to his release.

Unable to get out of prison, McCarthy held a far different view about all those people writing letters and signing petitions opposing his release. After three parole hearings, his frustration about this was ready to boil over.

Chapter 29

2015

BRIAN McCarthy's fourth parole hearing began, as before, with a polite greeting from a commissioner, giving the start of the proceeding a feel more like a job interview than a grilling of a convicted murderer.

"Good morning. How are you doing?" Christine Hernandez said after McCarthy took a seat in a conference room on Wednesday, April 15, 2015, at Marcy Correctional Facility.

"Good."

"What is your name, sir?"

"Brian McCarthy," he said.

Once again, his hearing would take place with just two commissioners. This time it was Hernandez, a former commissioner of the New York State Crime Victims Board, and James Ferguson, a former administrative law judge for the Division of Parole.

"How old are you today, sir?" she asked McCarthy.

"Excuse me?"

"How old are you today?"

"Fifty-two."

"How long have you been incarcerated?"

"This August will be twenty-nine years."

"What do you think about that?"

"I think I destroyed my life, as well as the destruction of many other people."

"Did you know the victim?" Hernandez asked.

"No, I didn't, not personally," McCarthy said. "I was aware of who she was, but I didn't personally know her."

"How were you aware of who she was?" Hernandez asked.

"I had a few interactions with her because of the facility campus. It was a college campus, and there was sports involved through hockey games, and some of the people that I knew in the dorm and of the town knew who she was, and I knew that she was on the campus, too."

McCarthy seemed to have forgotten his previous claims of an intimate relationship with Katy.

Hernandez noted McCarthy pleaded guilty to second-degree murder.

"Was there any sexual component to this?" she asked.

"There was an attempt on my behalf. I could not perform any sexual activity due to my use of drugs."

"Was she alive or conscious at the time?"

"She was alive."

"Was this (the attempted rape) before she was killed?"

"Yes."

Hernandez asked, "Why did you feel it was necessary to kill her?"

"It was not my intention. I didn't feel it was necessary," McCarthy answered. "I am not using it as an excuse. I was sexually molested (as a child), and I was a little angry about life, and I was not doing too good with it. I was involved in drugs. I am not using that as a crutch, but I didn't have ability for good reasoning. I didn't have tools to work with that. I needed to go to people that could help me, and I vented my anger by destructive behavior."

"Had you ever done anything like that?"

"Absolutely not," McCarthy said.

Hernandez pointed out there are "a lot of people who have had very unfortunate circumstances growing up, a lot of people under the influence of drugs or alcohol, and they don't go to the level that you went that day."

McCarthy responded, "I have asked that in the past—through psychologists and professional people that I have had personally and through the facility system—how you could go from a misdemeanor behavior to commit a heinous crime. I never understood that. I have some answers, some reasoning, but I don't have it all. It doesn't make sense to me."

Hernandez asked McCarthy how he thought Katy's murder affected those who knew her personally, as well as the Potsdam community and his own family.

"Starting with her family, I know I destroyed her family and future that she had. She was a college student. I took that away from her. . . . She was a popular person on campus." He said his crime also "destroyed her parents' relationship."

"They ended up not on good terms because of my destructive behavior," McCarthy said.

He was wrong about that. Katy's parents were divorced years before he killed their daughter. If anything, their shared grief brought the parents closer, as evidenced by their joint lawsuit in 1987 that won a $3.5 million judgment against him but had yet to retrieve a penny.

Hernandez noted there was "significant opposition to your release. I am sure you are aware of that."

"Yes, I am," McCarthy said.

Even in the cloistered world of prison life, McCarthy had felt the sting of being on the receiving end of social media outrage. When he went into prison in 1987, he could not have foreseen the day when users of Facebook, Twitter, online chat, iPhones, Reddit, web blogs, chat rooms, and online comments on news sites would play a role in whether he would get out. With the aid of the internet, the family's petition now had 7,407 signatures.

The state Department of Corrections and Community Supervision website (**doccs.ny.gov**) also offered the public an online portal to share their opinions about an inmate's possible parole, just by looking up his Department Identification Number (DIN), then filling out an online form.

When Hernandez noted that the parole file also had letters of support for him, McCarthy responded by grumbling about the other ones. "I think that the opposition against me is from people who don't know me today, compared me to what they know of the heinous crime that I committed 30 years ago."

Hernandez assured him that the panel would consider "everything statutory," including sentencing minutes and letters from the public.

However, McCarthy refused to let the matter drop.

"Okay," he said. "Is there any information that you derived from the internet or media to determine my release or denial of release?"

"Whatever is in this file, *sir*."

The sharp "sir" was Hernandez's way of letting McCarthy know that he had crossed the line in inquiring about the confidential information the board received from others.

McCarthy ignored the signal.

"Okay. I know there was a petition submitted and signed," he said. "The people that signed it from the last parole board, some of them out of state, which I didn't understand."

"Sir," Hernandez said, "whatever we have in the file we consider. People can write in, however. Whether they have or not, I am not going to discuss that with you today."

"Okay," McCarthy said, finally dropping the subject.

Hernandez asked McCarthy what he had been doing with his time in prison since 2013.

"I was a mobility assistant for a while," McCarthy said, referring to a prison job where he moved inmates in wheelchairs to various activities. He also spent time as a lawns and grounds machine operator at Marcy Correctional Facility.

"I was given the security clearance to operate the machinery. I was the only person in the facility to operate heavy equipment in this facility for early morning snow removal and/or kind of walkway care, spreading the salt with machines. It was very limited security that was keeping an eye on me, but it was approved to give to me, and I took it very serious as a responsibility. I also fix machinery. I am pretty good with my hands. I am very gifted. I have a second sense from my childhood that I really stay in tune with it. I look forward for a future job with it, but we'll see."

After briefly discussing COMPAS and other prison assessments, Hernandez asked McCarthy why he should get parole.

"All the years in prison, I see the guys come and go. I don't have that behavior anymore—the thinking capabilities, I don't have anymore. This is my change," he said.

"Where does the victim fit in?" she asked.

McCarthy said he wasn't sure how to answer. "I was going to ask, 'Which victim?' There is more than one."

"*Sir*," Hernandez said, "you took the life of a young victim who had her life ahead of her. You took the life of one victim. You are in prison for that."

Then she repeated her question: "Why do you believe you are a good candidate for parole?"

Instead of trying to repair the damage, left by his suggestion he considered himself a victim, McCarthy recited reasons he should be released, including staying out of trouble in prison.

"I have no misbehavior reports in seven years. I am not involved in drugs. I am not gang-affiliated. I don't have any assaults or weapons," he said. "Everything that I've done, I tried to be productive. College credits. I have multiple forms of credibility. Everything was productive that I tried to do. And to try to defend what I have done—I can't change what I have done. I acknowledged what I did and pled guilty to it. That is why I believe I am a good candidate for parole. I believe I have proven that I changed from the past and, since I have been incarcerated, my efforts are towards being a good member in society."

Asked where he would live if released, McCarthy said he would move in with his 64-year-old fiancée, who resided near Watertown.

"Are you married?"

"No, ma'am, I am not. I plan to be," McCarthy said.

"You do?"

"Yes."

Hernandez asked whether the fiancée knew why he was in prison.

"She knows my whole family. She knows everything," he said.

"What kind of work are you going to do?"

"I will do whatever they want me to do. I am certified air conditioning and refrigeration, machine operator. I worked on a dairy farm most of my life. I am not afraid of hard work. I have sign language in my abilities. Food service, there is a lot of that. I am not squeamish, and I am pretty physically fit.

"Some of the things that I look at—maybe, possibly volunteering to pay back some of the debt that I made on society, doing volunteer time through my religion. I am Catholic. My fiancée, she is a Eucharist minister, and there is a lot of good things that she can point out to me, being that I have been out of society for so long. I am hoping that I get some benefit from it."

Hernandez returned to questioning McCarthy about his behavior on the morning he fatally attacked Katy.

"How did the police come and find you? How did they know it was you?"

"I was unconscious on the ground when they found me," McCarthy said.

"Why was that?"

"I think I hit my head. I am not 100 percent sure, but I had head trauma. When they found me, they said, I was laying on the ground."

"Did you take responsibility when this happened?"

"Not at first, I didn't," McCarthy said. "I couldn't believe that I had done something like that. It didn't make sense to me."

Hernandez asked Commissioner Ferguson if he had any questions.

"Nothing additional. Thank you," he said.

She turned back to McCarthy.

Did he have anything to add?

After listing goals of getting a higher education and a job if released, McCarthy said he wanted "to establish community ties."

"I am not the same person that I was 29 years ago," he said. "I take full responsibility for my crime—I want to make that known. That is not something that I am . . . avoiding. That is something that I thought about many, many years. If I had a chance to go back in time and change it, I would. But I can't.

"Because I did what I did, it is going to be held against me for the rest of my life by myself and everybody else. I can only move forward. And the Hawelka family, too. I am not trying to be fictitious where I am trying to get over on people. I am trying to be true to myself. I hope that the parole board sees that I am deemed a good candidate for parole, and I hope that society can live with what I have done, and I will live within society's standards of the condition of parole that I am given, and I am just asking for a chance to prove it. I am hoping that I can prove that. It is something that I can only show you. Thank you."

Hernandez concluded the hearing after telling McCarthy, "We'll talk about your case and let you know in writing. Good luck."

Two days later, the panel in a 2-0 decision denied parole for McCarthy for the fourth time.

In the written explanation, Hernandez noted that Katy's murder was "a clear escalation in criminal conduct, for which you provided no reasonable explanation. Your actions, while long ago, exhibited complete disregard for the law and sanctity of human life."

The board also admonished McCarthy for feeling sorry for himself. "During your interview, you appeared to have a complete disconnect for how your actions have impacted the victim," Hernandez wrote. "When asked about the victim, you responded, which one? A vibrant young woman was violently and deliberately assaulted and murdered. She is the victim, Mr. McCarthy, not you. Your entitled attitude leaves much to be desired."

As he returned to his cubicle awaiting another parole hearing in 2017, McCarthy could at least take comfort that he presented the board with a prison record free of any disciplinary actions since 2008. But that was an illusion. As Katy's family would discover, the lack of new offenses on his official record didn't mean McCarthy had stayed out of trouble.

Chapter 30

2017

IN early 2016, Joseph Fahey resumed his previous role as a legal representative for Terry Taber. Because he had just retired as an Onondaga County Court judge, he could now act again as an advocate for Katy's family without it being a conflict of interest. His other reason for taking on the volunteer role had to do with his sister Mary, who needed to focus on some health issues. She came by one day to tell Terry that she was handing the job back to her brother, although Mary Fahey joked that she wasn't sure he'd do it as well as she did.

When he was a judge, within bounds of courtroom decorum, Fahey had not lost his passion for finely worded outrage, never more memorably than in 2009, when he sentenced Stacey Castor for murder. A jury in Syracuse convicted the upstate New York woman of fatally poisoning her second husband with antifreeze, then trying to kill her oldest daughter and frame her for his murder. Police also suspected Castor of using antifreeze to knock off her first husband. The scheme was so bizarre it inspired a 2020 Lifetime TV movie, "Poisoned Love." In sentencing Castor to life in prison, Fahey gave remarks so searing that the Lifetime film used them for a dramatic flourish at the end of the film. "In my 34 years in the criminal justice system," Fahey said, "I've seen murderers of every variety and stripe; but I have to say, Mrs. Castor, you are in a class by yourself."

Writing in his online blog (**joe-fahey.com**) in January 2017, Fahey had no trouble finding words to express similar disdain for McCarthy. Fahey wrote that, after reading the parole transcripts, he concluded that Katy's killer "hasn't given the victim any thought whatsoever." He noted, for example, how McCarthy repeatedly referred to Katy as "Kim Avadikian."

Fahey continued:

During the criminal court proceedings, Katy's mother told me she didn't want McCarthy executed because she wanted him to have to think about what he had done to her daughter every day for the rest of his life.

Clearly, he hasn't thought about her at all.

While discussing his claim of rehabilitation, he was asked, "Where does the victim fit in?" He replied, "I was going to ask which victim, there is more than one." This exchange reveals a stunning and callous level of narcissistic self-absorption to the degree that he believes himself to be a victim. . . .

McCarthy has repeatedly lied to the Board about the viciousness of his attack. He has slandered Katy in death by continuing to claim they had a prior intimate relationship. He has sought to minimize, rationalize and excuse his conduct by claiming to have been in an alcohol-, drug-induced state, contrary to what the police investigation revealed.

For the past nineteen years, I was an Onondaga County Court Judge and an Acting New York State Supreme Court Justice who presided over thousands of felony-level criminal cases and the annual reviews of civilly committed sex offenders pursuant to Article 10 of the Mental Hygiene Law. Because I was a member of the State Judiciary, I was prohibited from commenting about McCarthy during his prior parole appearances. I retired from that position on December 30, 2015. I now no longer have that restriction and plan to offer my opinion to the parole Board. It's not a difficult or complicated one to understand. He remains an unreconstructed, un-rehabilitated sociopath, who is a danger to women everywhere. . . .

It's been thirty years since Katy Hawelka was murdered.

She should never be forgotten.

Brian McCarthy should never be forgotten either.

In the blog post, Fahey included a link to the family's online petition, but he suggested that anyone who wanted "to do a little more" should write directly to the parole board.

As he and Katy's family awaited the next parole hearing, the number of petition signatures opposing McCarthy's release grew to more than 7,800.

On April 15, 2017, four days before McCarthy's scheduled parole hearing, Katy's family got the sad news that Mary Fahey died at age 64. Her obituary offered a long list of survivors and legal accomplishments, concluding that she "loved her family, her pets, politics and all things Irish." It encouraged donations to the SPCA in her memory.

Terry took the death hard. Mary Fahey had been a close friend and confidante who cheered up the family during the worst moments of the parole process, helped them to navigate through the requirements for filing impact statements, and never wavered in her commitment. "She seemed so hellbent on keeping him (McCarthy) in prison as much as I was," Terry said.

With Mary Fahey's help, the family learned to manage its role in the parole process, keep up on prison research, make sure to see a commissioner every two years, and know whom to contact for the panel's decision. Currently, the family expected to learn the outcome two or three days after a hearing by placing a telephone call to the state's newly created Office of Victim Services.

But as McCarthy's scheduled hearing date of Tuesday, April 18, 2017, came and went, there was silence. Carey Patton called that Friday and every day the following week to learn the parole board's decision, but the state officials had no news and no explanation why.

Katy's mother began to fear this was what happened when the board granted parole but wanted to hold off informing the victim's family.

As April was winding down, Joe Hawelka Jr. found a sympathetic ear in the Office of Victim Services who told him the hearing was postponed. Digging a little further, he learned McCarthy requested the delay while he appealed two disciplinary violations at Marcy Correctional Facility. On April 7, a sergeant at the prison had filed a Tier III ticket—the severest possible level—against McCarthy, one for "harassment" and one for "threats."

Joe Jr. was unable to learn further details. But prison records obtained much later under the Freedom of Information Law confirmed that, on April 19, officials canceled McCarthy's transfer to Bare Hill Correctional Facility in Malone, New York, with the notation "unsuit—no longer meets criteria."

Rather than go to the parole board and explain what happened, McCarthy was choosing to wipe the black mark off his record so his upcoming panel would never know about it.

Thinking that a sneaky way to avoid responsibility, Katy's brother countered that chess move with one of his own. On May 12, Joe Jr. sent the board an addendum to his March impact statement. In his letter, Joe Jr. shared what he heard about the April 7 disciplinary action and urged the commissioners to take this into account, even if McCarthy managed to wipe the violations off his record.

"He has been portraying himself as model prisoner," Joe Jr. wrote. "I would imagine the inmate did not want the violations on his record a mere ten days before his parole hearing. . . . Our family vehemently opposes his release and . . . in light of the current violations the inmate is facing, along with his pattern of violations and past actions, we do not feel that he should be considered for parole."

The family didn't know at the time, but this wasn't the first time McCarthy was in hot water since his 2015 parole hearing. The Freedom of Information request would also reveal a reference to McCarthy's "disruptive behavior" on April 13, 2016. The document stated McCarthy was the perpetrator in "use of body" as a weapon in a Marcy dormitory at approximately 6:30 p.m. However, no disciplinary action was listed in the records; it wasn't clear if McCarthy successfully appealed the violation, or if no ticket was issued.

While McCarthy awaited his next parole hearing, the prison system transferred him on May 17, 2017, to the general prison population at Riverview Correctional Facility, a medium-security prison in Ogdensburg, a city just 30 miles from Potsdam. His prison record listed "program purposes" as the reason for the transfer.

The family received notice in mid-May that the parole board rescheduled McCarthy's hearing for July 12. It also learned that McCarthy's appeal had been successful and that he would go before the board with a record clean of any new offenses. All Joe Jr. could do was hope that his letter found its way into McCarthy's parole file, although he had no idea if it would make any difference if it did.

It was morning when McCarthy's fifth parole hearing got underway on Wednesday, July 12, 2017. For the first time, he wasn't seeing commissioners in person. The hearing took place via a two-way video hookup between McCarthy at Riverview Correctional Facility and the panel members at Syracuse's parole office.

"Sir, are you Brian McCarthy?"

"Yes, sir. I am."

"Mr. McCarthy, I am Commissioner Ludlow. With me is Commissioner Coppola."

Back for his second hearing with McCarthy was G. Kevin Ludlow, the commissioner who heard the impact statements from Terry and Joe Jr. in 2009 and voted to reject McCarthy's parole in 2011. The only other commissioner this time was Marc Coppola, a former New York state senator from Western New York.

Ludlow and Coppola could see and hear McCarthy on a large TV mounted on a cart with video equipment underneath; McCarthy viewed them on a similar setup at Riverview. A stenographer in Syracuse transcribed the hearing.

After briefly asking McCarthy to confirm some details about his criminal history in New York and Virginia, Ludlow said, "We have some information in the file I would like to read and ask if it is accurate."

Ludlow noted Katy graduated near the top of her class at Henninger High School, where "she played in the school band and was well-liked by her peers and teachers." She attended Clarkson University with an eye at attending the Wharton School of Business and pursuing a career in finance. When her mother dropped off Katy at Clarkson to begin her sophomore year in August 1986, she believed her daughter was going to a school "safe from big-city crime."

Instead, Ludlow read, "Mr. McCarthy brutally attacked Katy by sexually assaulting her and kicking her head repeatedly. In spite of campus security witnessing what they thought were two college students in a romantic tryst, Mr. McCarthy continued on with the assault on Katy. He did not care who saw him. Because of her death resulting from this brutal attack, Katy was unable to give her last wish, that (her) organs be used to help others."

"Are those facts correct as you know them?" Ludlow asked.

"I believe the dates are pretty accurate, yes," McCarthy said.

"Okay," the commissioner said. "Anything you wish to say about the instant offense, sir?"

"Yes, I do," McCarthy said. "I'm not trying to blame it on alcohol or drugs, but I was involved as a youth almost 31 years ago in drugs, and that's what misled me in my life. And I also look at it where having exposure to a bad life, being abused sexually, gave me a bad outlook on life."

Without being asked, McCarthy added, "And I know that she was inebriated, too."

"How do you know that?" Ludlow asked.

"Because I smelled it."

"What did you smell?"

"Alcohol."

"How is that relevant to the attack?"

"Because we were both inebriated, and, initially, it was a consensual issue. But it was my fault," McCarthy said.

Ludlow asked, "Are you suggesting that you and the victim consumed alcohol together prior to the—"

McCarthy interrupted, "No, I'm not."

"—to the attack?"

"No, I'm not."

"I see, okay," Ludlow said. "Anything else you wish to say in response to the instant offense, sir?"

"Yes. I know I've caused a lot of pain to a lot of people. I have matured a lot. I've constantly been exposed to rehabilitation. I've taken every opportunity that I could. And in the issue that you just read, I can't reverse that. I can't go back and take that back. I wish I could, but I can't. I'm not the same person that I was."

Ludlow wanted to know if McCarthy was a native of Potsdam.

"Yes, I was."

"Have you ever killed anyone else?"

"No, sir."

"Have you ever assaulted, sexually or otherwise, any other victim?"

"No, sir. No, sir," McCarthy said.

McCarthy didn't acknowledge that he had been ticketed for assaulting other inmates at Attica, or that he had beaten insurance agent Leonard Page in Potsdam in 1986.

Ludlow asked McCarthy about his COMPAS assessment, which scored him as being a low risk to public safety.

"I agree with the COMPAS," McCarthy said. "I think that I am a low risk because I've tried throughout my incarceration to do everything I possibly could to rehabilitate the error that I made and the mistakes that I've also made in the institutions. I know that I've been exposed to some pretty negative behavior. I came from a good family. I wasn't taught to be like this. I wasn't taught to be an aggressive (person and to) assault people. It was nothing in my nature."

Ludlow stopped McCarthy.

"When you use the word 'error,' are you referring to the assault and the subsequent death of Miss Hawelka as an 'error'?"

"I'm talking about my judgment, my error in judgment being that I was involved in a bad lifestyle," McCarthy answered.

"I see."

"And I understand the things that I was exposed to were not healthy."

Ludlow turned to McCarthy's recent behavior in prison.

"Now, discipline-wise," Ludlow said, "no ticket since your prior appearance, correct, sir?"

"That is correct. I believe it's 10 years."

"I think I saw 2008 was your last ticket," Ludlow said.

"Okay," McCarthy said.

"Is that accurate?"

"That is accurate."

"Okay. According to the file, to be more specific, your last ticket was December 9th, 2008, at Livingston. And the file indicates nothing in the way of a disciplinary issue since that time; is that correct?"

"Yes, Mr. Ludlow."

From his pointed questions, it appeared that Ludlow had seen Joe Jr.'s letter, or otherwise knew why McCarthy's parole hearing was delayed. But with McCarthy's recent violations absent in the official record, and with the inmate refusing to volunteer the truth, Ludlow moved on.

After giving McCarthy a chance to talk about his participation in prison programs and what he would do when released, Ludlow asked if he had anything to add.

McCarthy said he had written a letter to Katy's family and placed it in the Department of Corrections and Community Supervision's "Apology Letter Bank." The repository was the state's method for inmates to express remorse for their actions without violating rules against directly contacting victims or their families. Only if the victim or the family agreed to accept the letter would the department mail them a copy or read it to them over the phone.

McCarthy also pointed out that he had arranged for Masses to be said for Katy "numerous times." At least one was at St. Ann's Catholic Church in Mooers Forks, New York, a hamlet about 215 miles northeast of Syracuse.

"I have done nothing but good since I have been incarcerated. I can't emphasize that point enough," McCarthy said. "There have been things that have been found. I've done things for staff that were out of the ordinary. I found keys; I turned them in. I've found different tools that could be turned into weapons. I don't have any criminal-mind thinking. I want to go home. And I think that I have a chance, and I hope that you consider me for parole."

"We appreciate that, sir," Ludlow said.

"Okay, I have a statement I'd like to read, Mr. Ludlow."

"How long is the statement, sir?"

"Just a couple of sentences. Not very long. Very brief."

"Okay, sir. Briefly, please. And we have a stenographic reporter here. We certainly want a totally accurate record. As such, please do not read too fast."

"Thank you," McCarthy said. "Thank you for considering all the factors towards my release. I know I am not the same person that I was 31 years ago. Everything I have tried to do is live the goal of forgiveness for all the people that I have hurt by such a selfish act. I'm really trying to be a better person. I would like to change. I would like the chance to prove that I have changed. Please see me as the person I am today and not as one who took someone's life almost 31 years ago."

Ludlow responded, "Mr. McCarthy, you're still a young man at 54. We want you to get your life turned around in a positive, constructive way. We wish you good luck in that regard. We'll advise you in writing. Good luck to you, sir."

Perhaps taking Ludlow's remarks to mean he had a sympathetic ear, McCarthy asked, "Is there anything I need to do to . . . certify some type of relief in the future, so that I'm earned eligibility for parole?"

"What do you mean 'relief'? I'm not clear on what you mean in terms of use of the word 'relief'," Ludlow said.

McCarthy repeated that he had a "clean disciplinary record" and had participated in various prison programs. He wanted to know what else he had to do to win parole.

"The question shows great insight on your part," Ludlow said. "However, the question calls for a conclusion. And, at this time, the interview is still open. Commissioner Coppola and I have yet to deliberate. And I have arrived at no conclusion. The panel has arrived at no conclusion. I appreciate the question. That's the best way I can answer it in response."

With that, Ludlow wrapped up the hearing with another, "Good luck to you, sir."

The board announced two days later that it denied McCarthy's parole in a 2-0 decision, which Ludlow explained in a brief statement addressed to the inmate.

"Your institutional programming indicates progress and achievement which is noted to your credit. Your disciplinary record appears clean since your prior appearance," Ludlow wrote, his choice of words again suggesting he knew McCarthy had successfully appealed the tickets. "The Panel notes your COMPAS risk score of low."

Ludlow added, however, that "the Panel acknowledges official opposition and significant and persuasive community opposition on file to your release. Required statutory factors have been considered, including your risk to the community, rehabilitation efforts, and your needs for successful community reentry. Your discretionary release at this time would, thus, not be compatible with the welfare of society at large and would tend to deprecate the seriousness of the instant offense and undermine respect for the law."

When she read the hearing transcript, Terry Taber thought it was very creepy for a killer to have Masses said for his victim. Besides, if McCarthy was sincere about making things right with God, she thought, he would not have used the gesture to win points with the parole board.

As for his letter to the apology bank, this was news to Terry. Out of curiosity, she called the Office of Victim Services and requested a copy.

When she received it in the mail, Terry noted it had been on file with the state since November 17, 2015.

Once again, McCarthy got Katherine Hawelka's name wrong. The letter began, "To the family and friends of Kathryn Hawelka":

This is a very difficult letter to write. I am sure that it will be equally hard for you to read, but I am hoping that you will choose to read this letter of apology. It is with true sincerity that I am writing this long overdue heartfelt letter that I have written many times in my head, but advised not to send until I recently learned about this repository. It is by no means meant to deliberately bring up painful memories, beg for forgiveness, or relieve my guilt.

What I want you to know is that I take full responsibility for causing the death of Kathryn and I am so very, very sorry. I am ashamed of my selfish, reckless actions caused so much pain and sorrow to you and to so many other people. Kathryn was taken from this earth well before her natural time. Your lives were forever changed. Community lives were changed forever. My life and family lives were also changed forever. Kathryn has never left my thoughts and prayers. As a Roman Catholic, I believe in the powers of the holy Mass. Each year I have a Mass said for her and will continue to do so.

During my incarceration, I have taken several programs that led me to face my childhood demons that caused me to turn to drugs and act out my frustrations, pain and shamefulness of being sexually abused as a child. This is not an excuse for what I did, nor is this confession to you a plea for forgiveness. It is always wrong to take the life of another. I was wrong to destroy Kathryn's and your family. I am also sorry for filling your heart with bitterness instead of happiness and love from Kathryn that you will never know. I hope that this letter of apology will help with your healing process and bring you some type of closure.

Thank you for taking the time to read my letter of apology. I cannot tell you enough how sorry I am.

Very sincerely, Brian McCarthy.

Terry read the letter once, folded the paper back up, put it away, and didn't look at it again until two years later when she shared a copy.

"I'm just glad they denied him again," she said with a sigh.

Following his parole hearing, McCarthy didn't remain for long at Riverview Correctional Facility. On October 12, 2017, the prison system transferred him from the Special Housing Unit at Riverview to the SHU at Gouverneur Correctional Facility about 30 miles away. Why he ended up in the two SHUs was unclear, as his official disciplinary record made no mention of any new infraction or another incident.

On November 7, 2017, McCarthy moved to the general prison population at Wyoming Correctional Facility near the Attica prison. There he remained until August 14, 2018, when prison officials transferred him to Cayuga Correctional Facility in Moravia, New York, just south of Auburn. "Subject now appears to be AOP (Assaultive Offender Program) eligible & is requesting placement," according to records explaining the transfer. It noted he had accepted a job as a prison porter.

In 2017, New York prisoner rights groups organized a "Parole Justice Call-In Day and Social Media Blast" to oppose the reappointments of commissioners Ludlow, James Ferguson, and Walter William Smith Jr. One activist described these three as "particularly punitive" toward prisoners seeking parole. Not long afterward, Governor Cuomo decided not to reappoint Ludlow and Ferguson. Smith, who had been a senior investigator for the state Crime Victims Board before becoming a commissioner in 1996, kept his post.

In March 2018, advocates for prisoners openly celebrated again when a panel—over strong opposition from police groups—granted parole to 70-year-old Herman Bell, who in 1971 fatally shot two police officers in New York City. To prisoner rights groups and some in the media, including the editorial board of *The New York Times*, the fact someone murdered cops wasn't enough reason by itself to keep an inmate behind bars forever.

"We believe every human that's incarcerated is redeemable," Jose Saldana, director of Release Aging People in Prison (RAPP), told the *Brooklyn Daily Eagle* in 2019. A year earlier, Saldana was released on parole after spending 38 years in prison for attempted murder.

Katy's brother was among those who disagreed that every inmate is redeemable, that every prisoner deserves a second chance. On that morning when McCarthy decided to beat, kick, rape, and strangle Katy, Joe Jr. said, he gave up his right to ever taste freedom again.

The next time McCarthy asked what he needed to do to win parole, Joe Jr. had a suggested response for the commissioners. "The last transcript, you can see, he's trying to fish for: 'What do I do?' He's asking them straight up: 'What else do I have to do?'

"Well, un-kill my sister. Let's start with that one. Make her rise from the dead, then we'll talk about you coming out."

Chapter 31

2019 and Beyond

A warm breeze brushed back curtains as it passed through open windows in Terry Taber's Syracuse home on a sunny morning in June 2018. At 74, Katy's mother was still living in the handsome Colonial where her second-oldest daughter had once lived, and which was now decorated with Oriental rugs over hardwood floors, comfortable furniture, a TV set in one corner of the living room, and shelves stacked with knickknacks and family photos. Be silent a moment, and a visitor might imagine echoes of Katy's hearty laugh or her feet racing up the narrow stairs to her bedroom to practice the clarinet or to study for a big exam.

When Terry pictures Katy in her mind, she is still the 19-year-old that she dropped off at Clarkson in August 1986. But there are moments when Terry imagines Katy as wife and mother, now approaching middle age, enjoying family life while still making her mark in the business world.

"Yeah, because she was a smart kid, and she had a really good head on her shoulders," Terry said. "Both of my other girls have done well, and my son has done well. So, I think really the sky was the limit for Katy, and she had the kind of personality she wasn't going to let anything get her down. I wonder about her being married and her having kids and a husband and a happy family type of thing . . . "

Terry's voiced trailed off until she added softly, "but not to be."

Over the years, Terry has attended social events where the small talk with someone she didn't know would result in the question, "How many kids do you have?"

Terry could say three children and avoid putting a damper on the conversation. But she always said "four," and if the person inquired more,

Terry wasn't afraid to add that Katy was murdered. Terry wasn't looking to make people uncomfortable, but she was never going to turn Katy into an afterthought.

A few years back, Terry went to a Syracuse suburb to watch her grand-children play soccer. While there, she spotted Sarah Kharas Salamino, one of Katy's friends in high school who was at the game with her children.

"Come visit me," Terry said.

Salamino came over to Terry's house for a chat about old times. Before long, Salamino asked if she could see Katy's bedroom again. There, tears poured out with the memories.

"Sarah and I sat in the room and cried. I hadn't done that in a long time, because I had kind of gotten over it and it not being Katy's room," Terry said.

For years after Katy died, Terry couldn't celebrate Thanksgiving without overwhelming sadness, knowing the November 1986 break was when she first expected to see her daughter home again from Potsdam. "Up until the last couple of years, Thanksgiving has always been my worst holiday. Thanksgiving is still a little tough," Terry said. "Some people were like, 'Isn't it good we're all together.' No, we're not all together. We got one missing."

With time, it has become easier for Terry to reflect on her daughter's murder without crying. But there is still no forgiving McCarthy, no matter how many apologies he writes or how many Masses he requests for Katy.

She insisted it isn't vengeance that drives her opposition to his parole, but rather her fear for anyone else who has the misfortune to meet McCarthy when he's in a bad mood.

"If he gets out at 90, maybe I don't have to worry about him," Terry said. "I just think, as long as he can stand on two feet and make a fist, he's dangerous."

Asked if she was still angry at McCarthy, Terry answered, "Not as much as I was. I'm just more sad than angry. I try not to think about him much. I don't want him to be that important in my life that I got to carry around a bunch of anger. When I do think about him, I'm just more sad for Katy than angry at him."

In 2017, Terry got a knock on her front door. Standing there were members of a film crew scouting Syracuse locations for the movie "Asher," an action thriller starring Ron Perlman as a hitman. They asked if they could shoot scenes inside the home. Terry welcomed them in, saying they could move things as they wished.

The crew decided to film in Carey's old bedroom. Terry noticed they decorated it to look like a 12-year-old girl was using it, placing on the dresser a brown box that the set decorator found in Terry's bedroom. It was the same box that held Katy's corsage from her senior ball. Not long before filming, Lisa Campolo had returned the box to Terry. Next to it, the crew placed a framed photo of Katy, taken around first grade.

Never once had Terry mentioned Katy's murder to the crew.

"The girl who was dressing the room—she had no idea about putting those two things together. It was just so bizarre," Terry said.

The scene shot in the bedroom didn't end up in the finished film, but Terry was left with the comforting thought that maybe Katy's spirit guided the crew's hands.

Something similarly eerie happened in 1989 when Terry had her house repainted. Afterward, she used an old camera to take photographs of the work. When the photos were developed, Terry discovered she accidentally double-exposed the film over shots taken years earlier. In one photo, she could see Katy's face superimposed over the window of her second-oldest daughter's old bedroom.

Over the years, Betsy McInerney had her own chilling experiences, such as watching a framed photo of Katy keep falling over, or a door repeatedly swing open on a desk holding Katy's picture.

For years, Betsy had struggled to hold onto a Catholic faith tested by unanswered questions on how God could allow someone so good and innocent as Katy to be murdered. In 2018, Betsy and a friend heard about a psychic medium from East Syracuse who carried on the traditions of a Catholic mystic, offering help in connecting with departed loved ones, angels, and saints in the afterlife. They set up an appointment and showed up with a healthy amount of skepticism.

In the very first visit, the mystic channeled messages from Katy that involved personal facts and events Betsy felt no one else knew, such as details from the Watertown hospital. Betsy decided then that those incidents with the framed photos falling over were "Katy trying to somehow get to us, to me."

The mystic described how, during McCarthy's attack, but before he sexually assaulted Katy, "she left her body. She didn't suffer," Betsy said.

However, Katy's spirit couldn't understand why no one came to her aid outside Walker Arena. "That's one of the things she struggles with," Betsy said, "that there were people there who could have helped her."

Before the session ended, Katy's spirit revealed she had been the family's guardian angel, looking out for them from heaven. As for McCarthy, Katy assured her sister, "He's not getting out."

A month before McCarthy's sixth parole hearing in April 2019, Joseph Fahey wrote again to the board, summarizing the case against granting McCarthy parole. This time the attorney attached a letter that Katy's mother had just received with a message of sympathy from a member of McCarthy's family. The note mentioned that McCarthy's father and siblings wanted nothing to do with him. It also said they hoped he remained in prison.

"The family has severed all ties with Brian and feel he should remain in custody for the rest of his life. Evil has no place in society," wrote the family member, declining to be interviewed for this book but asking that condolences be passed on to Katy's family.

Terry said she wondered what McCarthy—who had spent so much time trying to figure out who opposed his parole—would think about some from his own family being among them.

Fahey also shared with the parole board copies of recently uncovered court files from Virginia that showed how McCarthy had agreed to supervision when released on probation in 1985 but never followed through. "There is absolutely no reason to believe that McCarthy, if released (in 2019), would be amenable to supervision, given his history," Fahey wrote.

The tally of signatures on the petition opposing parole was 7,847 by April 2019. But Katy's family had reason to fear strong community opposition wouldn't be enough this time to offset growing demands by parole advocates to let more inmates out of prison.

Brian McCarthy's mug shot from 2017 and other details from his prison file obtained in 2018. (New York State Department of Corrections and Community Supervision.)

In fall 2018 elections, Republicans lost control of the state Senate, giving Democrats control of all three branches of state government, and with it greater power to ease parole restrictions and seek more commissioners sympathetic to releasing inmates.

In January 2019, parole reform advocates gathered at the state capitol to lobby lawmakers to pass legislation that would make 12,000 of the state's 51,000 inmates eligible for "presumptive parole." The measure would prohibit the board from denying parole to these inmates unless a panel gave a good reason, rather than putting the onus on the inmate to make his case. The activists also called for "elder parole" that would make just under 1,200 older inmates eligible for immediate parole hearings, including 310 serving sentences of life without parole.

While the measures, if passed, would not guarantee McCarthy's release, just the fact they were proposed added to a new paradigm in Albany: Parole board members who wanted to keep their jobs better have good reasons for refusing to release inmates.

Precisely a week before McCarthy's hearing, a parole panel voted 2-1 to release 69-year-old Judith Clark, the getaway driver for the 1981 Brink's armored car heist that killed three, including two police officers. In the board's written decision, commissioners Ellen Evans Alexander and Tana Agostini found that Clark had provided clear evidence of rehabilitation. They also noted her advanced age and her charitable work in prison.

Commissioner Walter William Smith Jr. was the sole dissenting voice, expressing concern for the families of the victims. "The sounds of their weeping will remain," he wrote.

McCarthy's sixth parole hearing got off to a routine start on Wednesday, April 24, 2019, once again through a video conferencing link, this time between Cayuga Correctional Facility and the parole office in Syracuse.

"Good afternoon, sir. Your name, please?"

"Brian McCarthy."

"Mr. McCarthy, I'm Commissioner Coppola. With me today, Commissioner Smith and Commissioner Drake."

Marc Coppola was back to consider McCarthy's parole for the second hearing in a row. The others were Tyece Drake, formerly a clinical supervisor at a halfway house for men who had been released from prison, and Smith, the commissioner who had just voted against granting parole to Judith Clark.

Shortly after the hearing got underway, McCarthy spoke up to say he might ask the commissioners to repeat a question because he could hear "echoes" from the video hookup.

"That's okay," Coppola said. "If it becomes a problem, I'll let you know."

Coppola noted he had taken time to read all of McCarthy's 1987 sentencing transcript and the "pretty thorough" presentencing report, not just the summaries provided to the parole board.

"At this point, do you have any questions or anything before I talk about the offense?"

"No," McCarthy said. "I would just like to state I pled guilty to what I did, and I know that it was a very bad crime, and I'm not the same person. I'm nowhere near the same person."

"Well, let's—we are going to get to that," Coppola said.

From reading the sentencing transcript, Coppola said, he discovered that the reason McCarthy received two years less than the maximum in 1987 was that a higher court had recommended giving defendants a break if they pleaded guilty. Coppola had now made it harder for McCarthy to insist he didn't know why he got a lesser sentence.

Coppola also reminded McCarthy that the record showed he sexually assaulted Katy after beating and kicking her, leaving her helpless.

"I think the actual cause of death was strangulation. Is that correct?" he added.

"I don't think it was," McCarthy said. "I think it was because of the angle that she was—her neck was pinched, and I think he (the medical examiner) said asphyxiation, maybe."

Coppola pointed out that he was just quoting from the presentencing report. "I'm assuming you have seen this document, is that right?"

"It has been a long time. But, yes, I have seen it," McCarthy said of the presentencing report, a copy of which he obtained after going to court in 2008.

Perhaps guided by Fahey's letter or the impact statements, Coppola continued to fact-check a long list of McCarthy's questionable testimony at previous parole hearings.

"It sounds like she was beaten unconscious, and therefore then the sex occurred. Is that correct?" Coppola asked.

"No, that is not correct at all."

"Okay. That is the way I read it," Coppola said of the report's conclusion that McCarthy had raped Katy while she was incapacitated.

"I guess that would be appropriate to accept it that way—the way it was written—but that is the presentence investigation. They are saying they assumed that is what happened. . . . Because I wouldn't talk to them. I willingly admitted to what I did. Do you understand what I mean, Commissioner Coppola?"

"Not really. I missed it," Coppola said.

"My intention was to have sex with this girl. We had an agreement. Her and I had an agreement, and being that she was incapacitated—drunk, as they say there—that is what you're assuming. Drinking, I couldn't perform.

I couldn't have the ability to have sexual intercourse. And in the process of that, she got mad at me, and she spit in my face. Then, that aggravated me, made me angry, so I struck her. I assaulted her."

Coppola asked if McCarthy was claiming the only reason Katy was "physically helpless" is because she was drunk, as opposed to being beaten.

"That could be, possibly," McCarthy said. "My contribution to that is, I did beat her. I'm not denying her—"

"Did you have sex with her at any point?"

"No, I did not. I tried, but I could not perform because I was inebriated."

"You are telling us what . . . instigated your rage was that she spit at you?"

"Yes."

"Did you know her at all? How did you meet her?" Coppola asked.

"I did, but at a distance. I knew who she was. I was kind of familiar, but I wasn't really familiar with her. It wasn't something that we were friends, but we knew each other, you know," McCarthy said. "It's kind of hard to explain that kind of relationship. But you just know somebody, and it wasn't something where you were dating them, you know what I mean? I don't know if I'm explaining it properly."

Coppola pressed for a better explanation.

"You weren't dating, so how well did you know her? Did you see her on a regular basis somehow? How did you know her?"

"I lived in the town, and I would go on the college campus because I knew a lot of people on the college campus," McCarthy said, avoiding a direct answer about how he knew Katy.

Coppola asked why he was outside Walker Arena at close to 3:30 in the morning.

McCarthy answered, "It was a shortcut you go through, instead of going on the main walkway through town, and you go to the college campuses, and that is where we ended up meeting up."

"Was this a pre-arranged meeting?"

"No."

"Okay. And you just ran into her, kind of?"

"Yes, I guess you could say that. It's something that, you understand, yes, I just kind of ran into her."

Professional decorum kept Coppola from calling out McCarthy as a liar. Instead, he asked McCarthy if he would be surprised if others didn't believe his claim that Katy consented to have sex with him.

"Probably."

"You would be surprised at that?"

"Yes, I would be."

"No one knows it but you and her, and she is not around," Coppola said. "So why would you be surprised if someone questioned that?"

"I'm just telling you what the facts were, that I remember," McCarthy said. "We weren't involved, is that I'm trying to get at. It wasn't a relationship. I would see her once in a while, and it would (be) like 'hi' and 'bye,' and that would be it. It wasn't something where I was purposely going out of my way to meet her."

Coppola asked McCarthy why he showed up at Clarkson at that hour.

"I was going to the college campus to see some friends that were on the college campus," McCarthy said.

At that point, Commissioner Smith jumped into the questioning.

Who were these "friends"? he asked.

"The ones that were college students on campus," McCarthy said evasively.

"What were the *names* of the college students?" Smith said.

"I only knew them by a first-name basis, because they were college students. I was only familiar with them because of the college and town we were in."

Smith persisted. "What were their first names?"

McCarthy offered three first names—all blacked out in the hearing transcript—one of which he described as "another girl that was involved." He said there "were a few names that were there and involved in my life that I was—I'm from that town."

Smith wanted to know if McCarthy was surprised that Katy, someone the inmate admitted he barely knew, supposedly wanted sex with him at 3:30 a.m. outside Walker Arena.

"No, not at all," he said. "I wasn't surprised at all, because I know there were—a lot of people were promiscuous. That is one of the things I looked at."

With that, Coppola decided to move on, but not before turning to Drake and asking if the commissioner had any questions.

"Not yet," Drake replied.

Because the general public cannot attend New York parole hearings, the only way it can find out what occurred is by reading a transcript made available weeks or months later, often with huge chunks blacked out for hard-to-fathom reasons. Such was the case for the 2019 hearing transcript, where even Katy's name and the location of the murder were redacted.

Some redactions made it hard to follow the exchange, such as in one section where McCarthy was asked about the morning he killed Katy.

"Why do you think you are still fuzzy about some of the details?" Coppola asked.

A parole censor would redact McCarthy's initial response. But it was clear from uncensored parts that followed that the commissioners didn't like his answer.

"I'm not avoiding it," McCarthy said. "I keep telling you, Mr. Coppola, I know what I did. I pled guilty to it myself, and I'm ashamed of myself. I'm not the same person. You're asking me questions that I can't answer, and I'm trying. If I can come up with answers that can satisfy you, they are the truth."

Coppola responded, "I don't want you to make up anything (or) fabricate. If you don't know, simply say, 'I don't know.' I'm not asking you to satisfy me. I'm asking you questions because I'm trying to get a picture of who you were that night. . . . If you don't know, tell me, and we will move on."

McCarthy said his memory might be flawed because he was under the influence of drugs and alcohol at the time of the murder. "And also, Mr. Coppola, I mean, I'm looking at things I never looked at before, when I'm looking at how bad a person I was and, how do I remember being that bad? Do I want to remember that? No, I don't. But you are asking me questions that make me realize I never thought about that."

Perhaps for the first time, McCarthy had a convincing explanation why his testimony was so often at odds with the official record: What he did to Katy was so horrible, so evil that McCarthy chose not to remember the truth of what happened.

Coppola turned to McCarthy's latest COMPAS risk assessment, which scored him as "highly probable" he would revert to drug abuse once released.

McCarthy said that made no sense.

"Mr. Coppola, I haven't done drugs in over 34 years," he said. "I pride myself on staying away from drugs. I was just given urinalysis a month before—or two months before I came to the parole board. I know what it was for, but I don't do any drugs, so I don't have any issues with that."

Coppola encouraged McCarthy not to worry about a COMPAS score, as the panel would make a decision based on a wide range of factors, including his conduct in prison.

"What do you do right now?" he asked, referring to McCarthy's prison job.

"I'm a dorm porter," a job that typically involves mopping, sweeping and cleaning. McCarthy said he chose "a minimal job" so that "I can work with my paperwork so that I can prepare for the parole board, so I can go outside and work out and stay healthy."

Commissioner Drake asked what McCarthy learned from his participation in the Sex Offender Program at Oneida Correctional Facility.

"You want the long or short answer?" McCarthy asked.

"I want the truth."

"How do I go from committing a minor larcenous behavior to taking another person's life?"

"What did you find out?" Drake asked.

McCarthy's immediate answer was redacted, although Drake's follow-up question indicated McCarthy claimed he felt threatened by Katy.

"So, you thought she was going to harm you again?"

"Yes."

"You thought your victim was going to harm you?" the commissioner repeated.

"Yes."

"In what way?"

"Because she spit in my face, and that precipitated me becoming angry, and then I became violent," McCarthy said. "Does that make sense?"

"To a certain degree," Drake said. "What harm could she have done? She is a woman. You are a man. You are stronger than her."

"What harm could she have done to me?" McCarthy said, who still had a habit of repeating a question, which some people do when they're stalling to come up with an answer.

"Yes."

"There is hatred in your head," McCarthy said. "If you have someone who is really a worthy person, it doesn't matter your strength or not. You can manipulate yourself to thinking that you are no good."

"Was that what it was?" Drake asked. "The hurt would have come in hurting, for lack of a better term, your ego?"

"Absolutely. That is a hundred percent on the mark."

"So she hurt your ego by spitting in your face?"

"Yes."

"What else did you perceive that she could have done to hurt you or your ego?" Drake asked.

"Talking to her friends and saying that I couldn't perform as a man," McCarthy said.

"So, it's safe to assume that you didn't want her to tell anyone that you could not perform?"

"In a sense of making me feel less of a person than I was."

Under persistent questioning, McCarthy finally gave a believable reason why he killed Katy: He wanted to silence her—but not for the bizarre reasons he gave. He had to know that Katy's death would keep her from possibly identifying him to the police as her attacker. Once he inflicted fatal injuries on Katy, McCarthy might have gotten away with murder had he not run into metal stairs trying to flee the scene.

Drake asked McCarthy if it was during therapy in the Oneida sex-offender program that he reached his conclusion that he injured Katy because she harmed his ego.

"I recognize it right now," McCarthy said.

Then, out of the blue, McCarthy offered that he didn't learn much from the SOP because the staff "ostracized" him for being a sex offender.

"I was looked at like scum, treated like scum, sent to The Box twice," McCarthy said, referring to Oneida Correctional Facility's Special Housing

Unit. "I was sticking up for a counselor. One of the inmates that was in the program was talking trash to the counselor trying to help us in a class/group setting, and I stood up and said something, and I got in trouble for that."

McCarthy was clearly angry now, and it didn't seem to matter to him that this was not a good look for an inmate trying to make a positive impression at a parole hearing. Furthermore, he had just spilled the beans that he had at least two disciplinary actions that weren't on his prison record.

Drake tried to cut him off, but McCarthy kept talking.

"Please, let me finish," McCarthy said. "This counselor was trying to give me information to help us, and I got sent to The Box. They beat me up, slapped me and put me in The Box under fictitious charges. I got a reversal on the charges, but after going through something like that, it was pretty traumatic. I shut my mouth. I didn't say anything. That is what I missed. I didn't get the opportunity to ask questions because the way they treated us. We were ostracized because of the SOP. I wanted help, and I couldn't get it. I was sent to The Box again, and I was beat up."

Drake gestured for McCarthy to be quiet. "My hands are up," the commissioner said. "It means stop."

"I understand what that means," McCarthy said, "but I need to tell you this."

"I need you to stop," Drake said. "I heard your story. I got it. I got it."

McCarthy, finally regaining his composure, uttered, "Thank you."

Coppola asked if McCarthy had anything else to add before the hearing ended.

"I'm trying to put my best foot forward, Commissioner Coppola. I don't know what else to say to you, but I am asking at a chance for parole."

"There is no magic answer," Coppola said. "Don't worry about that."

"I'm not trying to give you smooth-over answers," McCarthy said. "You asked me the tough questions. I gave you answers. I'm not wishy-washy. I have been in too long. I don't know what else to say to you. I hope I get a fair decision in the parole board hearing, and please look at who I am now, not the crime I committed that I can't ever change."

Coppola suggested that McCarthy keep in mind that others who opposed his parole also deserved a fair decision from the board.

"You said a fair shake," Coppola said. "That door swings both ways. I want to say that."

Coppola told McCarthy to expect a decision by the following week.

The next Monday, Betsy McInerney placed a call to the Office of Victim Services. Moments after hanging up, she immediately fired off an email to her family. "PAROLE DENIED!" she wrote. "It's a great day!"

In their 3-0 decision, written by Coppola, the commissioners offered McCarthy the most extended and explicit explanation any panel had given for rejecting his parole:

After a review of the record, interview and deliberation, the Panel has determined that if released at this time, there is a reasonable probability that you would not live and remain at liberty without again violating the law and that your release would so deprecate the serious nature of the crime as to undermine respect for the law. Parole is denied.

Required statutory factors have been considered, together with your institutional adjustment, including discipline and program participation, the risk and needs assessment, and needs for successful reentry into the community. Also considered are letters or statements in support of your release, or letters or statements opposed to your release. More compelling, however, are the following: Your instant of murder 2nd degree, you violating/assaulting your female victim to the point she became unconscious and helpless, and then engaged in sexual intercourse with her. The victim was then strangled, which was the actual cause of death. This description is according to the PSI (presentencing investigation) located in your DOCCS (Department of Corrections and Community Supervision) file. Your criminal history record reflects prior unlawful behavior, however the instant offense is a serious escalation of your criminal behavior.

The Panel has taken into consideration your parole packet submitted for review, which contained letters of support and reasonable assurance, as well as documents that are contained in your DOCCS folder; the results of your COMPAS Risk and Needs Assessment, including your independent assessments, and the low scores indicated therein. Your program completion, both mandatory and voluntary, were also considered, along with your improved disciplinary record since 12/08, however, discretionary release shall not be granted merely as a reward for good conduct or efficient performance of duties while confined.

Furthermore, the gravity of your actions should not be taken lightly. Your victim was beaten and ultimately killed by your hand. During the interview, the Panel tried to gain more information and insight into your frame of mind, motivation and interaction with the victim, yet your explanation of how and why you were interacting with her lacks credibility. Furthermore, the Panel felt that you still have yet to fully and adequately examine your motives that led to this terrible crime, which remains a concern to the Panel.

Therefore, based on all required factors in the file considered, discretionary release at this time is not appropriate.

(All Commissioners Concur.)

The panel placed McCarthy's release on hold until his next hearing in April 2021.

Several months after the decision, Fahey and Katy's family received a copy of the transcript, which at 63 pages was the lengthiest by far for any of McCarthy's hearings.

After reading it, Fahey gave high marks to the commissioners for doing their research and for challenging McCarthy on the facts.

"I do have to say that the parole commissioners who've heard this case over the years have performed in a way the family could admire," the attorney said. "They're the only ones who have done justice."

Fahey thought the defining moment of the 2019 hearing occurred late in the proceeding when McCarthy waved off Commissioner Drake's warnings to stop talking. It had to give pause to the parole panel that any inmate who rebelled at a parole hearing probably wasn't going to abide by supervision if released from prison.

Fahey would be the last to offer McCarthy advice on what he should do differently to win parole in the future. But it was clear to Fahey that the one person doing the most to damage McCarthy's chances at parole was McCarthy. Through six hearings, McCarthy had shown an unwillingness —perhaps an inability—to tell the truth, to show empathy for Katy and her family, and to provide the board with confidence he was no longer a threat if released.

One irony is that parole rights activists might be partly responsible for keeping McCarthy in prison in 2019—at least that's how Katy's mother saw it.

Terry Taber concluded that the commissioners had been forced to do more research and to ask better questions because, in the current political environment, they wanted a rock-solid record to support any decision they made.

"When he came up the first few times (for parole), they thought, we can keep this guy here, and nobody's going to give a rat's ass one way or another," Terry said. "This is the first time where it's like: We got to do due diligence to make sure we have covered a lot more bases than we have before and not let him skate like he has for the last 34 years."

Terry conceded there might be inmates in New York who deserve parole, who got a raw deal on sentencing for a nonviolent crime, who have truly reformed themselves in prison. But in her view, there are some like McCarthy who can never be rehabilitated, who are so genuinely evil, so inherently violent, that they remain a menace to society. She thought anyone who reads the parole transcripts would recognize that McCarthy was essentially the same man he was the morning he killed Katy.

But as McCarthy's 2021 hearing approached, she was aware that the parole board's decisions in the past had shown that there was always hope, even for murderers.

Just three months after McCarthy was denied parole in 2019, another panel voted to release convicted child-killer John Muggelberg after his seventh hearing and 36 years behind bars. Muggelberg was serving time for the 1983 slaying of 9-year-old Sandra Olejniczak, who was strangled as she walked home from a 7-Eleven to buy postage stamps in Amherst, New York. The commissioners said it granted parole after it weighed statements from the victim's family, Muggelberg's criminal history, his prison accomplishments, and an assessment on his ability to successfully reintegrate into the community.

After the board's decision, the mother of the slain girl could do nothing except express outrage. "As far as I'm concerned," Yvonne Olejniczak told WKBW-TV in Buffalo, "the only way he should be let out is in a pine box."

As much as she dislikes the cycle of parole hearings every two years, Katy's mother was ready to give impact statements for the rest of her life if that's what it took for some other mother not to suffer the loss of a child.

In 2020, Terry remained convinced that the criminal justice system meant "justice for the criminal." But after six parole hearings and six denials for McCarthy, she now believed that sometimes—maybe sometimes —it could also mean justice for Katy.

Epilogue

As Brian McCarthy neared his seventh parole hearing set for April 20, 2021, New York state officials advised Katy's family not to expect to learn the outcome until the following week. But on the morning of Friday, April 23, Joe Hawelka Jr. took a break from work and called the state's Office of Victim Services in hopes it had an early decision. A sympathetic staff member took a moment to check records before sharing the news: "He was denied." She added that McCarthy's next hearing was scheduled for April 2023.

That was all Joe Jr. needed to hear. He hung up and immediately made separate phone calls to his sisters, his mother, and family attorney Joe Fahey.

"I am starting to tear up, and I don't know why," Joe Jr. told his mother as he shared his unexpectedly emotional reaction to the good news.

"It's relief," Terry explained quietly, herself in tears. "We got two more years. At least he's in for two more years."

Even so, Terry was of the belief her family would have to press even harder in 2023 to persuade the parole board that McCarthy, who turns 60 in 2022, remained a danger to the public if released.

As it had for so many years, the family took comfort knowing that it would not stand alone in this fight, that community sentiment was overwhelmingly on its side. The president of Clarkson University was among those who, once again in 2021, wrote to the parole board opposing McCarthy's release from prison. The family's new Facebook page, **4KatyHawelka**, quickly drew hundreds of followers.

And there was the family's 12-year-old online petition, still going strong. By the time the latest parole hearing got underway, the petition had drawn

8,755 signatures, with more coming in after that. There was no shortage of people who agreed that denying parole to McCarthy was about the only shred of justice left for Katy Hawelka.

Afterword

WHEN I was a teenager in the 1970s, Brian McCarthy and his family resided a mile down the road from my parents' home in the town of Parishville, New York, along a rural stretch of Route 72 where everyone had a mailing address of Potsdam. He was five years younger than me, so we weren't close friends. But we attended the same rural district school, where his grandmother was one of my sixth-grade teachers. His family joined the small Catholic church where I was an altar boy. I even spent time at his house one evening when his parents needed a substitute babysitter. McCarthy was in high school when I graduated from SUNY Potsdam and left northern New York in 1979 to pursue a journalism career.

On August 29, 1986, while I was at work as a reporter for the Syracuse *Post-Standard*, my father telephoned to say that McCarthy had been arrested for a brutal attack on a young student on the Clarkson University campus. After she died three days later without regaining consciousness, I read her name for the first time: Katherine Hawelka.

As a reporter, I had covered numerous stories involving violent crimes, including murders, sex-related attacks, and other assaults. But I was shocked nonetheless to hear of this kind of violence between strangers in the North Country, where many residents felt so safe that they never bothered to lock their doors at night. I also found it deeply unsettling that someone raised by a wonderful family I knew could have committed such a heinous act.

I soon lost track of the case and didn't think much about it until 2009 when McCarthy became eligible for parole, and Katy's family stepped back into the media spotlight to speak out against his release from prison. Like many others, I was moved by how they put words to their sorrow, how Terry and her family had stood up to powerful institutions, and how they never gave up seeking justice for Katy. The more I read, the more I wanted to learn about Katy and her family and to tell their story in an in-depth way.

As a nation obsessed with tales of true crime, the media often turn killers into celebrities while giving only a passing thought to victims and the grieving families left behind. I never wanted to write that kind of book, or to impose on Katy's family and add to their suffering.

They blessed this project with the understanding I wanted this to be a book centered on Katy.

"I love to talk about Katy," Terry Taber told me. "She was just a special, special kid. She really was. Every mother says that, especially about the ones they lose. Well, she was. She was just a good girl with a good heart."

I am grateful to numerous individuals who helped in the research for this book. At the top of this long list is Katy's remarkable family: Terry, Betsy, Carey and Joe Jr. They granted me hours of their time for interviews, patiently answered my emailed questions, shared family photographs, and provided documents I would not have found otherwise. They also encouraged others to talk to me; more than one person agreed to be interviewed only after checking with Katy's family to determine if it was okay with them.

Retired Onondaga County Court Judge Joseph E. Fahey also was immensely generous with his time in recalling his work as an attorney for Katy's parents from 1986 to 1988 and as an advocate for them from 2016 to the present. Over our cups of coffee at the Freedom of Espresso in Fayetteville, New York, his exceptional memory and his immense legal knowledge were crucial as I tried to make sense of the criminal and civil proceedings from three decades ago and to understand the current parole process.

If we are to judge people by the company they kept, Katy chose well those friends who were closest to her. Endearing stories about Katy came from Syracuse high school friends Martha Gualtieri McLain, Lisa Campolo, Jim Damiano and Sarah Kharas Salamino. Clarkson University roommates Nanci Parks Gage and Nichole Caruso Pfeifer, and former Clarkson student Todd Kilburn were immensely helpful in sharing their memories about Katy in Potsdam.

Former Potsdam Police officers John Kaplan, Terry McKendree and John Perretta helped me to reconstruct details of the murder investigation, including their interactions with McCarthy on August 29, 1986. The Potsdam Police Department also gave me access to the original arrest file, which the department had preserved through a move to a new police station at 38 Main Street.

Brian E. Kurish, who was a member of the Potsdam Volunteer Rescue Squad in 1986, talked to me about the steps his crew took to keep Katy alive outside Walker Arena. He also offered first-hand recollections of events that morning at Canton-Potsdam Hospital as the medical staff revived Katy and as police scrambled to identify her.

The former district attorney, Charles Gardner, shared his memories of the prosecution of Brian McCarthy. Former state Supreme Court Justice Norman Mordue, now a federal judge, helped to explain the civil proceedings. Former New York state parole Commissioner G. Kevin Ludlow shared his insights on how parole hearings work.

Spokespersons for the state Department of Corrections and Community Supervision, the Jefferson County Medical Examiner's Office, Samaritan Medical Center (formerly the House of the Good Samaritan), and the St. Lawrence County Probation Department also helped in deciphering official documents. This included court records on file with the St. Lawrence County Clerk's Office, the Onondaga County Clerk's Office, and the Cayuga County Clerk's Office, and prison and parole records with the State of New York. The Clery Center helped to explain the Clery Act and to confirm other details about the center's founders. *The Post-Standard* in Syracuse, WSYR-TV (Channel 9) in Syracuse, and the *Watertown Daily Times* gave permission for me to use photos from their archives.

My son, John, a recent graduate of Clarkson, kept me straight on campus names and places while making sure I never lost sight of the many reasons that students loved their time at Clarkson. Former *Post-Standard* colleague and copy editor Kevin Hyland helped to edit the manuscript and offered a sounding board throughout the writing process. My wife, Kathleen, reviewed the many drafts of this book and gave me plenty of encouragement on days when I thought I would never see the light at the end of the tunnel.

I contacted McCarthy in prison, asking for an interview. He wrote back to say he remembered me and expressed happiness that "success has smiled on you." While he was sorry for what he did and prayed "daily for my salvation," McCarthy said, he didn't want to be interviewed.

"I think putting in print about the case and my history will bring the pain back to the surface of so many who don't deserve to have that happen," he wrote.

Former Clarkson University President Allan H. Clark also declined to be interviewed but emailed a six-page statement with his recollections. Several others employed by Clarkson at the time of Katy's murder declined to talk to me or failed to respond to requests for interviews. To try to offer their perspectives, I have turned to official records from the 1980s, as well as from interviews they gave to the *Watertown Daily Times*, *The Post-Standard*, the *Herald-Journal*, the Clarkson *Integrator*, the *Courier & Freeman*, the *Ogdensburg Journal*, the *Massena Observer* and other publications.

The best available summary of how Clarkson has improved campus safety in the past three decades is offered in the university's 2019 annual security report, which was required under the Clery Act.

According to the report, the university employs a Campus Safety & Security Department composed of "eight full-time security officers, one part-time security officer, three per-diem officers and the student agency, Emergency Medical Service (CU EMS). . . . During their patrol of University owned property, officers constantly monitor for criminal activity and evaluate campus safety and security." The security officers "submit to a detailed background check, complete the NYS Security Guard Course(s) and are licensed as security officers with the State of New York. Their training includes but is not limited to: effective communication, NYS Security Guard Course, Clery Act, Title IX, investigations, CPR/AED and first aid, defensive tactics, fire safety, domestic violence, sexual assaults, stalking, cultural diversity, and drug recognition to name a few. Our officers are Safety & Security officers and, therefore, are not sworn police officers and do not have authority/power to arrest. They can make immediate contact with local law enforcement officials as needed. In addition, the Village of Potsdam Police Department conducts patrols of our campus roadways and perimeter."

The report adds that it "is incumbent upon every member of the University to be alert to situations that require the attention of Campus Security & Safety." To assist with reporting crimes, the campus has installed 27 blue light and 18 yellow-red call box emergency phones. The security department also provides, upon request, a personal escort to any student walking from one university property to another."

While Katy's murder is not mentioned in the report, my son and anyone else who has enrolled at Clarkson since 1986 owe a debt of gratitude to Terry Taber and the late Joe Hawelka Sr., who helped to make the campus safer by holding the university accountable for its role in their daughter's death.

May this book about Katy and her courageous family offer its own legacy as enduring.

— William D. LaRue, January 2021

ABOUT THE AUTHOR

William D. LaRue is an award-winning journalist and former reporter for *The Post-Standard* in Syracuse, New York, and a former online producer for Advance Local's newspaper websites. A native of Potsdam, New York, he received a bachelor's degree in English from State University College at Potsdam and a master's degree in communications from Syracuse University. His previous books include 2015's *CANDY: True Tales of a 1st Cavalry Soldier in the Korean War and Occupied Japan,* co-written with his father, Kenneth J. LaRue; and 2018's *Captain Puckett: Sea Stories of a Former Panama Canal Pilot,* co-written with Kenneth P. Puckett. William, a father of two, lives in a suburb of Syracuse with his wife, Kathleen.

Made in the USA
Middletown, DE
15 August 2021